Another
FISHING
YEAR

Another
FISHING
YEAR

John Wilson's
FISHING DIARY

Green Umbrella
PUBLISHING

This book is for my good friend Norman Symonds who, although not an angler himself, has, through extraordinary vision and business acumen, created marvellous lakeland fishing for so many anglers.

This edition first published in the UK in 2006
By Green Umbrella

© Green Umbrella Publishing 2006

www.greenumbrella.co.uk

Publishers Jules Gammond, Tim Exell and Vanessa Gardner

The right of John Wilson to be identified as Author of this book has been asserted by him
in accordance with the Copyright, Designs and Patents Act 1988.

Printed and bound in Italy

ISBN 1-905009-37-2

CONTENTS

INTRODUCTION

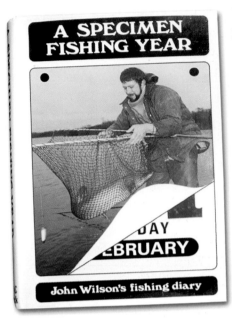

When I wrote my very first hardback book, *A Specimen Fishing Year*, published by A&C Black, way back in the heatwave year of 1976, little did I realise how much would change both in my personal life and in British freshwater fishing over these following three decades. Being then in my early 30s and now in my early 60s, I guess my hair was always going to change from dark brown to a mixture of grey and white. Like most of us however, I never contemplated divorce and remarrying. But eventually everything does settle down again, and becoming a real live 'granddad' to my daughter Lisa's two girls, Alisha and Lana, makes me feel extremely proud, as does watching my son Lee, who is a carpenter-joiner, work creatively with a length of wood.

I certainly hadn't visualised the amount of travel and exotic sports fishing that I would now be enjoying back in those early years of running a tackle shop in Norwich for six days a week, when the only way of fishing regularly enough to be able to write about it, was to grab 'dawn starts' two or sometimes three mornings a week before gunning the car back into Norwich to open the shop for 9 a.m. But I guess eventually selling the shop (John's Tackle Den) after 26 years became inevitable in order for me to concentrate upon angling journalism and TV commitments.

I have in fact during these past 30 years now penned over 30 angling books plus filmed some 130 television programmes and videos. My *Go Fishing* series made for Anglia Television (and shown on Channel Four for ten years) spanned 18 years and remains the longest running British angling series ever, something of which I am extremely proud. I have also been extremely privileged to have created a piece of natural history, from excavation to landscaping and stocking, in the shape of my own lakeland fishery, which nestles beside the house within sight of my beloved River Wensum. All would have been mere pipe dreams back in the mid 1970s.

Now while my 1976 diary essays mentioned a hidden fear for silver shoal species (although I was catching numerous big roach and dace at that time) not recruiting within the counties of Norfolk and Suffolk in the numbers they should have been, due mostly to cormorant predation, who could ever have predicted the kind of decimation we have since suffered, and continue to do so due to a totally 'gutless and ineffective' Ministry of Agriculture and Fisheries, and I might add, so far as the angler is concerned, a succession of 'head in the sand' governments, whose statute it is to protect both our salt and freshwater fisheries. When oh when, will the 'black death' as this bird is now known, be put where it well and truly belongs, at the head of the 'vermin list' along with rabbits, grey squirrels and rats, etc.? This one creature has obliterated the legacy of prolific river fishing that has always been handed down from one generation to another where children learnt to appreciate natural history by first trotting a float downstream for small silver shoal fishes, gudgeon and the like, before moving on to larger goals. And could anyone ever have foreseen back in 1976, that carp would become so prolific to eclipse roach both as Britain's most common and most popular species?

What about the weird and comparatively recent phenomenon of species like tench, bream, barbel and carp each now being caught at somewhere between 25-40% heavier than their respective record weights back in 1976. In those days 6lbs tench, 8lbs bream, 10lbs barbel and 30lbs carp were truly 'huge' fish for specialists like me to aim for. Nowadays, they are everyday catches on many waters up and down the country. Some say that global warming and our now mild winters are partly responsible for these particular species packing on weight, while others attribute the increase to fish being regularly and selectively fed large quantities of high nutritional value boilies and pelleted food. I think in addition, that because these species find themselves in many cases the 'dominant' species in rivers and lakes where they once had to share the natural food larder with vast shoals of roach and other silver shoal fish, due to cormorant predation, they no longer need to compete and subsequently grow fat as a consequence. The huge tench I caught back in June, with four of them heavier than the once British record, are a prime example.

Though primarily a book about a calendar year of specimen hunting around my home ground of Norfolk and Suffolk, including the trials and tribulations of endeavouring regularly to catch the whoppers, that 1976 year's diary also contained a number of side issues, from using the first prototype float rod manufactured entirely from super lightweight, carbon fibre, (which we now take for granted) to my scuba diving in local gravel pits during the 'then' close season, (why oh why did we pander to the greed of commercial fisheries and abolish it?) and playing with various ledger rigs on the bottom to find out why a simple fixed paternoster set up worked best. A method I still use incidentally for much of my ledgering.

Yes, those early years certainly provided a wonderful training ground and a platform for thinking, innovative anglers to voice their experiences. Sadly however, many fellow angling writers and friends like Doug Allen, Peter Stone, John Darling, Ivan Marks, Len Head, Colin Dyson, Trevor Housby, Bernard Venables and Dick Walker, who all contributed immensely to that period, have all passed on. Although we are all considerably more informed from their respective inputs, and freshwater angling today would just not be the same.

What you are about to read actually came about following a pike fishing session out afloat on the Norfolk Broads with good friend Nick Beardmore who informed me that a mate of his had just bid over £150 on eBay, to secure one of my 1976 *A Specimen Fishing Year* books, which originally retailed at just £4.75. I could not believe it. I was of course both flattered and flabbergasted, but then got to thinking about the unique comparisons that could be made from writing a sequel. So here it is. As in 1976, an open, honest account of each and every fishing trip both at home and abroad, with warts and all, including those inevitable 'blanks' that I made during the year of 2005.

But I doubt that I'll be around in another 30 years to see if 'this book' ever fetches over 30 times its original published price. Now there's a thought!

John Wilson
Great Witchingham, 2006

A NEW YEAR

Sunday, 2 January

Gusting, bitterly cold westerly wind. Bright sunshine all day.

It's certainly no coincidence that I chose to start this diary by boat fishing for pike with my dearest and oldest friend John (Jinx) Davey from Bungay in Suffolk, (we met when teenagers over 45 years ago, fishing the River Waveney for roach) on a lake near Norwich which I call 'The Conifers'. Because this exceptionally prolific pike water provided the very first entry in my first diary book back all those years ago in 1976, when my boat partner for the day was another old friend, the late Doug Allen.

Averaging between 10 and 14 feet deep, this lovely 'natural' lake is decidedly 'round' in shape and completely surrounded by tall, ivy covered fir trees, hence my nickname for it.

It is also quite unique in that of all the locations it has been my good fortune to fish within the counties of Norfolk and Suffolk over these past three decades, 'The Conifers' simply hasn't changed one iota, either in appearance or the fish it contains. And I cannot truthfully say that of anywhere else I fish, particularly the rivers. Its coloured water for instance, still produces a mountain of roach, perch, rudd and bream upon which preys a healthy stock of nicely proportioned double figure pike plus the occasional specimen over 20lbs. Even the old boat house is still there (though 'leaning' somewhat) despite gales having toppled huge trees all around it, and inside is the very same, ancient wooden boat (lovingly re-varnished and re-painted every so often) that I first fished from 30 years ago.

OK, enough nostalgia for this essay. How did Jinx and I fare in such appalling conditions with my estate car's thermometer showing an outside temperature of just 2°C on our 8 a.m. arrival? Wind chill alone from the force 6 westerly, gusting every now and then up to 7 and 8, actually gave us second thoughts about even taking the boat out, despite the forecast of a bright and sunny day ahead. But within half an hour we had rowed (well Jinx had) half way across the lake to a favourite spot 80 yards upwind from a thick line of tall reeds along the eastern, willow-clad shoreline and put the mud weights down, bows into the teeth of the wind.

Using three rods apiece our selection of smelt, mackerel and herring dead baits were fanned 30-50 yards out all around the boat, presented 'static' on the bottom. Both our downwind baits had floats set well over depth, while the others were free lined, with 3x2SSG shots pinched onto the traces below the swivel to hold them in position against the 'yawing' of the boat, and to provide a little resistance to a pike, in order that it moves off away from the rod and gives a positive indication. This is most important to alleviate possible unintentional deep hooking.

I was just about on the point of regaining feeling in the fingers of my left hand (why on earth don't I remove dead baits from the freezer earlier on the day before a trip?) and enjoying a cup of coffee, when the sensitively set free-spool ratchet on my Baitmaster reel started to sing. The float on the 'downwind' end rig must have shot away quickly because I didn't see it go, so I wound down instantly and heaved the rod back into a full bend. There then followed a spirited fight from a nicely marked and proportioned pike of around 10lbs which I chinned just clear of the surface with a gloved hand to remove the trebles, both of which were lodged in the scissors, before allowing it to crash-dive down to the bottom. Incidentally, when possible I always prefer to unhook pike without bringing them into the boat and especially without using the net, which is taken along 'only' in case a whopper turns up. Then I'll get the scales out, and weigh it in the landing net, deducting the weight of the net afterwards. For yours truly, those days of moving each and every fish from the landing net into a specialised sling have long gone. I simply cannot be doing with all the hassle of slime and cold fingers. I am perfectly happy 'guestimating' its size and I'm sure the fish would agree. In fact I don't use a weigh sling for any of my fishing in Britain. I do own a giant, reinforced weigh sling for the likes of Nile perch, Wels catfish and mahseer however. Besides, if the fish is already in a landing net, then it is already lying in the perfect receptacle for hoisting onto the scales.

After around an hour, with no further pick-ups, we decided to up with the mud weights and move around 80 yards across the lake in order to grid search as much of the bottom as possible. But as Jinx was about to reel in his last rod, a pike snuffed up the joey mackerel and fair sizzled line from the reel upon feeling the hooks. This particular fish put up an incredible scrap for such cold conditions and I rather think Jinx was expecting to see something larger than a long, lean machine of around 17lbs when it finally hit the surface in a shower of spray. Still, two doubles on a bitingly cold day in little more than an hour's fishing was perhaps more than we had expected.

We moved immediately afterwards, but had to wait a good hour and a half for the next piece of action, which strangely also happened just prior to our moving position again, when my float suddenly started zooming across the waves before sneaking beneath the surface and line peeling from the reel. Again an instant strike, (I'm always of the opinion that if the pike is any size at all, the hooks will be inside the jaws, which is why I only ever use comparatively small, whole or half-dead baits of between four and seven inches long) and my rod arched over to what felt a nice fish. Following much head shaking and several long, powerful runs, the 15lbs test line 'whistling' in the wind, alongside the boat came a superbly shaped and spotted pike of fully 15lbs. I gently eased out the duo of size 8 semi barb less trebles, and off she went.

Incidentally it may be interesting to note that throughout this winter I have been using pike traces made from a revolutionary new material, 30lbs test, titanium wire, which though noticeably thicker than the 30lbs test, easy twist 'stranded' wire that I would normally use for pike, but is still relatively supple, simply does not fray or kink, even after catching dozens and dozens of fish. These matt-black 18 inch long traces cost £5 and come fitted with two size 8, super strong and sharp Owner trebles, with a power swivel at the opposite end, and are available direct from Dunstable tackle manufacturer Mick Willis (tel. 01525 221968) whose customers have literally used the same trace all winter. And they say there's nothing new in fishing. But back to 'The Conifers' lake and those pike.

The session was now hotting up despite the cold westerly, and we moved once more, another 80 or so yards across the lake, always keeping within around the same distance upwind from the easterly shoreline. This time it was a run for Jinx, whose small roach was gobbled up by an equally small pike of around 5lbs.

The time by now was around 1 p.m. and we decided to make one last move and due to the cold, settle for a 2 p.m. finish. These days I'm pleased to say, and I don't care if it is to do with age (well, we are both over 60 after all) both Jinx and I know when we have had our fill. Reminds me of that famous Fred J. Taylor saying which goes, "I'll be glad when I've had enough of this." And it's so true.

Lo and behold at around three minutes to 2 p.m. (I swear) the ratchet on one of my multipliers presenting a free lined herring's head suddenly screeched into life, and from the moment of connecting, I suspected a big fish, because it felt really heavy and kept low to the bottom whilst I pumped it gently towards the boat. It then must have seen the dinghy's outline directly above and power-dived with incredible speed before turning around and zooming straight up to the surface beside the boat, performing a simply marvellous 'tail-walking' sequence. Jinx and I looked at each other totally flabbergasted. The last thing we expected from any of the pike in such cold water conditions (the lake had been frozen over only three days before) was an aerial display. And what an incredibly long fish it was too. Well over 20lbs 'long' but noticeably lean in the body. I just couldn't be bothered with net and scales, and so called her 19lbs, after chinning her beside the boat to remove the hooks and watching her disappear into the murky depths. What a great day's pike fishing against difficult odds and a wonderful start to 2005.

Tuesday, 4 January

Blustery southwesterly wind, heavily overcast, mild.

Following Sunday's pike action despite the cold, I was really looking forward to today. The wind had swung more southerly bringing in a decidedly mild air stream. Absolutely perfect conditions for pike fishing on a small private broad off the River Bure near Wroxham, which had been dredged several years back, but according to my boat partner Nick Beardmore, had not been fished since. A wonderful opportunity for Nick to show me the effectiveness of his 'special' homemade pike dead baits, which he calls 'mackreels'. These unique baits consist of several inches of pig's intestine packed full of minced mackerel and other oily fishes, plus various fish oils, tied off at both ends to resemble a sausage, or section of a thickish eel, hence their name.

Within an hour of dawn breaking we had the boat anchored up in the middle of the five acre broad, which is completely fringed by an impenetrable jungle of alder carr, willow and tall reeds, and, fishing three rods apiece, employed our most effective technique for Broadland pike, of fanning a selection of free lined dead baits all around the boat – smelt, herrings, and of course Nick's mackreels.

Now I'd love to say that during the following six hours before returning to the boathouse in mid-afternoon, those pike went crazy, but I would be lying. The plain, inexplicable truth was that we just couldn't buy a run on anything. Not even on Nick's smelly 'mackreels,' which benefit from a good stabbing with a sharp knife immediately prior to casting out, in order for the oils and juices to permeate through the water. They certainly leave an attractive 'slick' on the surface, and I shall definitely be trying them again, where on hard fished lakes, rivers and broads, I fancy they will have a real edge on all the more popular and regularly used dead baits.

So I have to chalk up the first 'blank' (you didn't assume I always catch, did you?) of the New Year. There is an inevitable 'high spot' to most fishing trips however, and ours was experiencing the rare sight, while walking back to the car, of a bittern getting up from a narrow, reedy dyke not ten yards away and flying over the marshes. And mere minutes later, a marsh harrier quartering the marshes beyond.

Unfortunately Norfolk pike fishing will have to take a back seat for the next couple of weeks. On Friday I'm off to fish in South America along Brazil's famous Rio Negro (part of the Amazon system) for the most colourful freshwater predator of them all, the peacock bass. And I can't wait.

Saturday, 8th January

Overcast with drizzle, followed by baking hot sunshine. Very humid.

Mention Brazil, and what comes to mind? Coffee? Pele? Anacondas? Well, hopefully, for Christine Slater of Tailor Made Holidays and me, plus our five British guests, it's going to be the totally unique sports fishing, with magnificently coloured peacock bass and huge catfish heading the long list of hard battling predatory adversaries.

Brazil is in fact the planet's fifth largest country behind Russia, Canada, China and the U.S.A. It is even bigger than Australia and covers almost half the continent of South America, bordering ten other countries plus the Atlantic Ocean. To the east and south are rugged mountains, fertile valleys and narrow, coastal plains, while the northeast consists mostly of semi-arid plateaux. The centre west is largely a vast plateau of savannah and rock escarpments, and the fabulous northwest contains the famous hot, humid and wet, rainforest-fed, basin of the Amazon, the world's second longest river, behind Africa's River Nile.

I previously visited this fascinating country back in 1993 to fish for the high-leaping golden dourado of the Parana River near Foz just below breathtaking Iguacu Falls, the borderline of Brazil, Argentina and Paraguay. And I not only became mesmerised by the sheer magnitude and beauty of it all, but also totally fascinated by a whole host of weird and colourful species from armoured catfish to the fearsome piranha. But I have to admit, by comparison with the Amazon system, in South America, the Parana is simply just another river.

Extending also into Peru, Bolivia, and Venezuela, this massive Amazon watershed is the largest on earth, dumping into the Atlantic Ocean one quarter of the world's fresh water in which live some 4000 species of fish, from the enigmatic arapaima to giant catfish, not forgetting the myriad of miniature and attractively coloured fishes kept by tropical aquarium enthusiasts. This is more species even than in the Pacific and Atlantic Oceans combined.

During its 4000 mile journey across South America the Amazon is fed by over 1000 tributaries, the largest being our chosen destination, the mysterious Rio Negro, which is up to 12 miles wide in parts, and itself containing a staggering 2000 different species, some of them more representative of saltwater tropicals, like garfish, barracuda and poisonous stingrays etc., to the hard hitting peacock bass and unusual fruit-eaters.

Following long hauls from Heathrow to Miami and then onto Manaus, our final 200 mile flight deposited us at Barcelos, followed by an hour's speedboat ride to the famous Rio Negro Lodge, which nestles amongst dense tropical jungle literally within spitting distance of the river. What a place! But were we knackered after such a lengthy journey.

Incidentally, fishing out from here and from both the Rio Arca Lodge and the *Amazon Queen*, an 85 foot long purpose-built houseboat (two alternative angling options), in fact the whole unique Amazon fishing experience, is the brainchild of owner and founder of Amazon Tours, ex-helicopter pilot Phil Marsteller, who originates from Ohio. Phil opened the Rio Negro Lodge in 1998, and its comfortable, air-conditioned accommodation provides immediate access to the vast maze of waterways and lagoons draining this upper Amazon rainforest, via fibreglass, shallow draft Nitro bass boats sporting 90hp outboards, zipping guests quickly along (two to a boat) at 50mph into the very heart of the Amazonas.

Having spotted vultures, giant terns and kingfishers, night herons, plovers, egrets and darters during our upriver journey, following a light lunch, we were all mega keen to get out

OVERLEAF
It's hard for us living on a tiny island to comprehend that Brazil's Rio Negro which winds through virgin rainforests and is itself up to 12 miles wide and full of spectacularly coloured peacock bass like this 13 pounder, John's first ever, is just one, of over a 1000 tributaries feeding the mighty Amazon River.

there and explore more of this veritable paradise, so after sorting out tackle we made directly for the boat dock where I was assigned an experienced local guide for the week's fishing, named Jim. Everything looked perfect except for the pair of tame, giant river otters playing amongst the boats. The male actually followed us up to the lodge and into the restaurant on our return, where everyone patted it as though it were a dog.

Now in recent years I have for good reason become, shall we say, rather disenchanted with otters. Due to faceless, 'do-gooders', who obviously haven't a clue about the current balance of nature, introducing them along beats of my local River Wensum where cormorants have ravaged the once-prolific shoals of roach and dace, and where runs of eels (once a large part of the otter's natural diet) are now pathetically low, you do not need to be a rocket scientist to understand why in the coldest part of our winter, especially should the river be in spate for week upon week, otters choose an easier option. They leave the river and chew their way through jumbo-sized carp in all the adjacent gravel pit fisheries. Mine in particular.

During the past few years I have lost dozens and dozens of double figure carp, grass carp and Wels catfish to otters. Resulting last summer in my spending exactly what my first family bungalow cost (30 years ago mind, but the figure rang a bell) on erecting a 235 yard long, six foot high chain-link fence in an effort to keep them out of my two-lake fishery. With two feet buried in the ground to alleviate their burrowing and an 18 inch 'angled' top, till now the fence seems to have done its job. So I'm keeping my fingers crossed.

But I have digressed. Back to the Rio Negro which translates to 'Black River'. It does look very dark, decidedly 'peaty' in fact and the colour of strong tea due apparently to the amount of tannin it constantly receives (from the hardwood trees), in which it is said, that mosquitoes cannot live. Strangely however, visibility is quite good, between two to four feet.

With just a few hours of the day remaining, guide Jim zipped Dave Nevatt and me several miles upstream from the lodge at 50mph (he drives flat out continually) into an off-river lagoon completely overhung around the margins by dense tropical vegetation, consisting mostly of tall trees and vines. Here we used Luhr Jensen, eight inch long, floating 'wood chopper' plugs to good effect for our first encounter with peacock bass. The technique was to work the structure-rich shorelines of fallen trees where the bass hide up, while Jim guided the boat silently along 60-70 yards out using the electric motor. This enabled Dave and I, each at opposite ends of the 17 foot boat, to cover the fringe of the fallen hardwood trees with 50 yard casts. 'Wood chopping,' as this technique is called, is however extremely tiring on wrists and forearms, slamming the rod tip sharply downwards before every successive crank of the reel handle in order to 'churn' the surface with the plugs rear propeller and bring a bass up to attack.

My first bass, a real beauty of around 13lbs was the most colourful freshwater fish I have ever seen, let alone caught, and it fought unbelievably hard, making run after run despite the 80lbs test Cortland braided reel line on my ABU 7001c multiplier and a tightly wound-down clutch.

Distinctly perch-like in shape and fin placement with two spotted dorsals, the first characteristically spiked and the second with soft rays, its mouth was huge and like all perch and bass, without canines. The back was olive-green, fusing down the flanks into spectacular golden-yellow, overlaid along the belly line with deep scarlet. The gill rakers, pelvic and anal fins and the lower half of its tail were also painted in scarlet. In the middle of the tail root a most distinct black 'eye' spot, fringed in yellow, immediately identifies the species. The top of the gill plate was overlaid with irregular patches of black, also fringed in yellow, while along the deep flanks, three wide, vertical bars of black finished the paint job. It's as though an artist has been given a commission to create the most breathtaking, outrageously coloured fish of all time.

In addition to peacocks, we caught paca (a spotted version) and butterfly bass, which instead of vertical bars have four large 'eye' spots evenly spaced along the lateral line, and turquoise-blue dorsal fins. These apparently are rarely caught into double figures whereas the peacock bass record, caught here from the Rio Negro weighed 27lbs. The peacock bass is in fact a member of the cichlid family and not a bass at all. We also caught bicuda, a tooth-laden version of the saltwater barracuda, and dogfish, a fully scaled, chub-like critter averaging 3lbs, possessing the most horrendous set of large canines. And they all hit our lures with real venom. The bass especially, rushing to the surface in a kaleidoscope of spray and making a distinct 'boff' sound on impact before crash-diving and ripping line away at real speed.

We also saw several beautifully spotted stingrays swimming over shallow, sandy flats, and caught a crocodile – well our guide did anyway. It was a small caiman of around four feet long, which made a grab for Jim's surface plug and became entangled in the braided line. This had obviously happened before because Jim purposefully drew it alongside the boat after a hectic scrap, and using the rod tip most deftly, wound the line several times around the croc's jaws before attempting to lift it into the boat, where it was carefully unhooked and released. What a start to day one. Can't wait for tomorrow.

Sunday, 9th January

Hot and humid. Bright sunshine all day.

There are exactly 40 guests staying at the lodge, all Yanks apart from our seven Brits, so grabbing breakfast for a 6 a.m. start and getting down to the boat dock is a hectic affair. Christine decided to accompany me today, and we were soon on our way at 50mph heading upstream to one of Jim's favourite lagoons, complete with packed lunches. After an hour's run, seeing macaws overhead and several pods of porpoises en route, Jim suddenly cut the motor and drifted silently into a shallow off-river channel which lead into a huge lagoon of around 200 acres. The amount of water here is simply mind-boggling and due to water levels being low at present a wide strip of sand several hundred yards long (once the river bed) separated river from our destination. This

ABOVE
ABOVE
Can there be a more beautiful, outrageously coloured freshwater species than the peacock bass, which is actually a cichlid. Weighing almost 20lbs, this monster (the world record is just 27lbs) provided a memorable battle for Dave Nevatt, having grabbed his 'wood-chopper' surface plug amongst the dense shoreline structure of fallen hardwood trees.

necessitated us leaving our 17 foot speed boat and carrying the icebox, rods, lures and a 5hp motor etc. across the dunes to where Jim kept a 14 foot, lightweight aluminium boat hidden amongst the dense jungle of vines and palms along the margins of the lagoon. What a pristine, wilderness setting if ever I saw one. That's what I like most about the Amazonas, total solitude where you don't see or hear another human being other than your guide and boat partner for the entire day's adventure. The guides at the lodge obviously go out of their way to explore different areas all week. Then at around 5 p.m. it's all back to the dock at 50mph.

Strangely for three hours absolutely nothing came to our surface lures worked between the fallen trees along the shallow margins. So we started trolling at around three knots through the deeper centre channel with smaller sub-surface artificials fished 50 yards behind the boat. Chris had on a four inch spoon and I, a five inch diving plug. Bingo! That's where the fish wanted to hit, three to four feet down, and throughout the remainder of the day we must have accounted for 30 or more fish (I simply lost count) of seven different species. Peacock bass, pacas, butterfly bass, bicudas, dogfish, piranhas and a weird, long and deep bodied but thin species, large scales and huge jaws called an arauana. No monsters however, our biggest being a 7lbs peacock bass for Christine.

A fabulous but extremely warm day in paradise. The temperature at 40°C with 90% humidity, this was by far the most uncomfortably hot place I have ever wet a line. Ice cold vodka and tonics with slices of fresh limes at the bar on our return, were more than welcome, as was the news that Dave Nevatt had taken a 19lbs peacock bass and Ian Jackson a 15 pounder. At least two of our party had struck gold. Well done the Brits!

Monday, 10th January

Hot, humid, bright sunshine, flat calm.

Today my boat partner was Dave Johnson from Hertfordshire, who has been on previous fishing safaris with me to the Zambezi River, the Florida Keys and to Canada. He particularly likes banging into big fish and so we decided to specifically target catfish, for which guide Jim had procured a large bag of fresh chicken heads – apparently 'the' local bait for big pussies.

But before we headed off, I just couldn't resist photographing a pair of giant river otters that had shown keen interest in our bag of chicken heads. These creatures have become so incredibly tame, one actually jumped up onto the boat.

LEFT
No wonder my boat partner Dave Johnson is smiling, this unbelievably tame, pair of Rio Negro 'wild' giant river otters, treated us to their playful antics every morning before we set off, by sampling our catfish bait. Fresh chicken heads.

Two rolls of film later Dave and I were on our way upriver. After about 30 miles Jim suddenly cut the motor and selected a particular tree which hung well out over the river from the tropical jungle upon which to tie our bows' rope. Anchors are either not used or unavailable locally. To angle the boat out as far as possible, directly over deep water some 30 or so feet from the bank, Jim then untied the long rope from the bows and re-tied it around the steering wheel. Perfecto! This is obviously the local way of doing away with expensive anchors, which only become snagged in the network of sunken hardwood trees lying on the river bed. When in Rome! It's so very true.

It was only now with the boat actually tied up that I realised how fast the Rio Negro is, with at least five knots of water above a depth of around 20 feet immediately downstream. I made up a couple of three foot, 100lbs test Kevlar traces with size 6/0 Maruto Eagle Wave hooks at the business end and with a two ounce running bomb above the swivel, Dave and I gently flipped our chicken heads (honestly) into the current and feathered them down to the bottom. Due to misinformed restrictions on baggage (I'll take my own gear next time) we were compelled to use the 80lbs test boat rods and multipliers provided by the lodge, and the reels were pathetically low on 80lbs line, something which cost us dearly later. But then you do live and learn, eh?

Literally within five minutes, Dave's chicken head was taken and he heaved the rod back into a beautifully coloured red tail catfish of about 25lbs, which fought strongly in the fast flow. Before I had time to pack the camera away and actually get my own bait in, he had recast and was fast into another pussy, which started to take line, but then the hook fell out. It was however, seemingly much larger than the first. I was on the point of wondering what the hell was wrong with my chicken head, when the rod top jerked over and line started to evaporate from the reel. I slammed the multiplier into gear, pointed the rod tip at the catfish and whacked it hard once the 80lbs line was starting to 'hum', and I have to say I was not ready for the brute force greeting me at the other end. A heavily tightened drag did nothing to stop this fish which after ripping 30 to 40 yards from the spool fortunately turned around and headed upstream directly towards me, and as it neared the boat I could feel the line grating. It had obviously gone beneath one or more of the hardwood trees littering the bottom, and to cut a long, exasperating story short, despite Jim untying from the tree so we could get a different angle on it by pulling from downstream, the result was inevitable. It was not coming out of that tree and so I had to wrap the line around a cleat and use the engine to break off. It is, incidentally, impossible to break 80lbs monofilament line from an anchored or tied up boat. There is far too much stretch.

Having caught more than my fair share of big fish over the years including 100lbs plus catfish, there is no way that lost pussy could have been any smaller. It felt truly awesome. But from this particular lair, for indeed that is what the swim was, there was one more bite to come, and when he struck, with the fish heading off downstream fast on a tight line, Dave was almost pulled off his feet and out of the boat. He did however manage to turn it eventually, though the outcome was the same as mine. It found sanctuary amongst those sunken hardwood trees that I am fast beginning to hate. Yet another monster lost.

Now for some staggering statistics. There are in fact at least five different species of tropical catfish inhabiting the mighty Rio Negro that can top 100lbs, possibly even seven with the amarillo and dourado. This, in my opinion, is what makes it so unique and a prime, 'virgin' location for European catfish enthusiasts who have topped out at between 140-180lbs with Wels in Spain for instance, and want to experience the power of much larger adversaries. Frankly this has got to be the most exciting, untapped river catfishing on this planet.

LEFT
A ledgered chicken head presented on a 6/0 hook produced this 25lbs red tailed catfish, netted by guide Jim, from a 20 foot deep and fast run close into the bank for Dave Johnson following a dogged scrap, despite the heavy, sea-strength tackle.

Ex helicopter pilot and the owner and founder of Amazon Tours Phil Marstellers who made wilderness angling possible in the heart of the Amazonas, lives beside the river. A man with immense vision.

So consider these three potential 100lbs plus species: the red tail, the surubin, and the striped catfish. Then we have the jau, which tops out at somewhere between 200-300lbs, and the massive and pelagic-like piraiba, that attains weights of up to 400lbs. What a river the Rio Negro is turning out to be, because save for the giant Mekong catfish of Thailand which is now so thin on the ground due to over fishing and actually considered an endangered species in the Mekong itself (it is in fact illegal to purposefully catch them in the river), South American pussies inhabiting the Amazon and its tributaries such as the Negro, offer simply unlimited potential for rod and line sport.

At around midday we gave up on the bank side structure-rich swims having tried several more, only to lose a mountain of terminal tackle amongst the sunken logs, without another run. Besides we were almost out of chicken heads. So we lure fished along a shallow, overgrown, off-river channel in search of fresh bait and in no time at all caught three dogfish. These are rather like a chub of around 3lbs, (that's their average weight) with the head of a bulldog. Their sculls are so tough it takes more than several clumps behind the head with the blunt edge of the guide's machete before they will even quieten down. But they make great catfish baits either filleted or used as cutlets.

After preparing these baits I decided we would try drifting with the flow for the catfish, well away from bank side snags, with our terminal rigs bumping gently along the sandy bottom behind the boat, instead of losing yet more gear amongst the trees. And using this technique, which apparently is not practised locally (I've used it to good effect for pussies in Africa on both the Zambezi and the Nile below magical Murchison Falls) Dave and I took three silver, spotted catfish of around 5lbs apiece. I am sure it will produce the whoppers here too. A most fascinating and enlightening day's fishing, made even brighter by the sight of colourful toucans and macaws. Apparently, the macaws, which are usually seen in pairs, mate for life. Phil Marstellers, owner of the lodge, has a most colourful (red, blue and yellow) pet macaw, which I photographed this evening in his garden that overlooks the river.

Tuesday, 11th January

Hot and humid. Bright sunshine. Flat calm.

In the company of my boat partner Ian Jackson from Hertfordshire, Jim sped us to an area some 40 miles due south of the lodge, to a galaxy of mouth-watering lagoons and backwaters. On the way we spotted several rather large caimans, so I wouldn't recommend wading here, and throughout the day both grey and pink porpoises. The latter are indeed a dirty pink. Quite unusual.

Unfortunately, few peacock bass were in a hitting mood and after several hours of working our top-water lures into dozens of mouth-watering, structure-rich swims in both river and lagoons, we had but one modest-sized bass apiece to show for our efforts, Ian taking a peacock bass of around 6lbs and I, a paca of a pound or so less. It would appear that one day these bass are really having it, and hitting aggressively, and the very next, completely uninterested.

Nonetheless, it was a fascinating day of serene beauty and apart from the occasional burst of chattering from birds and monkeys, a day of total solitude and silence. Great news when we arrived back at the dock at 5 p.m. from Dave Johnson whom I fished with yesterday. He caught a magnificent 21lbs peacock bass. Was he over the moon or what!

BELOW
Ian Jackson, who hails from Hertfordshire, displays a slightly different, yet breathtakingly coloured form of peacock bass, locally called 'paca'. Note the white spots along the top half of its back and fins.

Wednesday, 12th January

Mixture of showers and bright sunshine. Hot and humid, strong southerly wind.

Jim our guide sped Dave Nevatt and me way, way upriver to fish three remote lagoons. Exactly how far we travelled I'm not sure, but we left the dock at 50mph and one and a quarter hours later suddenly stopped. We had a second guide on board to help with the portage, and he pointed to a certain spot along the shoreline, which looked all the same to us. But lo and behold, hidden amongst the palms and vines was a folding 'porta-bote'. This we helped drag through the jungle for about a 100 yards to a completely secluded lagoon of around 15 acres. At this time of

the year when the Negro drops to its lowest levels, large concentrations of bass are virtually imprisoned in these off-river lagoons, till the heavy rains come and it rises again.

As we were preparing the boat however I could see an ominous disturbance over on the opposite side of the lagoon in the form of four giant river otters. Suffice to say that for all the hard work, we caught nought. So back to our 17 foot Nitro speedboat upon which was tied the porta-bote and off we sped to another lagoon, which produced just one small peacock bass for Dave on a woodchopper.

Fortunately, our third and final lagoon of the day did contain fair numbers of bass and dogfish, though all of modest size. Working both woodchoppers and zara spooks, 20 or so beautifully coloured bass, of all three species, came our way with the largest at around 7lbs. I was fascinated to see through the clear, shallow water of the lagoon several dozen plecostomus

LEFT
Just one of the uncountable, pristine and totally wilderness lagoons amongst the rainforest left by the falling waters of the Rio Negro in which numerous species including the hard-hitting peacock bass, become trapped until the river rises again. We had to pull our 'porta-bote' through 200 yards of swamps and dense jungle in order to fish this one.

I should have known better with the amount of travelling I do, and banged my boot hard on the floor before putting it on. Then I would not have panicked upon feeling this big and furry, poisonous? Spider scraping at my toes.

of between 3-5lbs, feeding upon algae on the bottom. Anyone who keeps tropical fish usually has one or two of these strange fishes amongst their aquarium inhabitants to keep the glass free of green algae, but I never knew they grew so large. Another spectacular day in paradise, and the only 140 mile round trip I've ever made whilst boat fishing in fresh water.

Had a real fright this evening when I put on my desert boots to go along for dinner. No sooner had I tied the laces on my right boot when I could feel something inside moving against my toes. Well! I couldn't get the boot off fast enough, and when I banged it against the inside of the sink, out fell one enormous, furry spider, the size of a tangerine. Phew! Half way through dinner my room partner Dave Nevatt went back to the room for some tablets. Apparently I had killed the spider knocking the boot so hard against the sink, so he eased it onto a leaf and deposited it outside. It left a brown residue in the sink, which Dave touched, and it burnt his finger. Guess I had one lucky escape.

Thursday 13th January

Hot and humid. Bright sunshine interspersed with torrential rain.

The multiplier spool beneath my thumb suddenly came to life as an unseen force ripped off the 80lbs monofilament at alarming speed. Yes, I was catfishing again, my boat partner being Terry Ashtin from Poole in Dorset, and we could not have been waiting for more than ten minutes, tied up to the overhanging branches of a bank side tree, before the action began. Sadly, as most of the guests staying at the lodge are Yanks and interested only in hooking up with trophy-sized peacock bass, little attention is paid to the amount of line on the four 80lbs class catfish outfits available. My Penn boat multiplier had probably less than 80 yards on the spool (how I wished I'd brought my own gear along) and when it was all gone I yelled at guide Jim to untie the boat. This he did, but as we hurtled downstream in the fast current I was unable to recover line fast enough with a near-empty spool, and so one brute of a monstrous catfish managed to find sanctuary in a log on the river bed. Without question, another 100lbs plus monster lost through inadequate tackle. Boy, was I gutted.

Half an hour later we had moved to another spot, and again my chicken head hook bait was greedily gobbled up. Fortunately this particular fish motored across the flow directly away from the entanglement of sunken hardwood trees littering the bottom along the margins, but after 30 seconds or so the hook inexplicably pulled free. Again we moved as we did every 20 minutes or so throughout the day, because if a run was to materialise it did so quickly or not at all, or the swim was full of piranhas, which picked the bait to bits in no time at all.

The next run came bang in the middle of a tropical deluge and was from a piraiba catfish (the largest species of all) of around 20lbs which felt absolutely tiny compared to those I'd lost. But it fought doggedly nonetheless. Terry then had a powerful run but the hook pulled after 30 seconds or so. And that was it really, although upon arriving back at the boat dock it was heartening to hear that one of our group had hit the jackpot, and it was Dave Johnson again, who experienced a monumental three quarters of an hour battle with a superb piraiba catfish weighing 125lbs. What's more, he lost an even bigger one. Well done indeed. The catfishing potential here is mind blowing to say the least.

BELOW
Dave Johnson and his guide are understandably unhappy about hoisting this heavyweight 'piraiba' catfish up for the camera. It fought for almost an hour having 'gobbled up' a chicken head (pun intended) from the river bed and was estimated at weighing around 125lbs. Note how parts of its fins are chewed away. The result of piranhas.

Friday, 14th January

Hot and humid. Bright, intense sunshine all day.

This, our last day's fishing had come round all too quickly, and following the fiasco of yesterday, I decided to remove the 'low-on-line' Penn multiplier (they had in fact run out of 80lbs mono at the lodge) from the 80lbs class boat rod, and use my ABU 7001c 'fully loaded' with 80lbs braid that I had been casting for bass with all week. Yes! It was catfish again, this time with Adrian Ricks from Esher in Surrey who, having never caught a catfish, fancied having a go. And would you believe, on only our second move, having motored just ten miles upstream from the lodge, I struck gold in the incredibly wide and deep-bodied shape of a huge red tail catfish.

Within seconds of my striking, and again the successful bait was a chicken head, Jim had untied the boat and 'thoughtfully' used the electric motor to quickly take us well out from the shoreline of sunken snags so I could play it without another mishap. So following a fabulous, extremely powerful scrap lasting fully ten minutes (but still nothing approaching the kind of power of those lost monsters) up it suddenly popped to the surface.

Jim and I hauled it on board and removed the 7/0 hook, with the chicken head still intact before taking the trophy shots. What a strange, incredibly coloured fish, possessing a large, bright red tail, with red edging to all its fins, and a blotchy, charcoal-grey and white belly. Its massively wide head and all along the back was yellowy-sandy brown, heavily overlaid with small black spots, and the lateral line was most distinct, below which fusing into the belly was a mixture of white and yellow. It was a real beauty of around 75-80lbs, its wide mouth sprouting a set of long whiskers.

With no more runs to follow we changed tack at around 10 a.m. and asked Jim to find us a shallow off-river lagoon for some fly-fishing action with bass. I had intended to use my fly rod regularly on this trip, but the fabulous catfishing has kind of taken over. Adrian wanted also to experience catching bass on the fly and would you believe we had an absolute field day working a long, shallow lagoon, taking 20 or so fish including piranhas (my first ever on fly), dogfish, bicudas, and all three bass species using floating lines and five foot leaders presenting 1/0 red deceivers. It was marvellous fun. But in the late afternoon to end the trip we returned to catfishing using cutlets from the dogfish, and on the last move of the day, first Adrian pulled out of a real 'biggy' followed by me doing likewise with just a modest-sized fish. Adrian then caught his very first catfish ever, a scrappy fish of around 14lbs. But don't ask me which species.

What a great end to a most enlightening six day research trip. I would have loved the opportunity of photographing more large peacock bass and indeed to have improved upon my 13 pounder. But everyone in our group caught at least one double which are considered 'benchmark' specimens, and I would not have missed the catfishing for anything. In the evening the lodge put on an extravagant floor show around the pool with local dancers as a finale to our experience in the Amazon jungle, and whilst enjoying the show I must have taken my eyes away from my steak dinner for a split second, because out stretched a long, furry arm and like lightning nicked the meat. It belonged to a tame woolly monkey that strolls around the grounds like he's one of the guests. But I could not take umbrage. I simply laughed my head off like everyone else.

BELOW
Fly fishing in off-river lagoons and especially beneath the overhanging jungle canopy along the margins of the river itself, produced several hard fighting species like this unusually painted butterfly bass for my boat partner Adrian Ricks from Esher in Surrey.

Thursday, 20th January

Blustery westerly wind accompanied by persistent rain all day.
Heavily overcast but mild.

Yes, following the lovely warmth and exotica of Brazil's Amazonas it's back to reality again and pike
fishing in Norfolk, on the River Bure in Wroxham to be precise, where friend Vic Brown has a
waterfront property comprising of two shallow, off-river lagoons and around 80 yards of river
frontage. Under more promising conditions (the river was low, without any flow and ridiculously
clear) I reckon that today I could have helped produce a few reasonable-sized pike for his two sons
Gary and Daniel, for the five foot deep, private lagoons overhung by mature willows and alders are
rarely fished and we had a good selection of dead baits in the way of lampreys and smelt. But save
for a 3lbs jack to Gary's rod at dawn and both pulling out of fair fish during the morning, we spent
the entire day including an hour or so into darkness without so much as another dropped run. How
I dislike heavily overcast conditions when attempting to catch predators.

Wednesday, 26th January

Light, bitterly cold northeasterly wind following sharp overnight frost.
Heavily overcast.

Today offered perhaps not the best weather for sitting out in an open boat, but then as I had promised Keith Lambert and Simon Clarke of the Catfish Conservation Group a session after pike on Oulton Broad near Lowestoft, I spent yesterday preparing tackle and getting my 14 foot aluminium boat ready. I was hoping that their two hour drive up from Hertfordshire to be at my Norfolk home for 6.30 a.m. this morning would indeed prove worthwhile.

Two hours later we were exploring Oulton Broad with the aid of my fish/depth finder, looking to mark down some heavy concentrations of baitfish shoals through the middle section where the depth varies (depending upon the tide) between seven and eight feet. Fortunately, some dense shoals of roach (and possibly skimmer bream) showed up on the display screen, as was the case during my previous trip on the Broad back in December last year with renowned wildlife photographer Hugh Miles and Martin Bowler, spent putting together some material for their proposed new TV series which has the working title of *Catching the Impossible.* And on that particular session we literally did pull the bunny out of the hat, when a beautiful, big 27½lbs pike gobbled up my lamprey-head static dead bait in the late afternoon, providing some spectacular video footage for the series.

Despite the inclement weather, I was kind of keeping my fingers crossed for Keith and Simon, so we motored upwind to the furthest extremity of the baitfish concentrations and put the mud weights down. This enabled us to reposition several times during the day, grid-searching style, simply by lifting the weights and drifting down with the wind to a virgin area without using the motor, my preferred tactics for fishing the Broads incidentally.

Using three rods apiece we soon had a selection of lamprey and smelt dead baits presented static all around the boat between 20 and 40 yards out, so Simon and I sat back in expectant mood while Keith put a pan full of sausages onto the gas stove.

Now I would like to report that something really special put in an appearance, but it was not to be. Although from a total of ten 'pick-ups' which came steadily throughout the day as we worked our way downwind, we did account for six, thick-set, nicely marked pike to around 19lbs, three of them doubles. I have used the royal 'we' here, because in point of fact Keith and

BELOW
No wonder buddy Simon Clarke has the smiles. He put six Oulton Broad pike to 19lbs in the boat, while Keith Lambert and I sat there blanking.

I both blanked after each, inexplicably, having two fish apiece come off, while Simon hit and landed all six of his runs. But to be fair, he did not rub salt into the wounds. That's probably because he's relying on my producing a prolific stretch of the River Wensum for tomorrow's chubbing session. A most productive day nonetheless taking into account the cold conditions, made complete on our return to the house by my wife Jo (she's a wonderful cook) who had gone to all the trouble of preparing a huge Indian meal to warm us up including beef Dansak, prawn Jalfresi, chicken Korma, plus some samosas and Peshwari naans etc., etc.

Thursday, 27th January

Blustery and biting northeasterly wind accompanied by intermittent rain.

I have to admit it, were Keith and Simon not due round at the house at dawn this morning, there is no way I would have bothered going chubbing in such appalling conditions. I guess I've been spoilt over the years by having the lovely River Wensum literally within walking distance of home, and so tend to 'pick' my sessions when conditions are ideal. Today the river was low and running fast, too clear by far (the bottom could be clearly seen through three feet of water) and so I rather expected a 'scratchy' session at best, even with the usually free-biting chub.

With next to no roach nor dace left in the river, compliments of cormorants, and the inability of those remaining to reproduce in sufficient numbers due to an excess of farming chemicals continually leeching into the river, resulting in blanket weed covering most of the 'once' clean gravel and sandy runs for much of the year, chub are now the river's major and dominant species, which of course is fine if you only ever want to catch chub, especially in these present, chilly conditions. But I would swap it all, including the fact that the river's chub, barbel and bream are now being caught at considerably larger weights, for a return to like it was in the 1970s when I could set off for a day's trotting and expect to catch numbers of specimen-sized roach and dace. Ah, if only!

After squeezing out a couple of bags of stale bread mash in the kitchen sink to use for our loose feed, and loading their 'roving' gear of just quiver tip rod, landing net and a chair apiece to join mine in the back of the estate, I drove Keith and Simon to a narrow and winding, but decidedly 'open' stretch of the river a couple of miles downstream from the house which is usually chub-friendly regardless of weather severity. And it was a good shout, although in the first three swims we tried, Simon fishing on his own while Keith and I shared the same run, we couldn't buy a bite on the favourite tipple of Wensum chub, quiver tip ledgered bread flake. A thumbnail-sized lump covering a size 10 hook.

I was even beginning to believe my worst fears, first suspected last summer, of there being far fewer chub about due to otter predation. Next to cormorants, otters are fast becoming a devastating problem along certain localised parts of the river, thanks to faceless do-gooders. But then Simon accounted for three nice chub of between 3 and 4lbs in quick succession from the same run, while Keith and I picked up a fish here and another there, as we slowly made our way downriver from swim to swim, leapfrogging Simon and then he us, to cover the river systematically. All put a good bend in our rods and tested our 6lbs reel lines to the full in the fast current. Keith even caught a personal best in the form of a beautifully conditioned chub of 5lbs 2oz, our best of the day. I was most pleased to see that he was still effectively using one of my early prototype rods, made over 25 years ago during my tackle shop days, and the forerunner to my 'twin-tip' Avon quiver tip rod marketed by Masterline International Ltd. for whom I have designed tackle during the past two decades. And this particular rod has been the best selling rod in the country, throughout the same period.

Bites throughout the day were noticeably spasmodic, and when the next fish I landed looked in a sorry state with its pelvic and anal fins almost bitten off and deep tooth marks along

its tail root, my original suspicions had been confirmed. In fact I'm sad to report that of the 14 chub we accounted for before calling it a day as dusk fell, (a good haul on a difficult day) no less than six had been mauled by otters, a percentage too high by far.

As I have witnessed on my own two-lake fishery, some of the fish grabbed by otters are simply 'played with' until they escape, whereupon they will recover through new fin growth and the bites scarring over. Those badly mutilated which manage to escape however, usually sink to the bottom and die slowly, where they 'gas up' and rise to the surface a few weeks later as 'stinkers'. And those, which are killed, partly eaten and left on the bank side, are either demolished a day later or, as is so often the case, are sniffed out by foxes and carried off that very night, a pile of scales being the only clue as to what has occurred.

LEFT
Happiness is obviously 'chub-shaped' for friends Keith Lambert (left) and Simon Clarke who usually pop up to Norfolk each winter to wander my local stretches of the River Wensum.

Tuesday, 1st February

Light northwesterly wind. Heavily overcast and mild.

As I am constantly studying weather patterns in relation to my domestic fishing, it's been pleasing to note that over the past two days the strong northwesterlies have dropped away to virtually nothing, overnight temperatures have not gone below 5°C, and a number of carp in my two-lake fishery adjacent to the house can be seen working the margins in less than two feet of water. A trip over to Buckinghamshire and the upper reaches of the Great Ouse after big perch was inevitable.

So I rang my good friend Jinx Davey who accounted for his best perch ever from the Ouse when I took him a few years back, a monster just three ounces short of 4lbs, to see if he fancied getting up early. No contest.

Having left Bungay in Suffolk at 4 a.m. Jinx was round at the house for 5 a.m. and we set off on the long drive across country, hopefully to be at the river for dawn. Some hopes! The traffic on the A14 around Cambridge and finally Milton Keynes was simply horrendous, and we arrived beside the Ouse a few miles downriver from Buckingham gone 9 a.m. Too late by far to capitalise on that often 'hot' dawn feeding spell.

It is in fact exactly, to the mile, a 250 mile round trip for me to enjoy a day's session after big perch on the upper Ouse. And so I try my best to go only when prospects are really promising. I don't even mind spending almost as many hours behind the wheel as I do actually fishing, because when the river is on form 3 and 4lbs monsters are very much on the cards, due to the extra food source they have in the way of the American signal crayfish which literally pave the bottom along these reaches of the Ouse. Back in the 1960s for instance the perch topped out at around 3½-3¾lbs along the very same parts of the river. And I am convinced that it is this extra rich food source in addition to all the small fishes which perch prey upon that has increased their potential optimum weight.

During the past few years I have notched up no less than eleven 4lbs plus perch (the largest 4lbs 8oz) plus dozens and dozens of 'threes' from this very stretch, and several 'multiple catches' of whoppers. The best being a catch of six perch weighing an ounce short of 24lbs, which included no less than four of over 4lbs. But I must admit that today, with the river low, barely moving and pathetically clear, I was not a happy bunny following such a frustratingly long drive. I could even see stones on the bottom three feet down. Not good at all. But I am also always of the opinion that the fish have got to be somewhere. It was up to us to find them.

Jinx made straight for the overhanging tree swim on the opposite bank, which produced his big fish before, while I spent a couple of hours exploring similar habitat-rich swims containing either sunken or overhanging trees or thick beds of marginal sedges and bulrushes. And like Jinx,

LEFT
Who's a happy bunny then? Well, who wouldn't be, having landed monster 'Great Ouse perch weighing 4lbs-10 ounces and 4lbs-2 ounces respectively, on successive casts? Part of my greatest perch haul ever. The humble lobworm can produce magical results.

I couldn't buy so much as a bite from any of them. The river, which is between just 30 to 40 feet across throughout these winding, upper reaches, so badly needed both flow and colour to get the perch foraging about after our quiver-tipped lobworms.

Eventually I decided to walk down to the very end of the fishery to the 'junction swim' where a fast flowing stream enters from the left-hand bank, providing that all important element of 'flow' and allowing the attractive juices of broken lobworms to permeate downriver and entice the perch into a feeding mood. At the end of the 40 yard run, which is around five foot deep, there is a huge overhanging willow directly opposite where I sat on a bed of sedges, and I started by catapulting out a couple of dozen broken lobs at varying distances down the swim. Then I positioned my two Masterline Avon quiver tip rods set low to the water on bite alarms, with clip-on bobbin indicators, pointing almost directly at the ledgered baits. I say almost, because I do like a slight 'angle' so the quiver tips take on a gentle curve, allowing me to visually identify the start of a bite, particularly drop-backs. And I much prefer the forgiving, cushioning action of quiver tip rods. More powerful ledger rods all too easily pull the hook from lightly hooked fish. A most important factor this, when targeting big perch.

The first bite came after about ten minutes and zoomed the bobbin up to the butt ring so fast I had absolutely no chance of connecting. But at least I knew that perch were present and better still, in an obliging mood. 20 minutes later one of the bobbins sailed confidently upwards as only a bite from big perch can, and my strike was met by solid, head-shaking resistance. This felt a very big fish indeed, and my heart was literally in my mouth as I pumped it slowly up the swim towards the net, praying the hook would hold. I could easily see its broad stripes, scarlet-orange fins and erect dorsal fins two feet below the surface, such was the water clarity. At the first attempt it fortunately slid straight into the net (how I dread those last minute dives) and I deposited it at the feet of Jinx who had wandered downstream to see how I was doing. "That's 5lbs John," he said with total conviction, but I wasn't so sure. It certainly was the deepest and thickest perch I'd ever caught, as was proved by the scales, which gave its weight at exactly 4lbs 10oz. A new personal best. Boy was I over the moon. Little did I know then however, that there was more, very much more to come.

Following a short photography session I recast both rods and catapulted out some more broken worms, while Jinx moved into a deep swim just 50 yards above the junction. Within 15 minutes up went one of the bobbins, and I was into a second big perch. Was it going to be one of those 'red letter' days I asked myself, as I slid the net beneath another monster, a fin-perfect beauty of 4lbs 2oz. I barely had time to ponder the outcome having slipped the fish into my 'catfish tube' to join the first, when up went the other bobbin, resulting in yet another wonderful perch of 3lbs 6oz. Incidentally, I rarely use a keepnet as such these days, much preferring the easy to transport catfish tube which has just four rings and which dries out in simply no time at all. It fits perfectly into my carryall too.

There then followed a definite 'lull' in perch activity as pike became most aggressive in the swim, and within an hour or so I accounted for no less then four of between 4 and 8lbs, plus being bitten off by another two. Now these are not by any means, as I have experienced on a number of past occasions, 'fluke' catches. These pike were specifically hunting out worms, (their gullets being crammed full of them) encouraged no doubt by my regular free baiting of broken

lobs. At least their presence in the swim was keeping the dreaded crayfish in their holes. In fact I did not get a single nibble from crayfish all day long, despite depositing on the river bed the best part of 150 lobworms.

My simple 6lbs test end rig consisted of a fixed paternoster ledger (tied using a four turn water knot) comprising of a 20 inch hook link (with a size 4 tied direct) and a ten inch shot link holding two size 3xSSGs. And my special 'perching' technique, I call 'back-ledgering', where as opposed to working progressively down the swim, I cast one rod to the very end of the run and the second to around halfway down. Then every 10-15 minutes or so, I raise the rod tips whilst cranking the reel handle a turn or two, which repositions each bait several feet back towards me. And the 'devastating' fluttering action of the worm as it lifts and free-falls down to the river bed, often brings a quick response from perch just sitting there in a non-committal mode. Rather like a cat that sits there with a mouse it has caught, daring it to move. It is a great way of 'searching' the swim with the absolute minimum of disturbance. Try it and see for yourself.

In mid-afternoon those perch, and there must have been at least a couple of dozen whoppers in the swim, if not more, started moving over the broken worms again in real earnest, resulting in my capturing still more specimens of 3lbs 2oz, 3lbs 4oz, 3lbs 4oz, 3lbs 8oz, 3lbs 10oz and 4lbs, plus bumping off on two more whoppers. It was truly mad, mad fishing and I pleaded with Jinx, who until now had not enjoyed so much as a chewed worm, to come and share my swim. This he reluctantly did for the last hour of the day and from four bites took a super perch of 3lbs 8oz. As the light faded fast I then landed the smallest fish of the day at 2lbs exactly. Dare I say, after such a plethora of monsters, it actually looked small! But as fast as it had begun, the feeding spell was over. What a truly memorable day, and my largest catch of specimen-sized stripies ever. Happily, we trudged back to my estate car in total darkness. And somehow the long drive back into deepest Norfolk didn't seem so arduous.

Thursday, 3rd February

Light westerly wind. Overcast, with the sun breaking through later.

I had been promising Nick Beardmore a pike fishing trip on Oulton Broad for ages, and asked him to be round at the house for 6 a.m. sharp. As it is a good hour's haul from the house, this resulted in us slipping in my 14 foot aluminium boat as dawn broke and putting the mud weights down at the 'town' end in around eight feet of water shortly afterwards. A perfect start to near perfect conditions with one of Nick's sardine, free lined dead baits being taken literally within 'minutes' of us getting all the baits fanned out between 30 and 60 yards around the boat. A nice fish it was too, making several powerful runs before it was under control and beside the boat ready for 'gloving' out. A superbly proportioned and spotted pike of exactly 19lbs. Nick was overjoyed.

This centre channel of the Broad where strong concentrations of baitfish shoals have shown up on the fish-finder display screen during recent trips is indeed a most prolific area as we were about to experience, with several runs coming to my rods during the next couple of hours all on lamprey heads, due I am certain to the high content of blood these fish contain, particularly in the 'head end'. And though we made just three moves throughout the day (with action at each) before finally raising the mud weights for the last time as dusk loomed over the Waveney valley, our total of no less than 12 pike from 15 runs was without doubt my best day ever on the Broad. Nick accounted for three fish including two doubles, and I, nine pike (one of them on one of Nick's 'mackreels') including seven doubles, the best going 19½lbs. I also pulled the hooks from an unseen, but what felt a very big fish indeed, when it dived beneath the boat.

A very dark horse indeed is Oulton Broad, and I certainly cannot think of when I last had seven doubles in a session.

What a great day.

Tuesday, 8th February

Sharp overnight frost with freezing fog. Hazy sunshine and southerly breeze later.

This was not exactly the weather that Nick Beardmore and I had hoped for to pike fish a secluded and shallow, 30 acre lake situated northeast of Norwich. I had in fact taken a beauty of 25lbs here way back in the 1980s and having not fished it since, was looking forward to the occasion. A little after our extremely chilly, dawn start we had a variety of free lined dead baits

including smelt, sardine, mackerel and lamprey heads fanned between 30 and 60 yards out from our position upon a boat staging (no boat available due to its annual refurbish) and so I sat back to wait after lighting the gas stove, and filling the pan with bacon and sausages, our favourite winter warmer.

Halfway through a bacon butty one of my rods was away and in came a mean looking jack of around 6lbs. Then it was Nick's turn with a zonking run that materialised into a chunky 15lbs pike which fought incredibly well, making several powerful runs and huge boils on the glass-like surface. By now we were well up for it, but save for another jack to my rod in mid-afternoon, nothing else materialised, and we reluctantly wound our baits in as dusk fell.

A disappointing day which I am sure could have been improved had the boat been available. So much of my Norfolk and Suffolk pike fishing on the Broads relies on maximum coverage, grid-searching fashion, provided by going afloat, and when attacking large waters from terra firma I inevitably feel at a disadvantage.

Wednesday, 9th February

Strong westerly wind. A mixture of cloud and intermittent sunshine. Mild.

Strangely, for me at least, yet another day's pike fishing from the bank, as Jinx Davey and I sampled a mature, 20 year old gravel pit trout fishery of around five acres close to where he lives in Bungay. And again, having caught just a couple of, albeit 'fat as butter' jacks to show for our efforts, the larger possibly weighing over 10lbs when it should have been no more than 6lbs, we suffered by not having access to a boat.

The fishery being almost 'square' with a large central, willow-clad island, surrounded by a deep trough, offered enormous potential, and has in fact produced at least one fish of over 30lbs in past years, compliments of the trout fishing syndicate who stock annually with more than

LEFT
Yes, whether boat or bank fishing for pike, I rarely leave home during the cold winter months without a cool bag and the frying pan. Trouble is, the pike know it and usually decide to suck my dead bait up from the bottom, 'just' when the sausages are browning nicely.

enough trout to go round. But due to a lack of access around much of the lake's overgrown perimeter, casting our ledgered dead baits out to search the deeper water was extremely limited. Definitely worth a second visit in the future though.

Thursday, 10th February

Overcast, gentle westerly wind and very mild.

Just couldn't resist a short, impromptu session along at a local mill pool this evening, the estate's outside thermometer saying 11°C, when I set off at 4.30 p.m. What strange, lovely weather for February, and though the River Wensum was running low and on the clear side, I felt that there was just possibly an outside chance of a barbel if I fished an hour or so into darkness. I've had them locally to close on 14lbs in recent seasons, and something bigger is always on the cards.

Unfortunately, the chub also respond to ideal conditions, and while I managed to shake the first one from my ledgered 18mm hair-rigged boilie, cast just to the side of the pool's main flush in about eight feet of water over a gravel bottom, the size 6 hook and three ounce lead bolt rig did its job on my second bite, which really thumped the rod over. The result was a surprisingly good scrap from a deep-bellied chub pushing 5lbs. I said surprisingly, because my barbel outfit consists of an 11½ foot, 1¾lbs test curve rod, and 15lbs mono on a small multiplier, my own Masterline 'six-shooter' to be exact.

I have in fact used small multipliers more and more in recent seasons for both carp and barbel inhabiting short to medium range swims, and especially for snaggy, hit and hold situations. With the line being transported directly onto the spool, as opposed to it passing at right angles around the bale arm of a fixed-spool reel, and taking into account the super smooth clutch of the multiplier, any ensuing battle is much more enjoyable. Plus the fact that you can play a big fish noticeably harder without the friction of a bale arm to worry about.

Several more thumps from chub followed as I fished for around an hour into darkness, but that slamming, rod-wrenching bite from a barbel never materialised. So I trotted off home to dinner.

Friday, 18th February

Chilly, westerly wind and overcast.

I was really looking forward to today's pike fishing. Nick Beardmore had arranged the boat on a secluded, 50 acre private broad fed by the tidal River Bure near Horning, so I picked him up en route for us to be pushing the boat out as dawn broke. This particularly shallow broad which deserved its nickname of 'The Flats' produced numbers of 20lbs plus specimens to 28½lbs back in the 1970s and '80s for my then regular boat partner, the late Doug Allen and me. In fact I caught my very first 'twenty' here, and on the same day had another. So I've good reason to love its irregular shape and marshy margins lined with alder carr, birch, tussock sedge and tall reeds, though in recent years it's fair to say that none of the Bure-fed Broads have produced the kind of numbers in big pike that they were once famous for.

RIGHT
During the coldest months there is simply nothing to beat long trotting for her ladyship the grayling amongst the clear and fast flowing currents of a southern chalk stream, as my long time friend Jinx Davey proves with this stunning specimen of 2lbs-6 ounces. His largest ever. Note the crimson in its dorsal and pelvic fins. There are none prettier than River Test grayling.

We decided to start at the western end and then spend the entire day working back down with the wind, so Nick, being a generation younger than me, got on the oars and headed the 12 foot dinghy into the wind. My mind instantly drifted back over 20 years ago to when I used to row Doug over the very same silty bottom, created like all Norfolk and Suffolk Broads as we know now, by peat diggers of the Middle Ages. I naturally pondered who would be rowing Nick over the Broad in another generation. Perhaps I'll even still be around and fishing. What a sad, silly sod I am at times.

Presenting a mixture of static, smelt, lamprey-head and mackerel dead baits on free line set-ups, we soon had all the rods fanned 360 degrees around the boat. It was time to put the stove on and fry up some square-shaped sausage-burger things purchased by Nick. And very welcome they were too.

During breakfast and that first hour (often a hot period) nothing came to our dead baits, but we were entertained by a particularly friendly heron that received one of Nick's dead baits every time he flew around the boat. The bird was well known to Nick and from a perch over 100 yards away on a willow branch it would respond to his whistling and waving of a fish overhead, just like the African fish eagles do on Lake Victoria and the River Nile itself. Absolute magic, and just one of the many, many reasons people like us love to sit out in the cold and wind waiting for a hungry pike to snuff up one of our baits.

After a good hour and just when we were thinking of repositioning, one of Nick's lines was away, but he missed on the strike. Mere seconds later, one of my multipliers screeched into action, so I knocked off the ratchet, waited for the line to fully tighten and whacked the rod back, fortunately into a goodish fish. Following a powerful tussle I steered the fish alongside the boat, and as there were no 'flying' hooks, I reached down and chinned out a lovely looking, thick-set fish of around 18lbs using a gloved hand. A great start, but no more runs were forthcoming, so we pulled up the mud weights and before searching down the full length of the Broad, decided, as the water was so clear, to work artificial lures across a huge bay at the very top of the western end. A wise move as it proved and a couple of hours of most entertaining action as jack after jack in the 4-8lbs range crashed into shallow diving plugs and five inch spoons, both at and below the surface. We literally lost count of those we hooked and released, but it must have been several apiece, the best of about 11lbs falling to Nick.

We then returned to presenting static dead baits again and worked steadily down the Broad at varying anchorages, in the hope of interesting a whopper. But although we accounted for at least a couple of fish at every move, none bettered 14lbs. We were even forced to stay later than usual when just before dusk the heavens opened to a mixture of torrential rain and sleet. The wind had now veered round and was blowing more from the north, with a decided 'bite' to it and a real promise of snow. It snowed continually all the very next day in fact.

Surprisingly, we even had runs and took three further fish during the worst of the rain, the best a 12 pounder. But the whoppers of 'The Flats' will have to wait for another time. We were more than content in landing over 20 pike in a day including six nice doubles, and happily returned to the boat dyke once the skies had cleared.

Tuesday, 22nd February

Bitter cold northeasterly wind. Intermittent snow showers and sunshine.

As sub-zero overnight temperatures and snow have been forecast all over southern England for the entire week, Jinx Davey and I booked a couple of overnights at our favourite hostelry in Stockbridge beside the clear flowing River Test, and made the 200 mile drive down to

LEFT
Centre pin reel, bait pouch, wide topped float that can be seen 50 yards downstream, and a chain of bulk shots 14-15 inches above the hook. These are some of the prerequisites for enjoying hard fighting grayling coming to the net. Jinx accounts for another 2lbs plus beauty.

Hampshire from Norfolk yesterday afternoon to avoid the subsequent chaos on the roads. In these weather conditions there is but one species worth targeting, 'her ladyship the grayling', which is always willing not only to feed, but to pull the float under boldly regardless of water temperature. In fact next to long trotting for big roach, now almost a non-event in my local Norfolk rivers even when the conditions turn mild, thanks to cormorant predation, a day's wandering the diminutive and delightful upper reaches of the River Test comes a very close second on my list of favourite running water techniques. And I endeavour to enjoy at least a couple of trips down south every winter.

I mentioned at the start of this book how 'The Conifers' lake in Norfolk had not changed one iota during the 30 years I had been pike fishing it. Well, these narrow and winding upper beats of the Test and its numerous side streams fall into the very same category, in that for the many years I have been making winter pilgrimages here, the grayling fishing has not altered either in quality or in the physical beauty of the surrounding water meadows. Due to experienced 'keepering' by men who love the valley and have spent much of their working life on the river, it always feels as though I am going back in time to when my old buddy the late Trevor Housby first introduced me to 'Terry the river keeper' back in the autumn of 1980.

I can remember Trevor's words as though it were yesterday. "I bet you're hating this Wilson," he would chortle from the next swim either up or downstream from where I was filling my boots with the most marvellous long trotting I'd ever known, taking jumbo-sized grayling to almost 2lbs, and barely a fish under the pound. And I found myself whispering the very same words into Jinx's ears this morning when I crept up on him slipping the net below a beauty pushing 2lbs that he'd hooked from a deep gully on an acute bend. As usual, double maggot on a size 14 hook tied direct to a 3lbs test reel line was the successful bait, although I have winkled a few specimens out over the years on orange-coloured sweet corn (which they could mistake for salmon eggs), bee grubs, and small red worms. But as our chosen beat covering around four miles of streams, main river and carriers is not regularly fished for grayling, they have little reason to become suspicious of maggots. And for an entire day's wandering from swim to swim, two pints emptied into bait pouch secured around the waist is usually enough. There is nothing worse than continually prising the lid from a bait box with freezing cold fingers.

Our usual plan of attack is to study all the grayling-holding swims (I wear yellow Polaroid glasses to this end) whilst walking upriver to the very top of the fishery, and then to leapfrog back downstream again, each searching different runs, but keeping in sight of each other to take pics when required. I tried in fact whilst walking upriver, to capture the comic actions of a roe deer doing its best to pretend it wasn't there amongst some tall tussock sedges on the opposite bank, not 30 yards away, but before I could frame up it shot off.

I really enjoy the challenge of working a short and chunky 'chubber' float carrying 3 swan shot (split up into a chain of six AA shot 14 inches above the hook with a no. 4 in between) down as many as maybe 40 or 50 different swims during the course of the day. Naturally, continually altering depth and ascertaining whether the bigger grayling 'on the day' want the bait running through or held gently back is truly both fascinating and extremely rewarding long trotting. Whilst the deeper runs around acute bends may shelve to four feet and be just a few yards in length, some of the long and shallow straights of half the depth could be over 50 yards and even longer. It simply depends on how far your eyesight can identify the float tip. Reason enough for using a 'wide-topped' chubber float.

Due to an overall lack of water this winter the river was the lowest I have ever seen it resulting in some good concentrations of fish occupying all the 'choice' swims between shallows,

RIGHT
I just love winter fly fishing down in Hampshire at famous Dever Springs day ticket trout fishery. Why? Because sizeable, triploid, rainbow trout, particularly during the colder months, are arguably, the most exciting and exhilarating to catch of all our British fresh water fish. After all, they originated from the cold waters of North America.

along of course with numbers of hefty, beautifully spotted brown trout in the 3-7lbs bracket, which don't half disturb the swim when you hook into them. The fishery is after all first and foremost, an exclusive, chalk stream brown trout haven, which just happens also to breed a few dace and roach, pike, and strong numbers of big grayling due to sheer water quality, and while I personally rate the grayling a better fighter pound for pound than trout, these big spotties are most reverently unhooked in the water, so they come to no harm.

From the deep run between an island at the very top of the beat I saw Jinx first bang into an enormous brownie the size of a salmon which became airborne twice before the hook came out, and on the very next cast he struck into his largest grayling ever. A real beauty of 2lbs 6oz, it lead him a merry song and dance before he was forced to follow it downstream below the swim to net it, or risk the hook pulling, such is the current speed of this wonderful river. Like all chalk stream grayling, the scarlet edging to the huge dorsal fin as it cut through the surface film, added a lovely splash of colour. It's what I instinctively look for (to distinguish between grayling and trout of identical size) when a fish hooked way downstream surfaces for the first time.

How many grayling we accounted for between us, during a strange weather pattern of snow showers and bright sunshine, it's difficult to say. A conservative estimate would I guess be around 30 to 40 fish each, and the vast majority of these were between 1¼ and 1¾lbs, including a number pushing 2lbs. My best weighed exactly 2lbs 2oz, and I was particularly pleased having taken them all on my new 13½ foot Masterline Signature System Trotter, which incorporates an 18 inch extension section, thus reducing overall length when required, to just 12 foot for trotting smaller streams. I tried the first prototype last autumn and following a little re-spacing of the standoff rings immediately above the handle (to accommodate centre pin, closed face and fixed spool reel enthusiasts) and shortening the handle, it is now lovely to use. Like all the rods I design for Masterline I really put this 'trotting special' through vigorous punishment, purposefully striking into grayling at (actually paced) up to 60 yards downstream. With modern carbon fibre rods it really is possible to create a decidedly 'crisp action' which is also 'forgiving' for maximum enjoyment of the fight.

What a fabulous day's trotting, made even more comfortable by the warmth of the pub and a bottle of easy drinking red put away whilst sharing our stories as dusk quickly engulfed Stockbridge and the Test Valley. The blustery snow showers could settle for all we cared.

Wednesday, 23rd February

Clear skies and a bitter cold northeasterly wind.

After spending most of yesterday trying purposefully NOT to catch trout, the trotting tackle was put away and replaced by ten foot, 6-weight fly rods. Our destination, following a hearty breakfast, was the fabulous Dever Springs, two-lake Trout Fishery in nearby Barton Stacey just off the 303 Andover road, (only a ten minute drive from Stockbridge) which, because only triploid trout are stocked, remains open all year through. How I wish more fishery owners adopted the 'triploid' syndrome, whereby because these silver-bodied trout come from heat-treated eggs and are 'sexless', they simply pack on fighting weight instead of developing either male or female tendencies which would put them into spawning condition and out of season at this time of the year. OK, so I accept that perhaps not everybody wants to be stripping in a fly

line between wet, freezing cold fingers, but as both brown and rainbow trout are more at home in cold water, I think they even fight more doggedly and for longer as a result, and I really look forward to some 'winter action'.

A new development at Dever Springs has added even more spice to the chance of hooking into a double figure rainbow, maybe a 20lbs specimen even, (something that is always on the cards here) in the shape of Atlantic salmon. These are now regularly stocked, and have recently been taken to over 20lbs. Fishery manager Neal informed me that introducing much larger salmon still is planned for the future. Quite what fly I would select to tempt an Atlantic salmon inhabiting a chalk stream-fed stillwater however, I'm not exactly sure, but it will be fun working it all out.

I've had some great sport at Dever over the years, using its incredibly clear water to shoot two of my *Go Fishing* TV series and several videos. I've caught some big fish too, including a rainbow of 15lbs 10oz, a blue rainbow of 11lbs 12oz and a brown trout, also weighing 11lbs 12oz. And I particularly enjoy stalking and sight casting to individual specimens during the warmer months.

Winter fishing differs in that most fish cannot be seen, despite the clear water. They tend to keep further out I think, and deeper down, but are of course responsive to the very same patterns of weighted, imitative nymphs that are effective throughout the warmer months. As Jinx and I really only had about three hours' fishing before heading back to Norfolk (I wanted to be on the road by 1 p.m. to avoid the dreaded rush hour of the M25) we decided to put our faith in lead-headed Fritz lures in hot orange, presented on 16 foot, 6lbs test leaders and to concentrate on the larger of the two lakes where there was a nice ripple, Jinx using a slow sinking line and I, a floating line.

Orange produced not the slightest interest, but on changing over to the same pattern in black, I banged into a rainbow of around 7lbs on my first cast. And didn't it fight hard, making run after run for the best part of ten minutes. Lovely stuff. My mind however was all about what I would do should I hook into a sizeable salmon. Unfortunately the situation did not arise, and we both had to settle for three nice rainbows apiece (all on black lead heads) weighing between 6 and 8lbs when our self-imposed time limit ran out, Jinx enjoying significantly more missed pulls on his sinking line which got the fly down deeper. A short, but interesting session.

Monday, 28th February

Bitter cold westerly wind. Early sunshine then overcast.

Following some heavy overnight snow flurries leaving a crisp, white topping on my two already frozen over lakes, today was far from ideal to go even chub fishing. But as my old friend and chub fanatic Bruce Vaughan was coming over to Norfolk anyway to discuss some new products (he is marketing manager for Masterline International Ltd.) we decided to venture out along the nearby River Wensum, our only concession to the appalling conditions being a rather late start at 9 a.m.

With the river bombing through, though actually starting to clear a little after all the snow melt of the previous week, we settled for a quiver-tipped ledgered bread flake, 'static bait' approach in conjunction with mash bread loose feed, and spent the first hour at a local mill pool. The flow was deceptively turbulent however and without so much as a knock, we moved a few miles downriver where a series of double s-bends provide slower water on the inside. It was still far from being easy chub fishing however and bites were hard to come by. Fish seemed loath to move upstream following the particles of mashed bread, as they usually do, so it was a case of casting further and further downstream (as far as I could throw 3x3SSG shots) until we literally banged a chub on the head, because when a bite did materialise, it came quickly after casting and really yanked the tip round. Not gentle half-inch pulls that we would have expected in freezing snow water.

Taken aback by its speed, I missed my first bite, but connected with the second, resulting in a modest fish of around 3lbs, but then I'm a firm believer in any fish being a good one when the chips are down.

With no further bites I moved swims and banged into a nice chub pushing 5lbs, literally within minutes of casting, but again, nothing to follow. Had I been on my own I would have called it a day there and then, such was the severity of wind chill. Being blessed with mile upon mile of superb chub fishing along my local reaches of the Upper Wensum I usually tend only to go in ideal conditions, not when it becomes painful, though I rather suspected that Bruce, who until early afternoon had not seen his quiver tip so much as 'twitch' wanted to see it out.

With two hours of daylight remaining and the temperature now little above freezing we drove to the bottom end of the fishery where lo and behold Bruce whacked into a good fish beneath an overhanging alder on his first cast. I was now seriously starting to contemplate a large glass of red back at the house, but alas, the quiver tip rod sprang back straight after only a few moments, as the hook pulled out. The look on Bruce's tortured face was priceless.

Having suffered a chronic chest infection for the last few days, (I'm still wheezing as I type this), Wilson was by now sitting in the car with the engine on and the heater turned up. I just knew Bruce wouldn't leave the river till he'd nobbled a chub, which I'm glad to say came at the very next swim beneath a line of overhanging alders. After missing a couple of bites the hook finally went in and out came a chub of around 1½lbs. To Bruce, it was as valuable in such conditions as a 6 pounder.

Friday, 4th March

Cold northwesterly wind with heavy snow showers.

We must be gluttons for punishment. At least those were my thoughts as Nick Beardmore and I drove towards Wroxham for a day's pike fishing with heavy snow starting to settle at just 7 a.m. We feared our destination, a series of shallow bays just off the main river, might be frozen over, and indeed it was. So much for global warming and the beginning of spring, and despite the odd daffodil out in the garden. These last two weeks of the river fishing season are usually noticeably milder, and a period I always very much look forward to, but right now Norfolk is more like Siberia with snow blizzards occurring every single day. In fact this must be the heaviest, most prolonged snow we have experienced for well over a decade, and I cannot say I am enjoying this 'delayed' winter one iota.

I turned the estate car around beside the River Bure in Wroxham and headed straight back to my beloved Wensum Valley and the house for a coffee and complete change of tackle. We swapped pike rods for quiver tip outfits and after watching the comical antics of a family of long tailed tits, a greater spotted woodpecker, two moorhens and two robins at the bird table outside the sun lounge window, (all after black sunflower seeds and peanuts) we took a bag of freshly made bread mash and a new white loaf, along to one of my favourite 'backend' swims immediately below a local River Wensum mill pool. I was determined that today would not be wasted.

What with having to drop Nick off at his house first and then waiting for him to return, by the time we moved into the head of a long, even paced, five foot deep run and introduced several 'golf balls' of mash, the time was gone 10 a.m. and the snow was still falling heavily. The river however was in fine trim and though quite fast, was not as yet, thickly coloured, with a visibility of around 18 inches. Ideal conditions really. Thank heavens for chub.

Sitting literally 'side by side' sharing the same loaf as well as the same swim, with the river running right to left, to cover a 40 yard long glide (and being the guest, I gave Nick the downstream slot) we plonked in our fresh bread flake offerings on size 10 hooks, just several yards downstream fairly close in and only a couple of yards apart, held static to the gravel bottom with 3x3SSG shots on the fixed paternoster links – my standard 'Wensum' cold water tactics. And boy, was I surprised when we both had bites, literally within minutes of casting.

Now being an out and out piking fanatic, Nick has over the years done very little chub fishing, and he admitted that the last time he quiver tipped was over 20 years ago, ironically, when I also took him along the Wensum, his previous best from those times weighing 3lbs 6oz. So naturally he was over the moon, following a great scrap, that his first fish today went 4½lbs. I missed my first bite, but connected with the next, resulting in a really deep-bellied beauty of

5lbs 2oz. It seemed that luckily, we had turned a bum day into something pleasurable after all, because on every single cast there was some kind of bite registration on our quiver tips. But many we missed, which was strange, and I should have perhaps seen the penny drop sooner, before Nick hit into a superbly proportioned roach that fought well in the strong flow and tipped the scales at an ounce short of 2lbs. Also a personal best.

Well, with most of the river suffering from a lack of roach due to cormorant predation and today being one of the coldest days of the entire winter, the last thing I expected was an isolated shoal of quality roach mingled in with the chub, but that's what we had occupying our swim nonetheless. A rarity indeed and no wonder we were missing so many presumed 'chub' bites. Apart from Nick foul hooking another big roach up the 'jacksy' which slipped the hook, we failed to put another on the score sheet, but continued getting frustratingly difficult to hit bites in between obvious 'chub' pull-rounds. It was fabulous fishing in such appalling conditions however. We even had a cheeky little robin turn up and hop from rod to rod whilst studying our loaf of bread before jumping to the ground to feed upon the crumbs. We also saw a grey wagtail. Having just flown over from Africa to breed here, like us, I bet it was surprised by the unspring-like weather.

We called it a day as the temperature started to drop rapidly and dusk loomed over the river having accounted for a dozen or so chub, with four of them just over or just under the 5lbs mark. We certainly could not have wished for a more fruitful 'replacement' venue, but I hope temperatures improve during this last, precious week of the season. I want more than another crack at those roach.

Tuesday, 8th March

Heavily overcast. Cold and blustery northerly wind accompanied by persistent rain.

I was sitting in the same swim fished by Nick and me last Friday as dawn broke at 6 a.m. this morning. Unfortunately the rain had washed all of the remaining snow into the river and it was a good foot higher in addition to being more coloured and noticeably faster. Mashed bread loose feed soon instigated bites however, to my usual offering of fresh white bread flake covering a size 10 hook and after missing a couple of 'clangers' I connected with what felt like a really hefty chub which zoomed off downstream screaming 6lbs line from the slipping clutch. Within a couple of minutes I had managed to slowly work it upstream to opposite where I sat and slipped the net out over the matt of marginal sedges in readiness, impatient to see its size. Then it shot straight towards me and buried the terminal gear amongst the subsurface entanglement of watercress and sedge roots. Sadly I eventually had to pull for a break, but I rather suspected that big chub (as they are past masters at doing) had left my hook in the snags anyway, before dashing back to tell his mates. Not the best of starts.

I then, just like the other day, missed more bites than I should have, before connecting with what initially felt like a big roach, but the fight was not 'dogged' enough and I subsequently netted a bream of around 3lbs which still gave a good account of itself in the fast flow. More finicky bites materialised and before long I realised that the majority were in fact from the dreaded signal crayfish, which over a decade ago unfortunately found their way into the Wensum from adjacent trout fisheries, having been stocked by the owners as a secondary crop.

Now when big bream, chub and perch (as on the Upper Great Ouse) are feeding aggressively the crayfish keep well out of the way, as indeed they did when I made that big catch of specimen perch a few weeks back, but this morning both the roach and chub became finicky early on, allowing the crayfish to become active in the swim, and of course by the time a roach has made up its mind to approach the ledgered bait, the crays have picked it to bits. So I packed up in mid-morning feeling not just a little frustrated, with nothing to follow the bream, and decidedly cold due to the rain and wind-chill factor.

RIGHT
I caught this superb 6¼lbs chub on quiver-tipped bread flake, during a short, impromptu session in the late afternoon from a favourite swim along the River Wensum close to home, after a powerful scrap lasting several minutes in the fast current.

Wednesday, 9th March

Overcast with a gentle westerly breeze.

Due to the day turning quite mild, at around 4 p.m. this afternoon I decided to terminate working on rebuilding swims around my two-lake fishery (there is always something to do) and return to the same swim of my previous two visits to see if I could winkle out a big roach by fishing on into darkness. In my 1976 *A Specimen Fishing Year* diary book, numbers of 2lbs plus roach featured in my catches from the Wensum whenever winter weather turned mild and the river ran coloured, but nowadays those rare roach that are left are greatly outnumbered and need to beat specimen-sized chub to quiver-tipped bread flake.

After loose feeding a couple of handfuls of mashed bread into the head of the swim I followed in with the hook bait, and literally within seconds of it settling on the river bed five

yards downstream, around clanged the tip to the tune of a 4lbs plus chub. It fought well in the fast flow too, though being able to easily see it shaking its head two feet down, I feared that the river had cleared too much for roach during daylight hours.

I missed the next bite but then connected with something sizeable, which fair sizzled line from the reel in a long, unstoppable run. Obviously a big chub, which by the feel of it was of similar stamp to the one I lost during my previous session, so I carefully and unhurriedly pumped it back upriver to where I sat. A couple more heavy chugs around the swim and up to the surface came the huge, open mouth of an exceptionally long chub, which fortunately slipped into my net instead of into the marginal growth entanglement. I unscrewed the net and hoisted it straight onto the scales. What a beauty. It weighed exactly 6lbs 4oz, after deducting the net, and came close to my best ever from the river of three ounces heavier.

I would now like to report that as darkness came so did the roach and that my first bite produced a whopper over 2lbs, but I would be lying. Actually, my only bite into darkness did produce a fish of around 2lbs, but it was another chub. Then I went home to dinner a happy bunny.

Thursday, 10th March

Overcast with a gentle westerly breeze. Mild.

As temperatures had not dropped below 3°C for three consecutive nights, I could not resist the temptation of making the long 250 mile round trip over to Buckinghamshire from my Norfolk home and the perch-rich upper reaches of the Great Ouse. So I set the alarm for 4 a.m. and headed for the same stretch of river that produced the catch of nine big perch between 2 and 4lbs 10oz for me on February 1st during a similarly mild spell. Unfortunately, upon my arrival the Ouse was noticeably lower than when I last fished and barely flowing. It was also painfully clear. Peering over two different road bridges at each end of the fishery, the bottom could be clearly seen through a depth of over five feet. Worse still, several other anglers were already fishing the area I had intended to. I had two choices: find another stretch with the reality that in such pathetically clear conditions I would no doubt sit there all day hoping for the odd bite or two as dusk fell, or, I could get straight back in the estate and drive back to the Wensum for some chubbing fun.

Yes, by 11 a.m. I had returned to the house (my wife Jo thought I was mad driving all that way for nothing) and swapped the huge box of lovingly looked-after lobworms, all 150 of them, for a bucket of mashed bread and a new loaf, and added my 13½ foot trotting rod to the quiver tip rod already in the motor. I decided to visit a stretch a few miles downriver from the house where the farmer had invited me to fish, but as yet I had not, now being a perfect time to sample this 'rarely fished' winding and quite shallow beat of the Wensum, which averages around four feet deep and runs fast between flat lying banks.

For a change and a bit of fun, I decided to quiver tip bread flake for a 'timed' 15 minutes in each swim, before long trotting, also for 15 minutes, to see which proved the most effective technique in these mild conditions. So I walked upstream for about three quarters of a mile to the top of the fishery and introduced, with the river running right to left, some mashed bread into a long glide immediately below an acute bend. I always enjoy wandering

RIGHT

Another 'Broadland twenty' for buddy Nick Beardmore, caught on float-fished static dead bait from a tiny, overgrown and ridiculously shallow off-river lagoon in Wroxham.

say, and just like the finish of the river fishing season, all good things must come to an end, because somehow, Nick managed to turn the engine off and the river at Wroxham suddenly became noisy with silence. What a day.

Friday, 18th March

Light westerly wind accompanied by a mixture of sunshine and cloud.

I dipped the rod tip at the end of the retrieve and lifted smoothly into the back cast. At that precise moment a huge bow wave suddenly appeared behind my black Fritz lead head. But I was too far into the cast to do anything about it, and watched helplessly and in total, gobsmacked awe, my casting arm stuck high up in the air with nowhere to go as a huge, incredibly long salmon tantalisingly charged at the fly and rolled over it not ten feet out, missing it by mere inches. The salmon was so close I could see it was a beautiful, silver cock fish of around 25lbs – a veritable monster. Boy, was I as sick as the proverbial parrot. So close and yet so far.

No, I was not on the mighty Tay or Tweed in Scotland, nor was I fishing an exclusive beat of a Norwegian river. I was hidden away in deepest Essex of all places, with good friend Brian Furzer, fishing Bean Mere, a four acre, clear water lake which is part of the famous Chigboro Fisheries complex in Heybridge near Maldon. And as I am at the National Carp Show for the next two days, just along the road at the Five Lakes Hotel and Leisure complex, I thought I would kill two birds with one stone and enjoy a day's trouting before meeting my angling public.

This really is day ticket fly fishing at its very best (tel. 07702 244440 for bookings) where in addition to the regular stocking of jumbo-sized rainbow and brown trout from 6lbs upwards into high double figures, small numbers of specimen-sized Atlantic salmon have also been introduced. And to think I very nearly had one. I'm still smarting at the thought, honestly. But then I did account for three nice rainbows of between 7 and 9lbs, which put up marvellous scraps all on the black Fritz presented on a long, 8lbs test leader and floating line.

As yet the lake has not cleared to its summer clarity (it literally goes as clear as gin) so stalking individual fish and sight casting to them was unfortunately not an option. So the order of the day was long casting into what little ripple the light wind brought along (few pulls came where the surface was calm) and allowing the weighted fly to freefall down deep before commencing an erratic retrieve. At least this is what produced for me on the day.

My partner Brian did even better than I, his largest rainbow weighing exactly 12lbs, and the most superbly coloured and proportioned double I have ever photographed, with perfect fins and a huge spade-like tail. It lead him a merry song and dance all over the lake too, which shelves down to 16 feet in places, before finally coming to the net after a spectacular battle lasting several minutes. We immediately celebrated its capture over a bottle of wine and lunch in the fishery's restaurant before starting the afternoon session (to book a table tel.

and searching a completely new stretch, and derive no small amount of satisfaction when the tip yanks round to the pull of a nice chub, which in this case fought strongly in the fast flow, a thickset, scale-perfect specimen of around 4lbs.

I then fixed up the trotting rod with a 3 swan shot 'chubber' float set slightly over depth, and tied a size 10 hook direct to the 3lbs test reel line on the centre pin. Instead of 3 swan shots for bulk, I pinched on a 'chain' of AAs about 14 inches above the hook with a BB shot in-between, to keep the bread flake hook bait close to the bottom. As when grayling fishing over a gravel or sandy river bed, I find that a 'chain' of shots literally 'bends' along the bottom (like a bathtub chain) whenever depth shallows up, thus stopping the float from pulling under.

The flow was so fast (more than walking pace) I needed to gently 'thumb' the drum of the centre pin to stop it from over running as the float took the bait 'expectantly' downstream. What an absolute joy to be long trotting the river again now the weather has turned mild and chub are most likely to intercept a moving bait. I seem to spend so much of the winter waiting for a static-ledgered bait to be eventually sucked up during freezing cold conditions.

After each of three trots down I pulled the float up a couple of inches, and must have finally got the depth just right, because on the fourth run through, a good 25 yards downstream the float sunk positively and the rod came alive in my hand to the pull of a good fish which also subsequently weighed around 4lbs following a lengthy, most enjoyable scrap. A fish to each method no less. So I moved swims to a series of slow eddies immediately below an alder on my own bank and this time trotted first, hitting into a nice chub on only the second run through after first introducing a few dollops of mashed bread. Well, that was enough for me, and I packed the quiver tip rod away to continue experiencing the immense sense of satisfaction I personally achieve from long trotting. All my good intentions of trying both techniques in every swim immediately went out the window in preference for the magic of seeing that float top disappear and the ensuing battle of sizeable chub in a strong current on just a 3lbs reel line and a delicate rod.

In truth, I'm sure I would have caught just as many chub had I continued varying tactics between moving and static baits, or simply quiver tipped all afternoon in the six or seven different swims that I fished, but then I doubt I would have packed up such a contented man when the light started to fade. I even failed to remember exactly how many chub I actually caught. A conservative estimate of 14 to 15 fish between 2 and 4½lbs won't be far out though. I do know that there were five chub resting in the landing net at the last swim I fished, a lovely long glide where at least two fish came from the best part of 40 yards downstream. Now that's 'long trotting'. What jubilation to see the float top vanish and strike at such range, with that split-second delay (when it could be a fish or the bottom) before feeling that throbbing, living resistance at the other end. Other bits may well be falling off and changing colour, but as yet there isn't any problem with this old boy's eyesight.

Monday, 14th March

Gentle westerly wind. Mild and sunny.

The last day of the river fishing season is usually mild and full of promise, and today was no exception. Nick Beardmore and I decided to visit the same collection of dykes and bays just off the River Bure at Wroxham, after big pike, that was frozen over a couple of weeks back which lead to our switching locations and that unexpected bumper haul of roach and chub from the River Wensum. So I picked him up as dawn broke at 5.45 a.m. and we were in his boat chugging along the river half an hour later, armed with a huge selection of both lures and dead baits.

Using an oar apiece (Indian style) it took us some time to navigate the 12 foot dinghy through a maze of shallow overgrown dykes, but eventually found ourselves in an irregular shaped, shallow lagoon of around two acres completely surrounded by alder carr, with numbers of fallen trees around the margins. It was like somewhere that time had forgotten, and just the kind of environment where big river pike choose to group up for their eventual spawning in April.

Within 15 minutes we had a selection of static dead baits fanned out around the boat and our breakfast of bacon and chipolata sausages sizzling away in the frying pan. Suddenly Nick said, " I'm away," so I turned the cooker off while he tightened up to one of his float rigs that was motoring steadily across the lagoon towards an entanglement of fallen and partly submerged willows. Fortunately, he managed to turn the fish on the strike and it immediately swirled angrily on the surface leaving a huge patch of bubbles and tail patterns. Obviously this was a 'biggy' so I put up the net top (we rarely bother with screwing the pole on) and leant over the gunnels to scoop it up when Nick brought it alongside. The pike was so immensely thick across the shoulders with a huge belly, and it slid into the net head first at the first attempt.

Without lifting it from the water I passed the net over to an ecstatic Nick, while I put the flashgun onto my Nikon F100, and following several shots of what was a superbly coloured pike that looked as though it had never previously been caught, Nick hoisted it onto the scales.

After allowing for the net, the pike weighed 21½lbs (I thought it was bigger) but the look on my friend's face said it all. What a great start, and didn't that breakfast taste good when we got the stove going again, both of us now brimming with confidence at what the rest of the day had in store from our newly found secret location of whoppers. Unfortunately however, like all fairy tales, ours never happened, and though we searched other areas all simply 'screaming' big pike, save for a few jacks of between 4 and 7lbs on lures and wobbled dead baits, not another big female was to come our way.

The flat calm conditions and strong sunlight, which raised temperatures almost into double figures by mid-afternoon, did not exactly further our cause, and so we decided to motor back to Wroxham for an early finish, where a crowd had gathered near the bridge to watch a crane lift a huge cruiser onto a trailer from the river. Little did I know however that we would be part of the late afternoon entertainment.

As we passed the cruiser, now in mid-air, I suddenly noticed Nick turn quickly around and with both hands grab the top casing of his outboard motor. Due no doubt to vibration and the fact that he had not tightened the two G clamps down enough, the engine was in fact slipping sideways off the transom. Had he let it go, it would have sunk still whining noisily away. But Nick had no intention of seeing his engine disappear into the Bure, so he hung on grimly with both hands, unable to release a finger to press the engine's 'off' button as the propeller rose like 'Excalibur' above the surface making an unbelievable clatter. We now had the attention of everyone who forgot about the airborne cruiser to watch a helpless Nick wrestle with his outboard motor, now totally out of control and clattering sideways along the gunnels of his dinghy with the ear splitting noise of a Formula One racing car.

I became totally spellbound by the spectacle, feeling a mixture of uncontrollable laughter, acute horror and no small amount of compassion for poor Nick who appeared as though he were endeavouring to demolish the dinghy with a chainsaw. At least that's what it looked like, and believe me, I cannot help grinning ear to ear at the memory of it all as I type this. But as they

say, and just like the finish of the river fishing season, all good things must come to an end, because somehow, Nick managed to turn the engine off and the river at Wroxham suddenly became noisy with silence. What a day.

Friday, 18th March

Light westerly wind accompanied by a mixture of sunshine and cloud.

I dipped the rod tip at the end of the retrieve and lifted smoothly into the back cast. At that precise moment a huge bow wave suddenly appeared behind my black Fritz lead head. But I was too far into the cast to do anything about it, and watched helplessly and in total, gobsmacked awe, my casting arm stuck high up in the air with nowhere to go as a huge, incredibly long salmon tantalisingly charged at the fly and rolled over it not ten feet out, missing it by mere inches. The salmon was so close I could see it was a beautiful, silver cock fish of around 25lbs – a veritable monster. Boy, was I as sick as the proverbial parrot. So close and yet so far.

No, I was not on the mighty Tay or Tweed in Scotland, nor was I fishing an exclusive beat of a Norwegian river. I was hidden away in deepest Essex of all places, with good friend Brian Furzer, fishing Bean Mere, a four acre, clear water lake which is part of the famous Chigboro Fisheries complex in Heybridge near Maldon. And as I am at the National Carp Show for the next two days, just along the road at the Five Lakes Hotel and Leisure complex, I thought I would kill two birds with one stone and enjoy a day's trouting before meeting my angling public.

This really is day ticket fly fishing at its very best (tel. 07702 244440 for bookings) where in addition to the regular stocking of jumbo-sized rainbow and brown trout from 6lbs upwards into high double figures, small numbers of specimen-sized Atlantic salmon have also been introduced. And to think I very nearly had one. I'm still smarting at the thought, honestly. But then I did account for three nice rainbows of between 7 and 9lbs, which put up marvellous scraps all on the black Fritz presented on a long, 8lbs test leader and floating line.

As yet the lake has not cleared to its summer clarity (it literally goes as clear as gin) so stalking individual fish and sight casting to them was unfortunately not an option. So the order of the day was long casting into what little ripple the light wind brought along (few pulls came where the surface was calm) and allowing the weighted fly to freefall down deep before commencing an erratic retrieve. At least this is what produced for me on the day.

My partner Brian did even better than I, his largest rainbow weighing exactly 12lbs, and the most superbly coloured and proportioned double I have ever photographed, with perfect fins and a huge spade-like tail. It lead him a merry song and dance all over the lake too, which shelves down to 16 feet in places, before finally coming to the net after a spectacular battle lasting several minutes. We immediately celebrated its capture over a bottle of wine and lunch in the fishery's restaurant before starting the afternoon session (to book a table tel.

01621 853590). That's what I most like about trouting here at Chigboro, it's all very civilised. There is even a smokehouse where your catch can be traditionally prepared using English oak and apple wood.

There are in fact three other day ticket trout lakes here, the largest being Home Water which is 16 acres and can be explored from either bank or boat, plus, four coarse fishing lakes, (open all year round) three available on day tickets and one for members only, containing carp to over 30lbs, and catfish to over 50lbs, plus specimen-sized tench, bream, and some truly giant eels.

Wednesday, 30th March

A gentle, calm day with hazy sunshine.

Spent a really lovely afternoon in the company of an old friend, gamekeeper Tony Smith, who also happens to manage Grove Water day ticket trout fishery, which is part of the Rainthorpe Estate just off the A140 road a few miles south of Norwich in the River Tas Valley. Tony justifiably feels extremely proud of his efforts over the past seven years which have seen a badly neglected and totally overgrown ¾ mile beat of the diminutive River Tas restored to a sparkling and fast flowing brown trout haven, where a selection of mouth-watering pools and glides, acute bends and undercuts offer the wandering dry fly enthusiast truly magical sport. In fact we spent the first hour after lunch simply meandering the banks of the Tas looking at the birds and for fish, where due to careful tree clearance the light now penetrates the water enabling long, flowing beds of weed to flourish and provide a wealth of aquatic insect life for the resident brownies which average between 1-2lbs, plus the occasional whopper.

This is superb stalking and sight casting, whilst upstream nymphing or dry fly-fishing on a catch and release basis, ideally suited to a tiny, size 3 or 4-brook rod outfit, because in parts, this forever winding little river is actually not much wider than the length of your rod. Only five permits are issued daily (weekdays only) at a cost of £20 and this includes fishing for rainbows, with a four fish limit, in a long, irregular-shaped three acre lake adjacent to the river, which is where Tony and I decided to spend the rest of a beautiful spring afternoon, sharing my eight foot, 5 weight floating line outfit after the rainbows which are stocked on a regular basis in the 1½-3lbs bracket along with a selection of larger specimens. Several years back Tony and I made one of my *Go Fishing* television programmes here, and if I remember correctly, my biggest fish of the day was a superb 8½lbs rainbow. There are also a few sizeable brownies in the lake, so there is always a surprise in store, though not during this recent session when we simply could not get past the attentions of smaller fish.

A size 14 black, beaded-buzzer presented on a long, 3lbs test leader accounted for a couple of fish, but I expected more takes, and it was not until we stood high above the water at the lake's narrow end and were able to observe through Polaroid glasses the trout's reaction to the traditional, slow, figure of eight retrieve, that it became apparent they in fact wanted to chase. Our catch rate then immediately improved threefold, to an erratic, fast retrieve, with rainbows shooting up to just beneath the surface from nowhere at incredible speed to grab hold and provide magical battles on the light outfit. A switch from buzzers to a damsel fly nymph even upped the amount of takes, and we enjoyed consistent sport and total solitude all afternoon with rainbows to around the 2lbs mark.

Thursday, 7th April

Blustery westerly wind with the occasional squall of rain.

I did in fact have a wrecking trip booked for this particular day, out of Rye in Sussex with old friend and skipper of 38 foot *Christyann*, Brian Joslin. But the gale force winds put paid to any big cod or pollack we might have caught, so I rang Roger Standen, editor of *The Freshwater Informer*, a monthly mag dedicated to anglers in the south, to see if he could throw up a trout water that I hadn't fished, and he recommended Hazel Copse, a fascinating little fishery near the village of Rudgwick on the Surrey/West Sussex border just off the A281 Guildford Road.

Owned and created by farmer Wilf Welch over 20 years ago, this day ticket fishery opens from 7.30 a.m. till dusk all year round and consists of two irregular shaped lakes, each with central tree-covered islands and depths to 12 feet. The larger is around three acres and the smaller about an acre and a half. The most exciting feature of all, is that in addition to both brown and tiger trout to around 5lbs, plus rainbows into double figures (best ever taken weighed 26¾lbs) Wilf has virtually pioneered the stocking of stillwater Atlantic salmon for the past 20 years, and regularly introduces whoppers averaging double figures. These are English salmon, farm reared from eggs, which remain in 'silver' condition and do not darken into breeding colours as one might expect, and they fight extremely powerfully. The best caught to date being a monster of 37lbs, and I'll wager that lead its captor a merry song and dance.

Wilf encourages catch and release for which an all day ticket costs £15. But those wishing to take home their supper can buy a four fish ticket (which includes the removal of one salmon) for £28, or a two fish ticket at £18 (tel. 01403 822878 for bookings). Personally, I think the catch and release ticket represents a great day's fishing, if like me, you don't want the bother of taking trout home. And I certainly enjoyed great sport throughout the day in both lakes, using a 6-weight rod and floating line combo with a long, 6lbs test leader, catching and gently releasing over a dozen spirited rainbows to around 3lbs. Due to the cold, blustery conditions and uncomfortable bouts of rain, exact presentation was difficult, to say the least, and perhaps at some point I should have switched over to an intermediate line in order to stop the surface movement from affecting the retrieve. I do so enjoy using a floating line and long leader set-up. Try as I may however and I must have offered several dozen different flies from tiny beaded buzzers to leaded mayfly nymphs and zonkers all at various depths, I couldn't raise any interest from a salmon, although I did put my fly in front of two silver whoppers that I saw cruising round. One looked around 10 or 12lbs, the other, twice as big. How I would have dearly loved to feel the power of either on the end of my line. A lovely day out followed by a short drive to Arundel where I stayed overnight in readiness to fish for trout again.

Friday, 8th April

Blustery northwesterly wind accompanied by persistent rain.

It always seems to rain when I visit Chalk Springs Trout Fishery in Arundel, West Sussex, which is a great pity, because first spotting through Polaroid glasses, and then sight casting a leaded bug or imitative nymph to one of the monster rainbow, blue rainbow or brown trout which are regularly stocked in excess of double figures into the four blue-clear lakes, is a technique I truly adore. It's the closest thing to bone fishing we are ever going to experience in the UK, but in overcast conditions with wind and rain ruffling the surface, the stalking enthusiast is at a distinct disadvantage. You either wait, without casting, for the wind and rain to abate every so often, as it did on my recent trip, permitting sight of the fly's descent to the trout's 'holding' level, followed by its reaction when you start the retrieve, or simply concentrate your efforts at the upwind end of each lake where for a distance of just a few yards, the surface is at least unruffled and by wearing HLT yellow-lensed Polaroid glasses, sight casting can be enjoyed.

Actually, despite the horrendous conditions I managed to induce a near-double figure rainbow into inhaling a leaded shrimp on only the second cast of the morning, and for several minutes it provided a spectacularly powerful battle, repeatedly cavorting across the surface and diving deep down through water which looks around eight feet but is in fact twice the depth, before the hook inexplicably fell out. I then took a succession of much smaller rainbows, all of which suddenly appeared from nowhere (as they do) a split second before the fly was grabbed by each intended whopper I had sight-cast to.

This really was as always, fascinating fishing which due to thoughtful management and stocking by owner Jonathan Glover and manager Darren Smith, has been maintained to an extremely high standard ever since I first visited the fishery ten years back. What's more, anyone can sample this most picturesque fishery for the price of a day ticket (tel. 01903 883742).

The larger of these small-water trout often follow a particular patrol route, and once I'd spotted a massive brownie that couldn't have weighed less than 15lbs, working along a deep gully close into the bank where I could observe its movements, I decided to spend the rest of the day in an effort to catch it. It was the most perfectly proportioned and beautifully spotted big brownie I have ever seen with a huge spade-like tail. It was also incredibly cute, as anglers who decry small water trouting seem to have trouble believing. Maybe because they never need to cast with pinpoint accuracy or actually ever get to see how many times 'their' artificial is refused before they eventually hook up in larger, more coloured waters. Who knows?

Personally, I cannot get enough of sight fishing, whether I'm watching a crafty carp inspect a floating dog biscuit presented in the surface film, or whether a selected giant tarpon or permit inhabiting a shallow flat covered by tropical saltwater, is eventually going to eat my free lined crab. And I was no less enthralled by this enormous brownie, which simply turned away in disgust, long before it got within chewing distance of my sinking artificial. On three separate occasions I managed to twitch a mahogany damsel fly nymph within inches of its snout, only for it to turn away at the last second. What a fish. And it's still there.

Thursday, 14th April

Light southwesterly wind accompanied by persistent rain.

With the Met Office promising light southwesterly winds in the English Channel, and nothing above a force 3 or 4, albeit accompanied by persistent rain, I finally got to make the near 400 mile round trip from my Norfolk home down to Rye in East Sussex for a much awaited wrecking trip with my old mate and skipper of 38 foot *Christyann*, Brian Joslin, (tel. 01424 814060 for bookings). After staying overnight in Rye I met Brian and his charter of five guys at the harbour shortly after 6 a.m. the following morning, and we were soon on our way heading in the direction of France to the first of two cod and pollack-laden wrecks that Brian fancied fishing, some 25 miles offshore.

In recent years, Brian and his guests have enjoyed no small amount of success by catching both cod and pollack whilst drifting over wrecks, not on traditional pirks, but on soft-bodied synthetic shads presented on clear mono, 4-8 foot traces with a plastic boom and 4-10oz lead above. These small lures have a tantalising wiggle in their tails and can be fished by slowly winding upwards a few turns once the lead has touched bottom close to the wreck, or by slowly raising the rod tip before allowing a little more line out in order to keep touch with the seabed, which is certainly far less tiring than working heavy pirks up and down all day long. And boy, are they effective! You don't even need to strike, simply wind smoothly into the fish when the rod top bends over positively. In fact a harsh strike is just as likely to pull the hook out.

I was truly amazed how time and time again, as I went through my entire arsenal of pirks, heavily leaded twin-tails and jigs etc. with only the occasional hit to show for my efforts, although I did pull out of two real 'lumps', anglers on either side of me were consistently winding into fish and on ridiculously small Storm shads of just three and four inches long. The kind of lures, with internally leaded heads and the hook point rigged on top so they won't snag on the bottom, that I use specifically to target freshwater species like zander and perch. And yet here 180 feet down on the bottom of the English Channel, cod of between 5 and 18lbs and pollack into double figures were all showing a distinct preference, over both of the wrecks we fished which were ten miles apart, for these tiny synthetic shad imitations. Most of which incidentally are impregnated with various scents and oils.

Brian put it down largely however, to the fact that everything was presently preoccupied with feeding upon sprats, great clouds of which filled the sonar screen around the wreck,

together with massive concentrations of pouting, and so even the largest predators were conditioned to feeding upon small fish. And I'm sure he was spot on.

   It was certainly a great learning curve for yours truly who 'honestly' loves the physical exertion of working pirks over deep-water wrecks. It is in fact one of my favourite techniques, but not when it fails to produce, and I soon switched over to the tiny shads provided by my new-found friends, on account, for the first time ever, of there not being anything 'small enough' amongst my extensive lure collection.

ANOTHER FISHING YEAR

Tuesday, 19th April

Clear skies and very hot. Water temperature 79°F.

Having met my safari party of eight anglers and Christine Slater of Tailor Made Holidays who came to wish us bon voyage at Heathrow's terminal 3 yesterday lunchtime, and following an EgyptAir flight to Luxor for overnight accommodation, we all finally arrived in Aswan airport at 8 a.m. this morning, where we met up with my old friends Nabil Abd el Moete and Tim Baily of African Angler. It certainly doesn't seem that I have been experiencing the heat, the solitude and the magical fishing for the Nile perch inhabiting massive Lake Nasser for the best part of a decade. My how the years fly. But it's always great to return and escort newcomers over this 300 mile long lake (one of the world's largest) which stretches from the high dam in Aswan all the way south to the Sudan, and watch their faces as a giant perch comes crashing through the surface film, because it is here that big fish dreams can become reality. I've certainly caught more 100lbs plus freshwater fish here than anywhere else with a personal best of 150lbs. There are however two other species in the lake capable of topping 100lbs, the vundu catfish and the sementundu catfish. And it is this awesome potential which brings anglers to the mystery of the land of the pharaohs, to spend a week on a 25 foot boat in temperatures over 100°F in a unique landscape of sand and rocky mountain tops.

The IGFA world record of 230lbs came from Lake Nasser, which is in fact the River Nile flooded over what was once the Nubian Desert, but there are stories of monsters caught commercially topping 300lbs. The truth is, no one really knows just how big Nile perch can grow. What visitors can be assured of however is that every sizeable perch hooked fights deep and doggedly with at least a couple of head-shaking, tail-walking lunges during and especially at the end of the fight, which is usually, if it is going to, when the artificial lure is thrown clear. A sickening sight when you have witnessed the vast size of your perch. But that's fishing.

I always tell everyone at the start of the safari that if all goes according to plan each should at least catch one perch of 40 to 50lbs plus lesser fish and maybe the odd tiger fish in the 3-10lbs range, while someone will no doubt hit the jackpot and boat a 'buffalo', the name we

ABOVE
The largest of
'African Angler's'
four supply boats,
'Nubian Queen'
aboard which guests
use [on the top
deck] at lunchtime
and for evening
dinner as both
restaurant and bar
whilst swapping
stories of monsters
caught and lost.
May I recommend
the local, chilled
'Rose' wine? It
compliments the
tasty meals
admirably.

give to 100lbs plus specimens, due to their hump-backed appearance. And believe it or not these statistics have run true to form on every single trip that I have taken. So everyone immediately had thoughts of their largest freshwater fish ever in mind as we started the safari at Garf Hussein on the lake's western shoreline, by boarding the supply boat for lunch and heading in a southerly direction following an hour and a half's road transfer from the airport.

After some delicious local dishes and a team talk about the 'dos and don'ts' of Lake Nasser from Tim Baily while yours truly dished out a trolling and a shore casting outfit to each of our guests, plus an assortment of various plugs and rubber shads (my collection fills one suitcase) we boarded the three fishing boats (three anglers to a boat) and set off along different routes with a view to all meeting up with the supply boat again at dusk for the evening meal. A system that works particularly well, where stories of fish lost and caught are swapped over dinner while sipping chilled beer or the local white, rosé or red wines which are surprisingly good. And everyone thinks we rough it when out afloat.

So that I get to fish with and to know all our guests, the two on my boat, which is called *Bahati* and guided by my good friend Mohammed, swap over daily with another, which in turn allows them to experience fishing with different guides. But everyone returns each evening to their original boat to sleep. Sounds complicated but it works fine.

Due to much of the lake's water being used for irrigation, though more so than usual this year, the level was around 20 feet lower than when I had last fished back in November. This unfortunately meant that little shore fishing was possible (which was a pity because there is nothing like whacking into a big perch from the shore) due to vast beds of weed sprouting up around the now shallow marginal ledges. Moreover, the perch were now largely concentrated offshore around sunken islands and pinnacles and over structure such as sunken trees and bushes where the normal depth of 40 feet was literally halved. This meant a complete rethink in lure selection for trolling with shallow running plugs such as Rapala's Super Shad Rap proving the most successful artificial by far. Even with these, which run at around seven to eight feet deep using a 30lbs test mono reel line, and up to two feet deeper if using low diameter braid, we were still hitting into beds of weed with more regularity than was pleasurable. But nothing grabs hold if the lure is weeded, so continually winding in to check was imperative when the rod tip was not vibrating quite like it should.

Wednesday 20th, Thursday 21st, Friday 22nd, Saturday 23rd April

Baking hot days and clear skies with temperatures over 100°F.

Apart from Friday evening when a huge sandstorm got up accompanied by thunder and lightning, and would you believe, if only for half an hour, heavy rain, the first I have experienced here in ten years, the weather was most pleasurable. Winds from both the north and south cooled us during the heat of the day, and despite a full moon the nights were wonderfully mild, with seemingly more stars in the unbelievably clear sky than I have seen anywhere else on this planet. That's the beauty of sleeping out in the open. It allows grown men to become boys again and relive some of those primal instincts and experiences which modern day city life suppresses.

Unfortunately, by Lake Nasser standards, and perhaps it was something to do with the full moon, as many anglers believe, sport was on the slow side. We covered vast areas in the middle of the lake and marked good concentrations of perch on the fish finders, particularly around sunken bushes and trees within a depth band of between 10 and 20 feet. But only now and then did those perch want to leave their ambush points and grab hold of our lures, even when we were living dangerously and literally bumping our lures against the sunken treetops.

RIGHT

Following a powerful dogged battle lasting for over 10 minutes I finally get to see my adversary as a huge head erupts through the surface film, followed by a spectacular, head-shaking, tail-walking leap. The most nerve shattering moment experienced by all Nile perch addicts like myself. Will the fish shake out the hooks of my large plug, or will I get to witness another 100lbs plus monster safely in the boat? I am afraid this particular fish spat the lure back at me mere seconds later.

Nevertheless everybody did manage to boat perch over 40lbs, and there were getting on for 20 taken between 50 and 80lbs. My best weighed 90lbs, while Ian Law who actually came over from Zimbabwe to join the safari hit the jackpot with a buffalo of exactly 100lbs. Due to a high water temperature of close on 80°F, which no doubt raised their metabolic level dramatically, every single perch fought like stink and repeatedly jumped, providing some truly memorable battles with every single guest catching his largest freshwater fish ever. So whilst I personally would like to have seen more fish caught, there were no complaints in the difficult conditions.

One of the week's highlights was when my guide Mohammed captured a three foot long monitor lizard in an old chicken wire tilapia trap left by the local fisherman, who were in fact off the lake as they are every year at this time due to the tilapia breeding season, but didn't fancy risking a painful bite removing it so I could take a photo. Fortunately, Tim Baily who originated from Kenya and spent no small amount of time big game hunting in his youth knew how to hold the monitor, and so Mohammed was saved the embarrassment.

Sunday, 24th April

Hot and sunny with a strong northerly wind.

This was my group's last day on the lake, and we trolled en route (taking a dozen or so perch to 45lbs) all the way up to Aswan where I said goodbye to everyone prior to their taking the train to Luxor and following overnight accommodation, a six hour EgyptAir flight back to Heathrow. I

OVERLEAF
Two of the numerous delights to be experienced by fishing Lake Nasser. A simply stunning sunset and one of the regular sightings, particularly on remote islands and shorelines. A monitor lizard, most carefully displayed by Tim Baily. Not something I would recommend as these, even the small one's can inflict a nasty bite.

was met by Nabil and taken to the Basma Hotel for a day's rest before my second safari party was due to arrive on Tuesday morning. Somehow, after the heat of the lake I couldn't face lying out next to the pool all day Monday, so I stayed watching films all day in my air-conditioned room and ordered food in before having dinner with Tim Baily in the evening.

Tuesday, 26th April

Baking hot and clear skies.

BELOW
Big John Smith gets a hand from guide Mohammed to show his 70lbs plus Nile perch to my camera. Just imagine the swallowing power of its huge mouth.

I joined the second safari party at the marina, and it was great to meet up again with John Smith, Derrick Carpenter and Mark Pickering each of whom have been on my 'Tailor Made' trips for several years, to Lake Kariba and on Lake Nasser. And from our 11 a.m. start at a spot called Military Island, after motoring 20 miles down the lake on the supply boat, I immediately knew that this was going to be a more prolific safari than last week's, although the weather appeared exactly the same. Though just seven perch were taken, two were over 70lbs. What a great start, and during dinner that evening camped at New Fox Island (so named for good reason) everyone's cameras were flashing at the eight or nine wild foxes that came alongside the supply boat to feed upon scraps thrown to them.

ABOVE
Derrick 'Del-boy' Carpenter brings a modest-sized perch to the boat, hooked on the troll around a group of sunken islands. Top hot-spots on the lake for numbers of perch.

Wednesday 27th, Thursday 28th April

Baking hot with clear skies.

Trolling similar areas, and in some cases the very same spots as last week through the Lake's centre region off the western shoreline we accounted for over 40 nice perch, many of which were in the 40-60lbs weight range, and as last week all on shallow running floating divers amongst sunken islands and bushes where the perch were grouped up. For me it was nice to see everyone hooking up and experiencing hectic action with big fish.

Friday, 29th April

Baking hot sunshine and clear skies.

This was by far the most productive of my two weeks on the lake, and I wish I could tell you why, but I can't. All three boats were working a huge area of shoreline and sunken islands interspersed with sunken trees and bushes covering thousands of acres, again within that all-important 10-20 foot depth band. An area called Gazelle, and one in fact that we tried last week with just the odd perch to show for our persistence. Yet now in a single day my boat alone accounted for 29 perch, the bulk of them weighing over 35lbs, with the best, a buffalo of 110lbs falling to Dickie Lee from Dorset. He caught it, by far his biggest fish ever, while we were slowly drifting across a huge bay some 200 yards from shore using one of my JW Masterline signature System 2¾lbs test curve carp rods, and just 20lbs monofilament.

Experience has taught us over the years that once a couple or so fish have been taken trolling over a particular area, it often pays to cut the engine and cast while drifting using our 'lighter' shore outfits. Not only is it more fun than repeatedly trolling up and down, drifting invariably produces more fish and you often actually get to see the fish you hook come up and grab the lure close to the boat. A wonderful sight in the clear water.

Dave Harding boated an 80lbs beauty, while my best weighed 90lbs. What a day and what remarkable scraps those big perch put up, each and every one of them repeatedly crashing across the surface with gills flared. They really wanted our artificials badly and 'big time'.

The other two boats fishing close by accounted for 12 and 20 fish apiece which included perch to 65lbs, while Tim Baily who actually put us onto the area in the first place took ten perch including a buffalo estimated at 120lbs. Fishing alone from his 14 foot aluminium 'stealth' boat he had no means of weighing the monster, but as Tim has caught simply dozens and dozens of big perch over the years to close on 200lbs his 'guestimation' was good enough. So in all, our party accounted for no less than 71 Nile perch in a day, with an average weight approaching the 50lbs mark. It really doesn't get any better than that. Well, not often.

Saturday, 30th April

Baking hot and clear skies.

All three boats naturally tried the very same area after breakfast, but those perch do learn to avoid lures quickly, and sport was nowhere near so hectic. Within an hour the other two boats left the bay to try elsewhere leaving us to persevere using a variety of different lures. I switched over to the extra casting weight of a fire tiger sinking depth raider and hooked into a couple of buffalos, both of which managed to shake out the hooks, but I did boat another 90 pounder. George Carslake however, who lives over in Spain for most of the year put yet another buffalo

in our boat with a superbly proportioned monster of 110lbs. This he said actually scrapped better than a 120lbs catfish he caught from Spain's River Ebro. It certainly provided me with several magnificent leaps to photograph with the surface as calm as a millpond. In fact I think the wind dropping right away was partly due to our lack of fish, although we did finish the day with 13 super perch including an 80lbs beauty for Devonshire publican Nigel Heath. His biggest fish ever.

Sunday, 1st May

Baking hot and clear skies.

Our last day, as we headed north back up the lake towards Aswan, trolling all the likely looking areas en route. But Lake Nasser had decided that we had perhaps caught sufficient. We managed only five fish (including perch to 50lbs) on our boat if you count the huge vundu, which must have been all of 60lbs, that we decided to release from one of the local fisherman's long lines. As commercial fishermen were not supposed to be on the lake we felt totally justified in doing this, having seen one of the gallon-sized bottle floats bobbing about and gained no small amount of pleasure watching this, one of my all time favourite species, dive down into the mysterious depths of a truly magical lake. I have another safari in November, and I cannot wait to return.

ANOTHER FISHING YEAR

Monday, 9th May

Hot and cloudy with first southerly and then westerly winds.

What I love most about carping and catfishing in Spain's Rivers Ebro, Segre and Cinca which all converge in the sleepy town of Mequinenza, just 130 miles due west from Barcelona, is that even from my house in deepest Norfolk it is but a two hour drive to Luton airport, followed by a two hour flight and then just a two hour drive. Hell, I cannot comfortably even reach Scotland in six hours let alone be ready to fish as soon as I arrive. Yet beautifully scaled carp, which can top 50lbs and are everyday catches in the 25-35lbs bracket, plus prolific numbers of monster Wels catfish to over 200lbs await those who visit what is without question Europe's premier location for big fish.

Simon Clarke of Catfish Pro and I arrived on the Sunday evening at the Bavarian Guiding Service which is situated on the banks of the Rio Segre in Mequinenza just above the wide junction where it merges with the mighty Rio Ebro, at around 7.30 p.m. and met up with good friend and top guide Gary Allen. On our behalf Gary had been baiting up a couple of carp swims in the Rio Segre just outside the camp, using a particle mix consisting mainly of stewed maize, wheat, hempseed and chick peas, all boiled up in a massive 20 gallon pot. He certainly doesn't mess about when it comes to pre-baiting, believe me, as our results with big carp over past years have proved. When I filmed one of my *Fishing Safari* programmes here for Discovery Television a couple of years back for instance, before noon we had accounted for, amongst several lesser fish, five carp of between 29 and 29½lbs plus a 31½lbs beauty. The programme was literally sorted in half a day. In fact we probably took longer filming a pair of storks on their huge nest on top of the church in Mequinenza the following day.

As we found out at 6.30 a.m. when we boarded Gary's boat at the floating stagings just outside the camp, having slept like logs in the pine chalet accommodation, the baited swims were on the opposite side of the River Segre along the drop off where the old river bed shelves down to around 12 feet deep. There is then around 150 yards of shallows between two to five feet deep (once orchards prior to the valley being dammed and flooded) to the eastern bank. The Segre at Mequinenza must be at least a quarter of a mile wide, and our first swim marked with a single reed stem, was obviously too far out for bank fishing. Bolt-rig fishing for carp from a boat however, was very much on and is an extremely pleasurable, if somewhat unique technique, that relies largely on an elaborate method of anchoring to stop the boat from yawing,

and it works like this. After running the bows into the current several yards upstream of the desired anchorage Gary lowers a heavy weight (you do need 'heavy' mud weights for this method to work (at least 50-60lbs) and pays out some 50 feet of rope. Whereupon the stern weight is then lowered and around 25 feet of rope is paid out while around half of the bows' rope is gently recovered. This anchors the boat halfway between the two ropes, which can each be pulled as tight as both wind and current strength will permit, before securing around a cleat. For extra stability in windy conditions a third heavy weight is lowered on a short rope and tied off at around midships. And that's that.

From Gary's beamy, 18 foot boat this allowed the three of us to fish two rods apiece, rested across the gunnels, one presenting our hook baits into deep water and the other into the shallows on the opposite side of the boat with the reels' bait runner levers engaged. When a carp ran off with one of our 20mm boilies or halibut pellets hair-rigged on size 6 hooks to three ounce in-line leads, the spool simply started singing. In fact, how nice it was not to mess about with indicators nor suffer the raucous noise of bite alarms. We added small PVA bags glugged in halibut oil to our hook baits, which varied from Dynamite source boilies to Mistral halibut boilies, and glugged halibut pellets. And we had runs on them all, whether one or two on the hair.

Even with the odd snag around in the form of woodwork from trees on the bottom (previous orchards remember) a 15lbs reel line proved quite adequate and nicely matched to our 12 foot 2¾lbs test curve rods. Since my last trip I had almost forgotten how much these big-river Spanish common carp fight, repeatedly making sizzling, clutch-screaming runs despite a firm drag setting, and my first which was around the 20lbs mark, I would have put larger had I lost it. I then accounted for a 24lbs beauty, while Gary and Simon had an equal share in six fish, also with two 20s apiece. What truly spectacular carping Spain has to offer, and all stunning looking, perfectly proportioned, fully scaled common carp. The original 'wild carp' no less, and today, exactly as it was when first stocked into European rivers during the Middle Ages, after being transported across Asia. You certainly never catch any of the lop-sided, pot-bellied, hernia-job monstrosities of mirror and leather carp that weigh half as much again as they should do, with which so many of our British waters are now blighted.

By 1 p.m. we were back in the camp where we met up with Jürgen, Marcus and Peter who run the Bavarian Guiding Service, and following a light lunch and a bottle of 'El Tinto' as I call it, Simon and I enjoyed a siesta till around 6 p.m. By 6.30 p.m., having left Gary ashore to sort his boat out for tomorrow (we are going catfishing way upriver on the Ebro which is dammed in several places above Mequinenza), Simon and I took one of the camp's boats (available to all guests) and anchored up in the same swim as before. But we hadn't looked at the heavy rain clouds coming over from the west together with a freshening wind, and after bumping off a good fish apiece, I managed to boat a couple of mid doubles before torrential rain spread along the valley.

Fortunately we had packed our waterproofs, but still got wet, the rain accompanied by thunder and lightning, was that heavy. Then, with an hour of daylight remaining it suddenly stopped and I became connected with a real train of a carp and our last of the session. Again, and weighing 27lbs, had I lost it, I would have estimated it significantly larger. A great start.

Tuesday, 10th May

Hot and sunny but hazy. Moderate southerly breeze.

Again we rose as dawn broke at 6.30 a.m. and after collecting our eel live baits from a plastic retainer tied to the boat stagings, loaded them into an aerated bucket along with all our other gear in the back of Gary's jeep. Simon was particularly interested in trying out some of his Catfish Pro company's latest products on upper Ebro pussies, like Eagle Wave hooks which come

in two wire thicknesses, CatLink Kevlar trace material, available in 150 and 220lbs test, and Rig Rattles, which are snap-on plastic spheres (with an internal ball bearing) that clip over the trace ten inches above the hook. These create extra, attractive sound waves as the eel moves around.

An hour later, following a mountainous drive we slipped the boat into a most striking stretch of the upper Ebro lined with tall reeds, birch and willows, where the chattering from finches and warblers filled the air. As we made our way upriver, a lone boat in a truly wilderness environment, we saw kites and the occasional buzzard overhead with storks high in the thermals, and several flocks of colourful bee-eaters. It was a twitchers' paradise and I cursed myself that my binoculars were still on the sun lounge window at home.

This entire section of the river, being quite narrow for the Ebro and varying between just 60 to 80 yards across with swirling pools and rapid shallows frequented by egrets and herons, followed by long runs up to 30 feet in depth, was more like the Wye and most reminiscent of a game fish river. Gary assured us however, that huge numbers of catfish were present (having spread both up and downriver from Mequinenza since their introduction by German anglers back in the early 1970s) and after going several miles upstream he finally cut the engine to anchor the

boat in a mouth-watering spot at the end of a long willow-clad island where two separate currents converged producing a tempting 'filter lane' of slower water immediately below the boat. It looked a classic barbel and chub swim to me, but when Gary's huge float supporting an eel on one of Simon's Eagle Wave 4/0 hooks set just three feet deep, trotted only five yards downstream, suddenly and violently disappeared leaving a swirling tail-pattern of water fully five feet across, I was in no doubt at all.

Gary had hooked up with a nice pussy, judging by the bend in his powerful rod, literally within a couple of minutes of casting. I hadn't even put my bait on. The ensuing battle was so exciting in the fast currents with great tail-slapping lunges and powerful runs from a beautifully marked fish that was all of 90lbs. What magnificent creatures, and what indiscriminate predators Wels catfish are. In its throat was one of its smaller brethren, a fish of about 4lbs, regurgitated whole and stinking like hell.

After a photography session we continued on downstream finding that pussies were cooperative, in most of the swims we tried, to eel live baits either trotted or held back as one works a stick float. Either way those catfish would zoom up from the bottom whether the depth was 20 or just five feet, and treat us to gloriously savage takes. It was utterly fascinating long trotting and I was glad I had reduced my multiplier reel line to 50lbs braid coupled to my Voyager rod for maximum enjoyment for pussies which as yet have not reached the massive weights of fish lower down the Ebro and Segre, though Gary assured us that fish between 100-130lbs were on the cards.

In some spots, particularly the deepest holes on the bends, cats would show up on the finder but seemed reluctant to hit. On several occasions however, usually just after we had anchored over a new spot, up

ANOTHER FISHING YEAR

would come a catfish and swirl right beside the boat as if to say "hello who are you?" They are by far the most curious freshwater predators that I have ever encountered anywhere.

From a total of 12 runs we ended up boating eight catfish. I had five between 25 and 40lbs, actually taking the first three on the same eel. They are so durable compared to other baits, which is why we use them, and Simon accounted for a brace of pussies the best around 45lbs. Gary bless him, after taking the first pussy which remained the best of the day, sat back and watched us enjoy ourselves like kids in a sweet shop. We are heading upriver again in the morning to yet another catfish stretch. I can't wait.

Wednesday, 11th May

Early sun followed by heavy cloud and intermittent rain. Very humid.

Today we left Mequinenza at 6.30 a.m. again and by 9 a.m. had slipped Gary's boat into a slow, narrow piece of the river immediately below a weir where the banks, like much of the upper river, are heavily tree-lined, and the depth varying between just five and ten feet. We were in fact over an hour late getting to the river on account of Gary's jeep over heating. Upon opening the bonnet, the radiator hose was badly split three inches from the clip and oozing fluid, so we cut the pipe back four inches and refitted the clip. Hey presto, we were on our way again, which

was just as well as we were miles from nowhere with next to no chance of a service call out, even if a replacement hose had been available.

This new part of the river was so very different again from yesterday's. I think that's what I personally love most about the entire Ebro system. It is forever changing and throwing up new and entirely different challenges. Unfortunately eels were not available from the bait supplier in Mequinenza but we managed to obtain 15 small carp, which worked extremely well, producing a total of nine catfish from around 15 savage takes. Like yesterday long trotting proved most successful, although every now and again a catfish would, right out of the blue, surface literally beside the boat to say hello. But could we get them to grab our baits? Could we hell. Nevertheless, with both Gary and Simon boating beauties of around 70-80lbs and me, a 50lbs fish, with the rest going between 20 and 40lbs, we were not complaining. The fights were simply marvellous from the very second our hooks found purchase, with lots of surface churning, tail-slapping action and many a powerful run.

At midday as we were on the point of running out of live baits, I made up my quiver tip rod and ledgered two grains of sweet corn, literally just a couple of yards downstream from our boat tied up to the marginal reeds, having first scattered a handful of corn over the area, to see if I could winkle out a few baits. But what did I catch in little over 20 minutes fishing? Three commons between 9-11lbs, and beautifully proportioned fish that had obviously never before seen a baited hook. What a river the Ebro is.

As yesterday we were treated to the sights of buzzards and kites high overhead, with swallows by the hundred sipping in hatching flies from just above the surface. We saw both grey and purple herons plus a couple of cuckoos, one of which repeatedly answered to Gary's excellent renditions. By 5 p.m. however a storm started blowing up and the skies turned slate grey. We instantly decided to call it a day. A good shout as it turned out, for within seconds of loading the boat onto the trailer and setting off to Mequinenza the heavens opened up and it rained all the way back.

Thursday, 12th May

Overcast and humid with a light southerly breeze.

Simon and I rose at dawn again to find the rain gone, so we took the boat out in front of the camp for a morning's carp fishing, promising to join Gary for lunch prior to our travelling way up the fast flowing River Cinca in search of more pussies in the afternoon, but we should have enjoyed a lie-in. Those carp, probably due to the storm, were in a most strange feeding mood, not really going off aggressively with our hook baits, for we lost no less than seven fish between us, all due to the hook pulling out. I played one veritable monster for a good ten minutes before the inevitable happened. A strange session indeed, to which there seemed no logical answer. And there still doesn't.

After lunch I helped Gary load a ten foot, red plastic boat onto the trailer and complete with a dozen or so eel live baits we set off for yet another new location, with Simon following behind in our hire car, the idea being to leave our car beside the River Cinca, by far the fastest

ABOVE
Perched precariously across the stern of our 10 foot plastic boat, 'Wilson' holds a 40lbs pussy hard in the strong flow. Luvly Jubbly! What simply marvellous long trotting for three men in a boat.

flowing of all local rivers, four miles downriver from where we were to slip the boat off Gary's trailer, in order that we had means of getting back to Gary's jeep once we had finished the afternoon's fishing. And very well it worked too, producing some of the most exciting river fishing for predators that I have ever experienced.

It started at the very first swim of our downriver safari, a long and deep back eddy on the opposite bank to where we put our little boat in, and to reach it, Simon and Gary had to paddle like mad across a set of rapids. Being the elder statesman of the trip (sad old git would perhaps be more appropriate) I sat up front giving directions and ready to lower the heavy mud weight, which like most of the weights at the camp are in fact foot-long sections of old railway track, and don't they hold well in a strong flow.

As usual Gary's float was the first to go and after a short but hectic scrap in came an angry pussy of around 30lbs. I followed up with one of around 60lbs, which went even better, and seconds later Gary hit into a biggy which inhaled his eel long-trotted fully 80 yards downstream along a narrow run between beds of rununculus. Despite his powerful rod and 100lbs test braided reel line this pussy really gave him a workout, making some gut-busting runs followed by huge, tail-slapping lunges on the surface. Not exactly the size of fish most anglers

RIGHT
This 100lbs pussy landed by Gary following a monumental tussle in and out of dense weed beds and in such strong currents was actually nearly as long as our boat. His smile says it all. Long trotting for such predators amongst turbulent water is totally mind-blowing.

sharing a ten foot dinghy would relish, because it looked every bit over 100lbs, and we had some real fun heaving it over the gunnels for a photo.

This kind of fishing is so vastly different from 'catting' in the UK or pursuing the big old girls on heavy tackle using buoy, or pellet-fishing techniques back in the wide, slow reaches of the Ebro and Segre around Mequinenza – monsters that could run anywhere up to and over 200lbs. I would however always personally prefer exploring fast flowing, more intimate-sized rivers for modest-sized fish, yet Gary's guests have actually landed fish pushing 170lbs from the Cinca in these turbulent upper reaches. Those of us in the UK, who think of 30lbs carp or 15lbs barbel as being 'big' river fish, just cannot comprehend such awesome prospects. More incredible still is the fact that the Cinca is not unlike a cross between the Hampshire Avon and the Border Esk.

Deliberately crash-casting our baits into small gaps in the weed and close beside overhanging trees sometimes brought an immediate response, the float simply not surfacing after hitting the water, such was the ferocity and speed of the takes. And while we drifted and paddled our way downriver trying every likely looking run we were treated to the sights of night herons, purple herons and bee-eaters, with kites overhead. What an afternoon's fishing. A veritable paradise, if ever there was one.

My best fish came from a huge, deep eddy in the middle of the river and was about 80-90lbs. What a song and dance it lead me too, repeatedly surging off on long, powerful runs trying to find sanctuary in a line of sunken trees along the opposite bank. But eventually I managed to work it into the shallows and with a gloved hand (essential for grabbing hold of pussies less you want scraped knuckles) haul it out for a photo. I actually got through four rolls of film that afternoon.

By the time we got back to our hire car, we had accounted for ten cats, missed a couple on the strike, and felt completely knackered. And I hadn't even picked up a paddle. What a memorable afternoon's fishing.

Friday, 13th May

Warm and sunny till noon then overcast and humid, with a gentle southerly breeze.

Unlucky for some maybe, but Friday 13th provided our best carp fishing of the week, after Gary had decided to change tactics and bait up a swim, (yesterday evening) right in the middle of the River Segre along the old river bed (prior to flooding) in a depth of around 12 feet. And from our 7 a.m. start in his 18 foot boat we just could not go wrong, although bites were somewhat spasmodic the carp coming in defined bursts every hour or so, with two and sometimes three rods all going at once.

The fish showed a definite preference for glugged 20mm halibut pellets, used in conjunction with small PVA mini-pellet-packed bags, and we took a total of ten beauties, plus a 10lbs catfish to Simon's rod before we wrapped for lunch. Simon had two carp including his best common ever at 27½lbs. I took three including a scale perfect beauty weighing 32lbs, while Gary (does he know his river or what?) accounted for seven fish including an absolutely stonking specimen that looked all of 40lbs, but which in fact pulled the scales down to 36½lbs. Having taken several 40s from the river Gary was also surprised. It put up a simply marvellous fight for

over ten minutes, repeatedly making long, unstoppable runs, and it was, like the majority of our fish, in absolute mint and scale perfect condition. The epitome of what a carp should look like.

After lunch and a siesta, Jürgen took Simon and me out in his boat over to the opposite bank of the Segre for some lure fishing in shallow water in the hope of a pussy or two. In recent years many cats including specimens topping 180lbs have in fact been landed on shads, plus of course many a zander for which the area has become renowned. But apart from a carp, which I foul hooked and which gave a good account of itself for several minutes before the hook pulled, we caught nothing. Then dark clouds came over and heavy rain set in, forcing us to return to camp for a beer or two, which is where we stayed till it was time to shower for dinner. The torrential rain in fact lasted till midnight.

Saturday, 14th May

Clear blue skies. Hot, with a light westerly breeze.

By far the nicest, warmest day of the week, with not the slightest hint of haziness, the photographer's nightmare. And would you believe it, we needed to be off the river by 10 a.m. in order to pack everything up and head for Barcelona Airport. From our 6.30 a.m. start however, fishing the same swim as yesterday, Simon and I managed to bag no less than 11 beautiful commons and pull the hooks from three more, before we reluctantly lifted the weights and motored back to the stagings. The best two came to my rods and weighed 25 and 28lbs. They

LEFT
Gary slips the net under my 32 pounder. Bolt-rig ledgering for carp from an anchored boat is not only fun, but extremely effective. Being 'on' the water, allows you to get much closer to the fish. And we didn't have a tangle between the three of us all week.

were really onto the bait now, giving zonk-off runs, followed by powerful fights, as only perfectly proportioned carp can. And I think we both could have done with at least a couple more hours of action. But then paradoxically, I find that it is always best leaving a location, looking forward to returning. And we certainly did that. Viva España!

Thursday, 26th May

Light southwesterly breeze. A mixture of hazy sunshine and cloud.

I've said it before and I'll say it again. There is absolutely no way I would wish to be an east coast skipper like my good friend Stewart Smalley for instance, who runs bass and wrecking trips out of Orford in Suffolk on 25 foot *Aldeburgh Angler II*. Just recently, due to strong winds, he literally could not get out and consequently earn his living for 25 consecutive days between the 1st and 25th May. And when I rang on the evening of the 25th to ascertain whether Thursday

ANOTHER FISHING YEAR

26th was a goer, I was of course expecting the worst. But no, miraculously, the Met Office had given 4-5 southwesterlies and Stewart said we were going. What luck.

Consequently I met Stewart and friend Mark Amoss at 8.30 a.m. the following morning at Orford Quay and soon we were heading down the river watching oystercatchers and avocets sifting a living from the shallows, while the largest colony of lesser black-backed gulls in Europe was settling down to the job of rearing their young all along Orford Island. A veritable twitchers' paradise is this entire area, where hares and foxes also abound.

Two hours later, we were over Stewart's favourite set of 'rips' 20 miles offshore where the sand and coarse shingle seabed dramatically rises in sets of pinnacles from a 100 foot to between just 50 and 60 feet of water, and just over the 'lip' is where we expected to contact the hard fighting bass, as we have for the past few years. After three drifts however, our frozen sand eel baits presented on size 4/0 hooks and long, 20lbs test monofilament traces, to 30lbs test braided reel lines, bumped along the bottom with a six ounce lead, remained untouched.

I could see the concerned look on Stewart's face, but on the very next drift, over went my rod in a most positive fashion. Instinctively, I lowered the tip to give line, and then lifted positively into a good fish, which for several minutes fought with immense power. I was in fact using my Masterline pike-system 9½ foot, lure rod, and what a workout this bass was giving it, 60 feet down over the lip. Most freshwater anglers would be totally gobsmacked at the kind of pressure even a 7-8lbs bass such as this can impart on a heavy pike outfit.

Ten minutes later I could see the relief on Stewart's face as he slid the net under my bass, a beautifully proportioned predator enamelled in blue and silver. The first of a new season, hopefully heralding yet another bumper year. And if our results were anything to go by, Stewart and his guests whenever he gets out are in for some spectacular sport, because from several more drifts Mark and I connected with numbers of hard fighting bass in the 5 to 7lbs range.

As the force went out of the flood tide, we decided to spend our last hour catching a supply of fresh bait for Stewart to freeze down, and though the poisonous weaver fish came readily to our sets of feathers, so did a plethora of launce and several mackerel. In fact that very evening when I arrived home, first on the barbeque was a brace of fresh mackerel. And didn't they taste lovely, heavily peppered, with some brown bread and butter.

Tuesday, 31st May

Hazy sunshine and a gentle southerly breeze.

A round trip from my house of exactly 390 miles down to the Dever Springs day ticket Trout Fishery in Hampshire, starting out at 4 a.m. and returning at 7 p.m. does seem one hell of a long way to go for what amounted to half a day's fly fishing, but I have always felt that it's worth the effort, despite traffic on the M3, M25, M11, and the dreaded A11 (will it ever be completely duelled in my lifetime) on the way home. One reason why I always endeavour to be setting off after lunch, which in this case was a roast beef, sit down affair in the lodge for a dozen guests, provided by our host and owner of Dever Springs, my good friend Con Wilson. And very nice it was too.

Fortunately, I had fellow writer Dick Brigham to natter with throughout the journey, and we met up with Brian Furzer from Essex at the service station at Popham on the 303 Andover

LEFT
My old 'bassing' pal and top skipper Stewart Smalley shows a superb specimen to the camera, caught by Mark Amoss (right) on a sand eel bumped over the lip of a 'rip'. One of several beauties we caught off Orford in Suffolk, that day. Fish to 8lbs from depths between 60 and 90 feet really gave my pike rod a thorough testing.

road for a much-welcomed fry up, before arriving at the Fishery shortly before 8 a.m.

Instantly we could see how clear the water was, actually observing individual trout moving whilst driving beside the two lakes towards the car park. But then stalking and sight casting to individual fish and observing their reactions to your artificial is very much part of the magic at Dever Springs (tel. 01264 720592 for bookings) where the water is so crystal clear, areas that look around eight feet deep, are nearly twice the depth. From the off however and after several casts to cruising rainbows which seemed totally oblivious to our weighted nymphs, we realised that something about conditions on the day was affecting their feeding. And Brian Furzer, who wears a huge barometer-sports watch, came up with an answer immediately. Apparently, after taking several readings, barometric pressure was going up and down like a yo-yo, which accurately portrayed our subsequent success, and lack of it.

Throughout the entire morning those trout seemed to be on one minute and then decidedly off the next. Resulting in just short 'windows' of action, when they were really willing to give chase and possibly 'take' for several casts, followed by not the slightest interest being shown, no matter how many times we switched artificials. Moreover, only a few fish really hit hard and turned away with the fly, to aid hooking. So many simply came up, inhaled the nymph, and spat it out with equal speed, making a solid hook up virtually impossible. To improve the ratio of fish missed to those hooked, and both Dick and I were certainly missing our fair share, I went all suicidal and even scaled down to a 4lbs leader and tiny size 12 bug. Not really a good idea seeing as Dever is stocked with rainbows that can run anywhere between 5 and over 20lbs, plus Atlantic salmon over 20lbs.

Frankly, I don't think it had any effect anyway. It was a marked case of barometric pressure affecting whether fish feed or not, something we all suffer from, perhaps more regularly than we think. But of course we are usually not to know. Best fish of the day weighed 11lbs, whilst Dick and I returned to Norfolk with some nice rainbows to around the 8lbs mark, (and didn't they go through the clear water) decidedly more enlightened than we had started out. Brian's watch has certainly given me food for thought.

Sunday, 5th June

Heavily overcast with lashing rain and a strong westerly wind.

Not exactly the kind of conditions I'd hoped for to start my three day break on the island of Jersey in the Channel Islands. Skipper of *Theseus II*, Dave Nuth, who has been taking out charter trips here for over 20 years, picked me up from the airport on the Saturday evening following a Flybe flight of just one hour from Norwich Airport (would you believe, my first ever flight from Norwich) and deposited me at The Shakespeare Hotel on the Samares Coast Road in St. Clement, which is but a ten minute drive from the marina in St. Helier. Jennifer Ellinger of the Tourist Board had certainly done a good job. But it was a pity about the weather.

It was however, great to meet up again with Dave whom I had not seen for over ten years since I came over with Dave Lewis, Neil Mackellow, Mel Russ and others from EMAP's *Sea Angler* magazine to film two one hour videos, a boat fishing adventure called *The Sequel* and a long distance shore casting spectacular called *Mastercast*. These had proven immensely popular, and as I recall, were great fun to make. I thought then, that the fishing potential around the island of Jersey was phenomenal, and Dave Nuth (who operates one of just two sports fishing boats out from Collette Yacht Marina in St. Helier, so over fishing is hardly a problem) had assured me that things had not changed one iota. We had simply both got ten years older, that's all.

After a 'full English' and tactical discussion at the hotel, Dave drove me to the marina where I met our 'mate' for the next three days, 26 year old local enthusiast Mark André, and within minutes we were off, out of the harbour and into a very lumpy 4/5 sea brought about by a strong westerly wind accompanied by persistent rain. But we were there to do a job and produce some fish, so personal comfort went out the window immediately and on went all the foul weather gear I had brought along.

Fresh bait being the first consideration, Dave pointed *Theseus II*, which is a 38 foot Interceptor, equipped incidentally with a stern door to facilitate wheelchair anglers and the easy landing of big fish, in the direction of a 150 foot deep bank consisting of broken ground interspersed with sandy humps, to secure enough sand eels and mackerel for both today's and tomorrow's fishing. Onto our light rods (who said bait catching couldn't be fun) went sets of five Shakespeare super flash lures (in medium-size 6 hooks) plus reflective 'yans' to

get them down, and we soon started to hit into bait whilst jigging on the drift. There were good concentrations of mackerel and the occasional garfish in the upper water layers with both launce and scad, plus the odd pouting just above bottom. We also caught a pilchard, while Mark boated a sizeable pollack for good measure. And within what seemed like mere minutes, no less than five different sea birds were feeding around the boat: fulmars, herring gulls, greater black backs, shearwaters and gannets. Watching the gannets dive-bombing and plummeting down deep beneath the surface for sinking pieces of fish that we had purposefully thrown in was indeed mesmerising to watch. And people say to me how can you sit there fishing in the rain?

When we had caught our fill and with the rain still falling heavily, Dave motored to a mark situated to the west of St. Helier, where on our 12lbs test outfits using braided reel lines we set up six foot long mono traces and size 5/0 hooks below a boom and six ounce lead rigs to drift for bass over banks of shingle and sand in depths varying between 130 and 160 feet. This produced several nice bass, the best going 9½lbs, and didn't they go in the strong tide.

ABOVE
Bass, two at a time to nearly 10lbs on our first day out, certainly gave ace, Jersey skipper Dave Nuth and I something to smile about. Great fun on light tackle too, in the strong tides, deep down over banks in 130 feet of water.

Dave however was not happy about the amount of pick-ups and suggested we move further north to a favourite steeply shelving bank of shingle, in order to attract a turbot or a brill before calling it a day, which is more or less what happened. Does Dave know his local fishing or what? I was so impressed by his willingness to instantly try a new tack or new technique when things were not happening. That old adage about life in that 'you make your own luck' is so very true. Or put another way, the harder you work, the luckier you get.

Using fresh strips of both mackerel and launce we did in fact catch one modest-sized turbot and a reasonable brill on the drift plus the inevitable 'doggies'. Dogfish must literally 'pave' the seabed around the Channel Islands, and can become a real nuisance. By 6.30 p.m. and completely soaked through, we had not only caught over ten species, I had actually got through two rolls of film. So for day one it was mission accomplished and a return to harbour was in order.

RIGHT
Tope have immense
strength and are
sometimes more
difficult to control
out of the water
than in it. This 49
lbs female (my
largest ever) was
obviously unaware
she was being
returned to fight
another day.
Bless her.

Monday, 6th June

Heavily overcast with a strong westerly breeze and persistent rain.

Had an alarm call for 3.30 a.m. as Dave was picking me up from the hotel at 3.45 a.m. which he did dead on time, accompanied by a gusting westerly and lashing rain. The thought of angling for a living is not always fun, believe me, but Dave was insistent on leaving early in order to be around the other side of the island right at the top of the tide, which is when the tope are most likely to be caught. This weather is giving us a real battering. Fortunately Dave's wife Maria put my sodden gortex waterproofs into their tumble drier overnight, so at least I started the day dry.

Due to the Met Office giving a change in wind direction from westerlies to an easterly blow later in the day, Dave suggested that we take the tray of mackerel we caught yesterday (kept on ice overnight) around to his favourite tope mark about a mile off shore to the northeast of the island, before the promised easterly made fishing there impossible. And I could not agree

more. In fact that's what I most like about fishing in Jersey. Whatever the wind, there is usually a productive mark that you can snuggle into. So as dawn broke with the rain still sheeting down we headed around the island in an anticlockwise, northeasterly direction, and within an hour, at around 6 a.m. had anchored up over a boulder-strewn gully in around 140 feet of water. The weather was cold, wet, and truly abysmal.

During the first hour or so, at the very top of the flood, doggies were a real nuisance, ripping our mackerel flappers to shreds, but as the ebb came they were replaced by our target species, and a tope of around 20lbs was the first fish on board. Again, Dave knew exactly where and when.

I was using my own Masterline JW System seven foot boat rod, which comes with a separate handle and three slim and lightweight carbon tips in 12lbs, 20lbs and 30lbs line classes. I chose the 30lbs tip and a 30lbs braided reel line, which was just as well because my next run came from a big fish which headed straight down tide, ripping line speedily from the reel despite a firmly set drag. Following several minutes of heavy pumping, interspersed with powerful dives, I finally managed to bring the tope uptide and as it neared the boat it came up in the water to within a couple of feet of the surface (a great sight to witness through the clear water) and veered along our starboard side, looking a very long fish indeed. When it surfaced beside the stern Dave quickly opened the door and netted it out at the first attempt. A superb female fully five feet long and weighing exactly 49lbs. My biggest ever, (following a string of low 40 pounders over the years) and the best on Dave's boat for two seasons, so everybody was over the moon. And what a great fight it gave on my little rod.

What a result despite the incessant rain and overcast conditions, but save for another modest-sized tope of around 25lbs a little later on, there was nothing to follow, not even doggies. Soon the ebb tide was so strong, 2lbs of lead were necessary to hold bottom and so Dave suggested that we up anchor and continue heading anti-clockwise around Jersey's 9 miles long x 5 miles wide coastline to a 150 foot deep mark at the western end where we could drift for turbot and brill, Mark taking a 5lbs brill on the very first drift using mackerel strip. But it proved to be our only worthwhile catch. As everywhere else, doggies were a pain in the proverbial, so tired and sopping wet through yet again we came back to the marina having feathered up a tray full of fresh mackerel for tomorrow's planned assault over one of Dave's favourite conger marks to the southwest of the island. And 'yippee!' the weather forecast is for clear skies and sunshine.

Tuesday 7th June

Stiff easterly breeze and clear blue skies. Sunny all day.

My third and final day's fishing out of St. Helier started at 4.45 a.m. with Dave picking me up from the hotel following a heavy night out at a local restaurant (apparently there are over 200 on the island) organised by Jennifer Ellenger of Jersey Tourism, and by 6 a.m. we were anchored up over a favoured conger mark, with four rods presenting mackerel flappers in 130 feet of water over heavily broken ground which according to Dave, holds numbers of congers which hide amongst the honeycombed bottom. Not your average conger habitat, but then conger eels are unbelievably common around the Channel Islands over every type of ground imaginable. Why, nobody knows, but it's great news for eel enthusiasts.

During our first hour, which was the last of the flood, we took a few small 'strap' congers around 8-10lbs, and Mark lost what Dave thought was a large undulate ray, the hook inexplicably pulling free when the fish was only half way up. I then went and boated a surprise tope of around 25lbs, and when the tide turned and the ebb started to pull strongly, necessitating our changing from 1lb up to 2lbs of lead to hold bottom, the larger eels started to show, Mark and I catching several between 25-35lbs, all on mackerel flappers and a size 8/0 hook to a 150lbs mono trace. These provided great sport in the strong flow.

While Mark and I concentrated upon the eels, Dave put two smaller hooks down baited with small squid heads on a light outfit and instantly started getting into sizeable black bream. Beautiful, deep-bodied specimens up to the 4lbs mark which really tested his sporting outfit in

the fast flow. I could not resist a go whilst waiting for the congers and my first drop down produced a red gurnard, surely one of the most striking fish around the Channel Islands, next only to the blue and yellow painted cuckoo wrasse.

Then my conger rod lurched over and I found myself connected to what turned out to be the heaviest eel of the day, following a lengthy gut-busting session of pumping and winding, a shortish, disproportionately thick and angry conger eel of 45lbs.

At midday we moved inshore opposite the Corbiere Lighthouse and anchored up in a huge 50 foot deep eddy between two reefs, where Dave said (he forgot to mention doggies) there was every chance of a blonde or small-eyed ray. And as usual he was right with Mark catching a nice small-eyed ray of 6½lbs, plus a couple of chunky ballan wrasse.

In all, my three days' fishing around the island had produced no fewer than 18 different species, and I can't think of anywhere else I could have achieved that, especially against such temperamental weather, (which in most locations would not even have allowed us to put to sea). Can't wait to return. And thanks a bunch Dave.

Thursday, 16th June

Chilly northeasterly wind overnight, changing to southwesterly. Mixture of sun and heavy clouds.

I always look forward to the new coarse fishing season. I know that I can now legally fish in still waters during what used to be the 'old close season', between 14th March and June 16th, but I rarely do. Somehow it's just not the same. So I'm kind of glad that as yet, we still have to endure a close season to go river fishing. This saw me on the morning of the glorious 16th, as it's become known over the years, getting up at 1 a.m. and positioning myself amongst the marginal sedges of a local River Wensum mill pool. A pool I had been baiting up incidentally, with a couple of handfuls of 20mm boilies for several days, with a big barbel in mind. Trouble was no one told the barbel.

Nevertheless I sat there expectantly from 2 a.m. till 9 a.m., despite a chilly northeasterly breeze accompanied by heavy clouds, with just one chub of around 4lbs to show for my loss of beauty sleep. I did bang into a really big chub mind, which is hardly 'cricket' on barbel gear consisting of a 15lbs test reel line and a three ounce bolt rig ledger set up, but it slipped the hook anyway, though it looked the best part of 6lbs.

I put the complete lack of interest from both the barbel and large bream that also inhabit the pool, down to the current weather pattern of continual 'lows'. It was as though someone had flicked an 'off' switch. So I went home and had a large fried breakfast, before starting to arrange a huge rockery in front of the house. Having had ten tons of sandstone delivered I've more than got my work cut out for the next few weeks at least, and after a couple of hours heaving chunks of it around I decided that today was not the best time to start on account of my lack of sleep. So with my wife Jo about to go out for the day, I slipped a video into the TV and lay down on the settee with the idea of nodding off.

Two hours later I woke up sweating with bright sunshine streaming through the windows. Immediately, I could feel the weather had broken, and changed for the good. I went outside and noticed that the air was now humid and the wind had swung around to the southwest. Even better! I got straight into the estate and popped along to a local gravel pit where I had been hedging my bets for the 16th by also prebaiting a deep, marginal tench swim with 10mm pellets.

My 13 foot float rod was already rigged with 6lbs test on the centre pin reel and a light waggler float set up with a size 10 hook tied direct, and broken down with an elastic band at both ends. I was thus fishing literally within minutes, delighted to see that clusters of bubbles were erupting on the surface of the 12 foot deep gully only 20 feet out, even in the middle of the day, once I'd introduced a handful of pellets. Those tench were hungry alright.

Onto the hook went a ¾ inch section of elastic band (try it and see) and to this I super glued on two pellets. Quite literally, within a couple of minutes of the float settling, under it went, and over went the rod tip to the pulsating, dogged fight of a big tench. How I love playing large fish on a centre pin reel. Their each and every movement is felt beneath the thumb which brakes the drum as gently or as powerfully as you like. There really is no finer or more exact method of float fishing, and this tench wasn't having any. For several minutes it stayed deep down chugging away close to the bottom sending up to the surface great clumps of Canadian pondweed, and every so often making long, powerful runs of up to several yards at a time. Long before I netted it I thought this was a 'biggy' and indeed it was. A beautifully deep bellied

female of 8lbs 12oz to be exact. What a result. I popped her into a soft retaining tube several yards along the bank and noticed that a heron and a pair of oystercatchers were sharing the same overhanging willow branch about 50 yards away. What a lovely sight. But there was more to come.

My second and last bite some 20 minutes later resulted in an even larger tench. A really dark fish this one, which strangely, didn't fight for as hard or as long as the first, but weighing in at 9lbs 5oz, (my largest ever incidentally) what did I care. At an ounce over 18lbs, this was by far my best brace of tench ever, and on the float rod to boot. I had managed to make a great 'traditional' start after all.

Friday, 17th June

Warm southwesterly breeze. Very humid. A mixture of sunshine and cloud.

After losing so much sleep yesterday I didn't even bother putting the alarm on for this morning, I was that knackered. I still woke naturally at 6 a.m. however to a gloriously warm and sunny day. Looks like summer has arrived at last. Within half an hour I was sitting in the same tench swim as yesterday, thinking that I'd better make hay while the sun shines. With such big fish around, a double figure tench looks to be on the cards, and I honestly thought that my first bite had connected me with one, such was the power of this particular fish which stayed deep throughout a lengthy battle. Again it came to double pellet laid on, and again it was another whopper pulling the dial of the scales round to 8lbs 14oz. What incredible fishing, and all so immensely enjoyable on the centre pin.

I then had to wait an hour or more for the next bite despite the fact that several groups of bubbles were continually erupting in the swim. It seemed as though I should have been getting far more bites considering their feeding was so intense. But then when I netted an even larger fish of 9lbs 1oz following yet another arm-wrenching fight, I kind of sobered up. These are truly monstrous tench for the county of Norfolk.

I sat there till midday, but not another bite came my way after 8.30 a.m. and I went back to the house an incredibly happy bunny.

Saturday, 18th June

Warm southwesterly breeze. Cloudy and very humid.

There is no surprise in guessing where I was sitting at 5 a.m. this morning, but though the same swim was erupting with feeding bubbles, those tench were decidedly finicky. Could they have become suspicious with my catching just four of their brethren?

I think they had, and not until I scaled down from a 10 to a size 12 hook with a single pellet super glued to the hook shank, did I encourage a couple of bites. And again I accounted for two tench, though I can hardly count the first, which was a feisty male of around 5lbs, foul hooked in one of its pectorals. But did it give me the run around for a good five minutes, or what? At one stage I really thought I'd hit a double.

The second fish was another beautiful big female weighing exactly 7½lbs, which was pure delight both to play and admire. Those dark, olive green flanks and that little red eye are childhood impressions that have stayed with me for over half a century. Wild images that I simply never tire of. Unfortunately I'm forced to give the swim and its tench a week's long rest on account of taking my 32 year old daughter Lisa to a sharking competition out from Montauk Point, Long Island in New York over on the other side of the pond, and we have to check in at Heathrow's terminal 3 at 6.30 a.m. tomorrow morning. So I'm in for yet another early start. We shall have to leave Norfolk at around 3 a.m. to be precise.

Monday, 20th June

Light westerly wind. Warm and sunny all day.

Lisa and I together with 15 other Brits, some of whom brought their wives along, all arrived safely at JFK airport yesterday evening following a six hour flight, and three hours later our coach deposited us due north of the city at Montauk Yacht Club close to Montauk Point at the very tip of Long Island, overlooking the Atlantic Ocean. This is the most famous sharking location on this planet, and for good reason. 30 years ago Montauk was epitomised in Peter Benchley's famous book, and later during the shooting of the motion picture *Jaws*, and so it's only fitting I guess, (what better location is there?) that for the following three days it will host the third, and annual Brits vs Yanks Hook & Release Shark Fishing Tournament. Incidentally, though much of the location filming for *Jaws* was completed along the coast at Martha's Vineyard, which became the town of *Amity* for the film, it was Captain Frank Mundus, known affectionately as the 'Monster Man', and his boat *Cricket II* operating out of Montauk, whom the film's character 'Flint' actually portrayed. Frank caught in 1964 (a decade before *Jaws*) and just 15 miles out from Montauk in 180 feet of water, the largest great white ever taken. Weighing a staggering 4,500 lbs, the monster was 17½ feet long and 13

RIGHT
Troy Louis (left) shows his monstrous 30lbs striped bass to the camera, whilst crewman Dave Schleifer of 35 foot 'Halfback', displays one of the several 25 pounders hauled in by my daughter Lisa. Part of a 30 fish haul we made trolling parachute jigs close to the bottom in 40 feet of water, in the prolific seas off Montauk Point, Long Island, New York.

feet in girth. This and many other monster-shark encounters and captures are all recorded in Frank's own book *Monster Man*, published by Avery Publishing Company. The ISBN number is 0-9703568-0-3. It is fascinating reading.

The Brits vs Yanks competition which is open to everyone is the brainchild of my good friend Christine Slater of Tailor Made Holidays and American angling author and broadcaster the late Stephen Sloan who sadly passed away just a few weeks ago.

Last year during the same week over the three days, 48 competitors sharing 24 boats, with a Brit and a Yank on each, accounted for close on 900 sharks, including over 800 blues to over 300lbs, 17 makos to 400lbs and five threshers to over 400lbs. Everyone including all the local skippers who took part said they had never known a competition so full of sharks. What's more, we Brits won too. So this year everybody is out for some hectic action and a repeat performance, though I doubt anywhere near so many sharks will be taken as 2004 was quite out of the ordinary even for Montauk.

With today however, not being part of the competition, I chartered skipper Art Cortes's famous boat *Half Back*, which is a 35 foot Viking that cruises at 25 knots, and is renowned for holding the IGFA world record for blue shark of 528lbs caught by Joe Siedel on 9 th August

ABOVE
Amongst the stripers, every so often a 'lunker' blue fish grabs hold. This 12lbs beauty held by Dave Schleifer gave Troy Louis a real workout, despite the wire line and heavy tackle required to get a parachute jig down on the troll to the 'hitting' depth.

2001. Taken on 80lbs class gear, this monster was his first ever shark, would you believe, but then Montauk is certainly a place where dreams can come true.

Along with fellow Brits Stan Povey, Troy Louis and Dave Nevatt, Lisa and I were using this first day to flex our muscles and get into the sharking slowly by hitting into some big striped bass. Incidentally, I had some beauties last year to over 25lbs, so we made an early start by leaving the marina at 6 a.m. following a short discussion with Art and his mate Dave Schleifer about the day's prospects, which with settled weather, looked most promising. The beauty of Montauk as an inshore location for bluefish, fluke and stripers, plus false albacore and blue fin tuna later on is that literally within 15 minutes the rods can be put out, the favoured area for stripers being from just a mile off Montauk Lighthouse to Block Island, (discovered by Dutch explorer Adrian Block in 1600) which is 14 miles out.

The most effective technique for big stripers is to troll an 8/0 parachute jig (which simulates the pulsating swimming action of squid) at somewhere between two and three knots, up to 100 yards behind the boat. To ensure the jigs (only two rods are used at the same time) work close to the bottom in between 25 and 40 feet of water over rips, heavy stainless steel wire is used on a 4/0 high speed, metal spooled multiplier, and the line marked off with coloured telephone wire at regular intervals. Red is at 100 feet, 150 feet is white, 200 feet is blue, 250 feet is yellow and 300 feet is green. This is so the skipper can yell out what length of line he wants out so the jigs are presented just above bottom. In the autumn, more sporting techniques are used such as drifting over the same rips with live bait, just like British bass fishing. But right now 'parachute jigs' on the troll produce the best results by far.

Incidentally, special wire-line rods are also used. These have Carbaloid rings that do not groove. Ordinary rings last no time at all. The leader is 25-30 feet of 60-80lbs mono, and to work the jig, without question the most exhausting technique I have ever experienced, you hold the seven foot rod pointed at the lure with one hand above and one below the reel which should be beneath the rod, and deftly jig the tip down towards the boat's stern every three or four seconds until you feel a bass grab hold, or till your forearms feel like lead. There is certainly no mistaking a hit, because the rod is almost wrenched from your grasp by fish in the 20-30lbs bracket. What a 50 or 60 pounder feels like (stripers can top 70lbs) I can only imagine.

Taking it in turns to work the two rods, beautiful big stripers (strikingly enamelled in black horizontal stripes similar to mullet and tiger fish) started to come

with surprising ease right at what skipper Art said was the best time, at the start of the flood tide. We caught so many I cannot remember who took the first. Not that it matters anyway. What I do remember however is that daughter Lisa heaved out a couple of splendid 25lbs specimens. I was so proud of the aggressive way she pumped them in. She will certainly have no problems with the sharks tomorrow.

At around 10 a.m. having boated around 20 bass between 5 and 25lbs and several bluefish getting on for 10lbs, sport started to slow up some and on the skipper's advice we enjoyed drifting for fluke, which are a large, very aggressive flounder that can reach over 20lbs. Using flowing mono traces below an eight ounce lead and the 1/0 hook baited with a mixture of squid and whitebait we accounted for a dozen or more fluke to around 4lbs plus several thornback rays to 8lbs from a 50 foot deep mark where the seabed consisted of banks of shingle.

LEFT
During slack water Skipper of 'Halfback' Art Cortes suggested we have a break and try flounder fishing on the drift for a while. And who do you think caught the largest? My 'ear to ear grin' daughter, Lisa of course. I'm so proud of her.

After an hour's fun we resumed jigging for bass over the rips and banged into some beauties almost immediately, Lisa having to relinquish her morning's top fish to Troy who boated a thickset deep-bellied monster getting on for 30lbs. A particular fish I played right to the boat would have beaten it, so Dave the mate said, but the hook pulled free when the four foot long striper was within sight of the net. But so it goes. What truly marvellous fishing Montauk has to offer. We certainly returned to the Yacht Club a happy bunch at around 3 p.m. having lost count of how many fish over 20lbs we'd boated, a conservative estimate being well into the high teens. And to think that in the autumn these stripers tend to run significantly bigger, 40 pounders being everyday encounters.

JUNE

RIGHT
Tournament charter boats, having left the marina, pass Montauk Point early each morning within sight of 'Jaws country' and the deep blue, shark-prolific waters of the Atlantic Ocean. Can you hear that unmistakable music from the motion picture reaching a crescendo?

FAR RIGHT
My first shark of the tournament, a small blue, is drawn to the boat for unhooking and release. Note the partially inflated 'balloon' float, and large plastic bucket full of drilled holes which releases a steady 'chum' slick down tide. Imperative for attracting sharks up to the baits.

Tuesday, 21st June

Light westerly wind. Blue skies and bright sunshine.

There was much excitement when all 34 competitors and 34 skippers and mates gathered around the pool restaurant this morning at 5.30 a.m. to pick up their packed lunch boxes and to see who was fishing with whom. I had been allocated 36 foot *Masterpiece* skippered by Mark Assogna with mate Joe Vish to crew. My American counterpart was John Epifanio from Chicago who is director for the Centre of Aquatic Ecology in the Illinois Natural History Survey, specialising in the genetics of fisheries biology, so there was plenty to talk about.

Soon we were on board and out into open sea cruising at over 20 knots in a flat calm, heading southeast of Montauk. When around 25 miles out without another boat in sight the skipper cut the engines and set *Masterpiece* on a steady if somewhat slow drift over an area of peaks and pinnacles varying in depth between 200 and 240 feet. A huge bucket of chum was lowered over the side, resulting in a continual slick of minced fish and oils drifting downtide, and we sat back patiently to wait for sharks to follow the chum line up to our four rods, (a 30lbs and a 50lbs class outfit each), each set at different distances from the boat presenting a large, fresh mackerel on size 10/0 hooks to 200lbs test single strand wire, suspended beneath a partially inflated balloon, set at varying depths from 20 to 50 feet.

Within minutes the chum line had attracted several different birds including storm petrels and shearwaters, plus a huge sunfish that must have weighed getting on for half a ton which swam slowly around the boat for several minutes before leaving. What strange creatures they are. Water temperature was 61°F and everything looked good, but two hours later not a single shark had materialised.

Then quite suddenly one of my floats started moving positively away, so I banged the hook home immediately and subsequently pumped a modest-sized blue shark of around 80lbs to the boat following a lively scrap. Half an hour later one of my companion's floats shot off and he too was into a shark. Again it was a blue, slightly smaller than mine. And as we both hooked up on our 50lbs class outfits (350 points if you hook up on the 30lbs class gear) we scored 250 points each, which unfortunately was where it stayed till we wound the lines in at the official end of day one come 3 p.m. A draw and not exactly a hectic start to the competition.

Back at the Yacht Club however others had fared much better, my daughter Lisa catching her first two sharks and missing out on another two chances. She was over the moon. In fact apart from her wedding and the births of her two daughters, I cannot remember her being so animated and bubbly since she was a nipper. She really made her father's day. Some of the other Brits had also done well and when all the points were added up we were in the lead by what amounted to a couple or three sharks, so there was still everything to play for.

Wednesday, 22nd June

Light westerly wind. Sunny and humid.

Another 5.30 a.m. start and day two of the competition, which for me at least, produced virtually a repeat of yesterday in that my only run produced a blue shark of around 75lbs. As it took the bait on my 50lbs test outfit I scored 250 points again, which was only marginally better than my American counterpart Alan Kenter from New Jersey who hooked a really big blue estimated at around 250lbs, but lost it due to the hook inexplicably pulling free. So all he scored was 100 points for 'hooking up'. And those two runs provided our only excitement.

Strange really, because everything looked so good as our 40 foot boat *Windy*, skippered by Jack Passie and crewed by Mike Aylmer got off to a flying start when we pulled out a whole bunch of fresh bait in the way of 2-3lbs bluefish on trolled umbrella rigs close to Montauk Lighthouse over broken, rocky ground in 120 feet of water. We then headed southeast for 26 miles, and were in fact the first boat to arrive at the sharking grounds and get the 'rubby dubby' over the side and a healthy slick going. Obviously no one told the sharks.

I felt particularly sorry for camera lady Ann Bailey from the Sky TV angling programme *Tight Lines* who came on board hoping for some hectic action. Mind, so were we.

But there was always the chatter back at the poolside bar to look forward to and to see how Lisa and the rest of the Brits had fared. And for the second day running Lisa had thrashed her dad, (she was loving it) whilst the rest of the team managed enough points to keep us Brits in front.

Thursday, 23rd June

Northeasterly wind. Clear blue skies, bright and sunny.

I am pleased to report that today, the third and final day of the competition, several sharks managed to work their way along our rubby dubby slick and onto our hooks. Our boat *Oh Brother*, a 39 foot BHM, captained by Robbie, and his mate Billy to crew, sped us out 28 miles to the sharking grounds in over 200 feet of water, once we had trolled up enough bluefish inshore for fresh bait. Used as both hook bait fillets and as chunks for periodically throwing into the slick trail, it's hard to find a more attractive fish than bluefish which can grow to 20lbs and provide great sport themselves on light tackle.

Within an hour of starting to drift, there were several species of birds feeding from the slick, including shearwaters, sooty shearwaters, storm petrels, herring gulls and greater black backs. And the first action in the form of a 75lbs blue came to my rod. My Yank partner Jack Mylott from Florida then banged into a larger blue, certainly over 100lbs, while I heaved too hard into what the skipper guessed to be a big mako, and promptly snapped the 30lbs line at the reel. I then brought a blue well over 100lbs to the boat following a lively fight, as simultaneously Jack found himself connected to a lovely big thresher. Talk about hectic action, and all within the space of an hour or so. This fish really did give him the run around for a good 20 minutes, before we even saw what it was, the skipper skilfully manoeuvring the boat so Jack could keep his line directly off the stern. Billy the mate held it tight when it hit the surface allowing me to crank off an entire roll of film. What a truly awesome shark, with a scythe-like tail two thirds of its body length. It was so long that once I needed to duck in order not to be swiped around the head when it came alongside the stern.

Robbie estimated it at around 250lbs, and cheers went up all round. Threshers are now an endangered species all around the world's oceans and it was indeed a privilege to seen one in the flesh. Jack and I then took another modest-sized blue apiece and that was our action over, Jack easily beating me by 1600 points to 950. His thresher alone was worth 650 points. But what a great day out with great people. And I guess that's what we Brits bring back with us from this tournament, firm friendships and some wonderful memories. I'll never forget that look on Lisa's face when I met her walking back from the dock. Yes! For the third day running she had beaten dad. What's more, when all the scores were added up us Brits had totalled 45,450 points to the Yanks 44,650, thus winning for the second year running. But with a mere thousand or so points (just three or four sharks) separating the two teams it was a close call.

During the three days of the competition 34 anglers had landed a total of 247 blue sharks to over 200lbs, 15 makos to 400lbs, and two threshers of 250 and 400lbs. And my Lisa had come 5th in the Brits and 11th overall. I was so incredibly proud of her. Don't ask her dad where he came.

Friday, 24th June

Westerly wind. Sunny all day.

Today being a 'free' day after the tournament before we all set off back across the pond, and because Lisa decided to go horse riding, I asked Dave Nevatt if he fancied joining me for a day's fly fishing for striped bass with British guide and interior designer Matthew Miller who operates a 23 foot Deep V Parker which has an 8½ foot beam, out of Sag Harbour, not far from Montauk, and knows the coastline with its series of rocks, reefs and rips extremely well indeed, as we were to find out.

His season goes from May through till the beginning of December, starting with stripers, bluefish and weakfish on the fly with the odd bottom fishing trip for fluke thrown in, and steps up a notch between July and August when bonito, plus blue fin tuna in the 20-60lbs range and the occasional yellow fin, can be taken on the fly rod just 12-24 miles offshore. Also available from May till August incidentally, is 'Florida' style skiff fishing over the shallow inshore flats in crystal clear water between 1-4 feet deep, sight casting into the bays for stripers and bluefish. And if you can't put out a fly, soft plastic 'sluggo'-type lures work well on light spinning gear.

From the beginning of September false albacore in the 8-20lbs bracket are added to terrific runs of big bass and bluefish. This period in the autumn, known as the 'Blitz' when bay anchovies collect in bulk due to the structure and currents around Montauk, sees the bluefish and stripers bulking up for spawning, and is prime time for hitting into trophy bass on the fly.

After the autumn blitzes, from November through to the first two weeks into December, the bluefish disappear leaving monstrous-sized stripers (Matthew has taken them to over 40lbs on the fly) which feed specifically upon blue backed herring. What a season. No wonder Matthew needs a vacation afterwards.

Before Christine Slater of Tailor Made Holidays organised the first Brits vs Yanks shark competition here three years ago, I had no idea what truly fabulous and varied light tackle action was available around Montauk, in addition to the sharking and summer trolling for giant tuna, and all only a 100 miles north of the city of New York. It's a whole different ball game to the sea fishing potential I have at my disposal living close to the Norfolk coastline, around the same distance north of London. Just shows how much we have raped the North Sea, doesn't it?

Matthew takes his fly fishing for stripers and blues with refreshing professionalism, something, from one guide to another, I was pleased to compliment him on. For starters, he had on board the choice of four different top of the range ten foot outfits from 8-10 weight, with disc drag reels and both intermediate and sink tip lines. And I particularly liked the way he continually dished out pieces of information about the particular rips we were drifting over, such as the rock formations etc. and exactly where the fish were lying. As the species we were after, both stripers and bluefish, were pushing tiny sand eels up to the surface (denoted by huge flocks of terns feeding upon them which we were continually chasing) Matthew's fly selection was based upon representing sand eels with long, sparsely-tied Clouser Minnow patterns in white and green and white, his favourite all-terrain pattern being a Maryland Crab Clouser which worked particularly well close inshore around huge kelp-covered boulders and rocks.

In fact by far the prettiest area we fished was along the southern, extremely rocky shoreline of Plum Island which is owned by the government and private. Subsequently the beaches and rocks are never fished from the shore. This allowed Matthew to work his boat in some areas, literally to within 30 yards of the beach so I could double-haul my fly, using a clear mono intermediate line and 15lbs test leader almost onto the sand before retrieving using a fast, erratic strip. This produced some unbelievably hard takes from both bluefish and striped bass up to around the 7-8lbs mark, many of which I actually saw scream out of nowhere to grab hold through the clear water, Matthew immediately and skilfully reversing his boat backwards through the maze of boulders so I could enjoy the ensuing fight. And didn't

BELOW
Some of our new found friends and part of the American team.

BOTTOM
Most of the competitors in our victorious and most patriotic British team.

those fish go. I haven't enjoyed battles with saltwater fish on the fly so much since I last bone fished in the Bahamas.

Every now and again a seal would pop up to the surface and look us over, and literally within telephoto lens distance, there was an osprey's nest on top of a telephone pole, with the female clearly visible. Dave Nevatt, who also enjoyed the fishing whilst working shallow diving plugs in addition to taking shots on my camera, certainly thought it

was close enough to film, and got out his 300mm lens. What a stunning location to fly fish.

After several drifts along the boulder-strewn shoreline we concentrated on the birds working around 200 yards offshore. Using the 'intermediate' line outfit with the fly only a couple of feet below the surface resulted in a plethora of bluefish between 3-5lbs which simply do not stop shaking their heads and repeatedly crash-dive. Matthew however, was certain that bass were feeding below the 'blues' and suggested I switch over to a heavier fly on the sink tip line outfit. And he was so right. Almost immediately I banged into a nice striper of around 8lbs, and then managed to pull the hook from a whopper, certainly a fish into double figures. I felt even sicker when Matthew informed me that one of his guests took a 20lbs striper from this very spot only two weeks back. But in the words of 'Arnie' I will be back.

ABOVE
With help from our guide Matthew Miller, Dave Nevatt (left) hooked into numerous hard-battling blue fish between 5 and 8lbs using a light weight lure outfit and shallow diving plugs. And didn't they scrap. Just a 5lbs blue fish fights with the power of a double figure pike.

LEFT
Striped bass such as this provide unbelievably good sport on the fly rod, all around the seas off Montauk. A 10 foot, 9 or 10 weight outfit and disc drag reel outfit is ideal. But you need plenty of backing. They can reach weights of 50lbs plus.

Wednesday, 29th June

Gentle southerly wind. Overcast, with spasmodic bouts of sunshine.

Following torrential overnight rain accompanied by thunder and lightning which kept our dogs in a continual state of unrest throughout the early hours, I was not exactly optimistic about my guest Lee Rickwood's chances of catching too many carp when he pulled up beside the summer house adjacent to my two-lake fishery at 5 a.m. this morning. Light values were incredibly low and nothing seemed to be moving or feeding in the dank, early morning air. After baiting up several close-in swims with 10mm pellets however, and seeing a few bubbles erupting on the surface in two of them, Lee, who works in the publishing industry, settled in to the first with me by his side to assist in the technicalities of lift-method float fishing for carp. Not having purposefully float-fished for carp before Lee was amazed at just how close they can be caught through being stealthy, observing tail patterns and bubbles etc. and by sitting several feet back from the water's edge, as I put the net beneath his first hard fighting carp, a beautiful, golden metallic common of around 9lbs.

The fish had certainly been affected by the overnight storms and were incredibly finicky for so early in the season, when more aggressive bites are usually expected. But through the perseverance of holding the 11 foot Avon rod expectantly, yet in a relaxed mode all day long, and accurate, but sparse loose feeding of pellets just beyond the peacock quill float (where the double pellet hair-rigged to a size 10 was lying) there was enough action throughout the day for Lee to drive back to his home in Andover in Hampshire a happy man, and I hope, a wiser carp fisherman having put eight fish on the bank into double figures, some of them providing arm-wrenching battles in and out of the lilies on the 8lbs test reel line, plus a 1¼lbs rudd, which was his first ever.

Friday, 1st July

Overcast. Light westerly wind.

Living just a few miles away in Aylsham, Nigel Meyer was round at my two-lake carp fishery at 5 a.m. sharp, having been surprised only the day before with a 'fish-in' with me as a birthday present from his wife, and most eager to have his string well and truly pulled.

Presently, most of the carp are not feeding anywhere near as aggressively as they should be at this time of the year due I think for two reasons. Their spawning was both late and spasmodic, coupled to a recent and unusual weather pattern comprising of several consecutive 'lows', and I explained to Nigel that in these overcast mornings little seemed to be moving and feeding in earnest. Nevertheless I loose fed a mixture of 10mm source boilies and 10mm pellets (just a handful or two) into several favourite 'close-in' swims with trees overhead, as I walked him stealthily around, purposefully picking up our feet like a chicken so as not to spook carp along the margins, before running through the fundamental principles of 'lift-method' float fishing.

Apart from a few small 'wildies' Nigel had not before encountered sizeable carp or used a float in their pursuit, so he was the perfect pupil. Firstly I showed him how my 11 foot Avon rod, coupled to a fixed spool reel loaded with 8lbs test, is best supported with the handle along his knee and thigh directly beneath his forearm, with two fingers around the reel stem. Most important this, because it permits a fast, upwards and powerful strike in order to pick up and straighten the right angle of line between rod tip and bait, in order to set the hook into carp not belting off with the bait.

With today's, heavy-lead, bolt-rig scene of course, which the majority of 'carpers' use, most fish are hooked before the angler even picks up his rod from the rests, whereas float fishing, where you hold the rod throughout, is entirely different. In addition, with two fingers each side of the reel stem, your forefinger is perfectly placed not only for picking up line in readiness for casting when the bale arm is opened, but also for applying gentle pressure to the side of the spool to slow down powerful fish. And I was hoping my guest would feel the strength of at least a few double-figure carp, in and out of the lilies which form 'movement' areas in most swims just a couple of rod lengths out from the banks.

Then I explained to Nigel that short underarm 'flick' casts were all that was needed to fish each and every close range swim around the two lakes. I purposefully maintain them 'overgrown' anyway to encourage carp along the margins. So all was set. I then ran through the simple float rig with a four inch length of peacock quill attached to the line by a band of silicon rubber set a foot over depth, (lock a float to the line with a shot either side and the line snaps when a carp runs through weed or lilies) with a single swan shot pinched onto the line five inches from the size 10 hook, hair-rigged to accommodate two small boilies or pellets.

From the first four swims we fished not a single bite materialised, but at least it gave me a chance to explain why the rig should be cast well beyond the baited area and then quickly wound back with the float well clear of the surface (so the bare hook doesn't catch on bottom detritus) and finally lowered down so that the hook comes to lie beyond the shot and the shot

beyond the float. Then loose feed can be thrown a couple of feet beyond the float, (using a cupped hand and underarm throw for accuracy) with the minimal chance of line bites. Although when float fishing for carp line bites are of course unavoidable, and to alleviate striking into thin air or foul hooking fish, I often fish with the float 'flat' on the surface and not 'cocked'. I explained to Nigel that with a fair amount of fish movement in the swim, with the float cocked as though we were tench fishing, with just a quarter of the tip showing, the slightest nudge by a carp against the line would result in false registrations and our striking, whereas with the 'flat float' only its cocking and disappearing beneath the surface should be struck. So I suggested that he do the same to avoid confusion. After all it was his first session ever after carp on the float.

What did he catch? Well considering the conditions I reckon Nigel was more than pleased with his five carp averaging double figures, the best being a long, powerful common of around 14lbs. The prettiest however was an absolutely stunning (there are only a few in the lakes) black and red koi of around 9lbs. He also took a beautiful golden metallic common of around 11lbs, his first fish of the day incidentally, and a couple of sizeable roach. At various times whenever the sun broke through and a few fish started moving on the surface, I got Nigel into 'floater fishing' using a controller rig and mixer held onto the size 10 hook with a silicon bait band. And he almost did the business in the form of a beautiful big common, all of 16-17lbs, from an entanglement of lilies. But sadly, when the fish was just a couple of yards away from the net the hook pulled. I reckon my latest prodigy is going to be seriously float-fishing for carp from now on.

ANOTHER FISHING YEAR

Wednesday, 6th July

Cool and blustery westerly wind, mostly cloudy.

David Barnes and I have known each other for over 30 years, since he first came into my Norwich tackle shop in fact, as a rep for Richard Forshaw the tackle company back in 1971. Like me he has worked for Masterline International for these past 20 years, but it was only last summer when we actually got around to sharing a day's fishing. And very nice it was too. David had booked a punt on the famous Blenheim Palace Lake in Oxfordshire (anyone can do this by contacting their estates department) for a tenching session, and if I remember correctly, we had

a 'field day' landing some 27 tench and bream between 4 and 6lbs on float fished sweet corn and small cubes of luncheon meat. So a return trip was in order, which is why I drove down to Royston to stay overnight at his house yesterday evening, with David doing the driving to Blenheim this morning.

Unfortunately, this tremendously prolific fishery was having an 'off' day, big time, because try as we may, and we tried, moving several times all around the 25 acre lake from our 7 a.m. start till mid-afternoon, we had just the occasional small perch on worms to show for our efforts. And like most of the other boats out, not a single tench came our way. I rather think that the intermittent spawning fish have suffered this summer, along with lengthy bouts of low pressure, the subsequent chilly and rainy weather which has for the present precluded any chance of aggressive feeding. Our one and only tench suddenly coming on a single kernel of sweet corn to my rod at 4.30 p.m. for no apparent reason, though I suspect it was the only one in the swim. It was a male tench of around 4lbs which though it fought strongly was grossly disfigured having been chewed around the dorsal fin area by an otter or the world's biggest pike. A lovely day out nonetheless.

Friday, 8th July

Light westerly wind, cool and overcast with bouts of drizzle.

When oh when will this weather break and these depressing 'lows' be replaced by what we used to call summer? I must however admit, following the day's events, to feeling extremely elated right now, not from what I caught, but what six year old Ryan Seeber managed to catch from our two-lake fishery in just an hour before and an hour after lunch along at my local pub the Bridge Public House in Lenwade. The trip was in fact arranged some while back through the Starlight Children's Foundation for young Ryan who sadly has a very rare disorder called Hunter's Syndrome, and because he is always watching my programmes on TV, his parents Bob and Rachel thought he might like to meet me. But the pleasure, as is so often the case, turned out to be entirely mine.

There is so much joy to be gleaned from watching the look on a child's face as he or she marvels at the silver and gold enamelling of small roach and rudd, in which the lakes are ridiculously prolific, and within minutes of the family arriving young Ryan was hauling them out wholesale on float-fished sweet corn, with his dad Bob helping to steady the rod. I rummaged through the garage especially to find this particular rod because I made it purposefully, several

LEFT
Picturesque Blenheim Palace Lake, in Oxfordshire, designed with astute vision, like all his projects by Capability Brown, usually throws up a mountain of sizeable tench and bream during the warmer months, providing superlative close range sport on the float from a punt. This lone, late afternoon tench however, was scant reward for Dave Barnes and me.

RIGHT
My youngest guest of the year, six year old Ryan Seeber from Harrogate, aided and accompanied by dad 'Bob' was justifiably overwhelmed by the size of this lovely common carp. All morning he had been perfectly content whacking out roach and rudd weighing a few ounces, and then, suddenly, had never felt such power on the end of his line before. But he soon settled down again.

years ago for my granddaughter from eight foot two piece 6-weight fly rod blanks, which being super lightweight with a forgiving, all-through action, is so easy for a child to hold, yet long enough to control the float rig. Most so-called youngsters' rods on the market are either too short (for sufficient line to be taken up on the strike – remember kids have short arms) or as stiff as a broomstick, whereas in conjunction with a miniature fixed spool reel and a 3lbs test line, using this lightweight rod, Ryan really enjoyed every thrash, dive and wiggle of all the roach and rudd he caught which were all in the absolute mint of condition, 'like new pins' as the saying goes and varied in size between two and ten ounces. I put them all straight into a large white bucket half filled with water, so that every so often he could simply look at them with fascination.

While all this was going on, on account of Ryan continually mentioning 'carp', yes he's only six, but dad Bob is an ardent carper and fly fisherman, I put out a heavier 'sleeper' rod with an 18mm boilie hair rigged on the business end, close up to a patch of dense lilies to the right of where we were float fishing and scattered a few freebies around it, after first putting the reel into free-spool mode. And within half an hour of returning from lunch and casting it out again, the reel started to sing like a canary. Quickly I lifted the rod and put Ryan's right hand around the handle whist he cranked away furiously with his left. And with a little extra help from dad Bob supporting the rod while I grabbed the landing net, and with mum Rachel shooting away on the camcorder, collectively we willed that carp into the net, thankfully at the first attempt. A lovely and lively, bronze-backed common carp pushing double figures. Ryan, understandably, became most excited and was almost lost for words. Then it was immediately back to a roach or a rudd on the float again, before his retention span eventually started to wane and it was time to leave. What a truly lovely, memorable day, and I didn't catch a thing.

Tuesday, 12th July

Heavily overcast, replaced by sunshine from midday. Light, northeasterly wind.

As my guest today, Dave Reynolds from Harlow in Essex, had never caught a carp or a tench, it was only fitting that his first fish, presenting a hair-rigged pellet on a 'lift-float' rig, shortly after our start at 5 a.m., was a tench of around 3lbs. There are in fact very few tench in my two-lake fishery, which is stocked with both king and grass carp averaging double figures, plus catfish to over 20lbs and a few surprises including big chub, golden orfe and eels, plus hoards of roach and rudd to over the pound. So Dave of course was over the moon with his tench, and the several superb roach he caught throughout the day to around 1½lbs plus six double figure carp to 14lbs.

A couple of these coming in the late afternoon to floating mixer biscuits presented on a 'controller-rig' amongst dense lilies.

He really enjoyed the 'visual' experience of watching carp slurp down floaters and the ensuing 'hit and hold' battles which followed, with me shouting directions and encouragement till each fish was on the surface ready for netting. He also enjoyed creeping up on the kingfishers' nest in the steep banking along the opposite side of the 'old lake' and listening to the 'chirps' from the young inside. We had in fact been watching the parents flying through the trees and into the nest, back with fresh food for the young all morning, so to actually witness the entrance to the nest, a slime-covered hole (due to the excrement of liquidised fish running out) in a vertical wall of gravel banking beneath a canopy of dense brambles, and hear those young, really made his day. And I have no doubt that Dave drove back to Harlow a very happy bunny.

Thursday, 14th July

Humid, overcast followed by bright sunshine. Light westerly wind.

Due to the night being so incredibly warm, I just couldn't resist putting the alarm clock on for 3 a.m. which had me comfortably seated behind a screen of tall bulrushes and sweet rush in one of my favourite barbel haunts at a nearby River Wensum mill pool as dawn broke. And with a

This big, scale-perfect common carp was the largest of six doubles (plus his first ever Wels catfish) taken by ex-miner Owen Brown from Nottinghamshire during a day trip to my two-lake Norfolk fishery. And all came by float fishing close into the marginal features.

20mm source boilie hair-rigged onto a size 6 hook, anchored to the river bed with a two ounce lead, I was confident of instigating a few bites. But as so often happens when specifically targeting barbel, other species come along by default rather than by design, and during this particular session I just could not thwart the attentions from ever-hungry chub. I must have had a good 20 or so 'klonking' bites where the rod top clanged round savagely a foot or so, and inevitably, though I refrained from pulling into these obvious 'chub' bites, two fish, both beauties over 4lbs, eventually turned downstream with the bait so aggressively, they hooked themselves.

As the light increased I could easily make out their dark shapes moving up and down the three foot deep, gravel-bottomed run, tilting their heads down every so often to inhale a loose-fed boilie or one of the 10mm halibut pellets I introduced by the handful every few minutes in the hope of drawing a barbel or two from the dense beds of streamer weed at the end of the run. Had I wanted to OD on specimen chub, then this would indeed have been the morning to do it, because the commotion of playing and subsequently landing fish from the relatively shallow swim seemed not to bother the others one iota, and a couple of them looked to be well over 5lbs if not larger.

Then quite suddenly a goodish barbel, possibly the better side of 10lbs came steadily upstream out of the streamer weed and foraged around the bottom, definitely sucking up some of my loose feed, before disappearing into a depression immediately below a thick bed of weed, further across the river than I had been feeding. Naturally, I then placed my ledgered boilie at the head of the depression and sat back to await events.

Five minutes later around went the rod top as something belted off with my bait and shot downstream at a rate of knots, just like a barbel, ripping line from the slipping clutch. Trouble was, it materialised into a really thick-set, dark coloured bream of around 7-8lbs which, although it gave a good account of itself by turning those deep flanks side on to the fast flow, was really no match for my barbel outfit. What I've got to do to extract a barbel from the river at present, I just don't know. Go bream fishing perhaps?

Friday, 15th July

Humid and overcast. After a light shower, bright sunshine all day. Light westerly wind.

One of the joys in accompanying anglers around my two-lake fishery is that through their efforts and results I get an enormous 'buzz' even though I may not actually fish myself. Take this morning for instance when ex-miner Owen Brown from Mansfield in Nottinghamshire, caught a Wels catfish using two 10mm pellets presented beneath a peacock quill float using the 'lift' method

ANOTHER FISHING YEAR

on his very first cast. It was in fact a 'kitten' of around 4lbs and his first pussy ever, fighting incredibly strongly despite the 8lbs test line and Avon rod set up for carp in mind. Boy was he over the moon!

He then took a succession of super roach ranging from 8oz up to 1½lbs, all on two 10mm source boilies hair-rigged to a size 10 hook, before a carp finally turned up, a nice, fully scaled mirror pushing 10lbs. I think he could have packed up there and then a happy man, but we had the entire day ahead, and Owen went on to finish up with several more pound-plus roach and rudd plus six carp averaging double figures, the best a stonking, scale perfect common of exactly 16lbs.

What struck me most about the session apart from my guest enjoying some memorable sport, was the number of quality roach he caught from my little lakes which together amount to less than three acres of water, and in which roach happily thrive and grow large despite competing with carp, grass carp and catfish for the available natural food source. When less than 100 yards away the seemingly lush and clear flowing upper reaches of my beloved River Wensum are now virtually incapable of producing roach to match. It is to me so very, very sad. Due to the severe and I'm loathe to say, 'ongoing' cormorant predation of its once prolific roach and dace the river is now nothing like when I first moved to Norfolk and opened up my tackle shop in Norwich way back in the summer of 1971, when I quickly made a name for myself by accounting for numbers of 2lbs plus roach, mostly by long trotting the River Wensum. Many of these wonderful catches are recorded in my diary book, *A Specimen Fishing Year*, written during that heatwave year of 1976, and the forerunner, albeit 30 years back, to this very book you are now reading.

The Ministry of Agriculture and Fisheries (now called D.E.F.R.A.) whose statutory obligation it is to protect and maintain our inland fisheries (what a joke – but I'm not laughing) has not only let down at least two generations of anglers, but by not taking upon itself to nationally organise the culling of cormorants, or at least put them on the 'vermin' list, has obliterated a legacy of quality river fishing for our children, not only in East Anglia but in flowing water and lakeland fisheries up and down the country. I cannot possibly put into words the contempt I feel for this governmental department. Its lack of action is scandalous.

My guest Owen knew exactly how I feel because the catching of so many good roach from my lakes (where cormorants are not allowed to ravage) prompted him to recall his late father stick-float trotting on their local River Trent and catching monstrous bags of roach including specimens to over 2lbs. Something, which like my local rivers is also sadly no more.

How I should like to be a benign dictator for just one year, and to put everything right in the UK and our now 'Nanny State' that has been allowed to go wrong. Yes, and you can add to cormorant culling, harsher prison sentences, more prisons, zero tolerance shown to those who steal, mug and maim, and I would make car boot sales illegal. They are the biggest market place of stolen goods by far. I would also make it just as hard for people to enter our overcrowded shores as Britons themselves now experience when wanting to emigrate abroad, and I would employ the Army to put in place inner city areas of lawlessness where aggressive youngsters roam the street to frighten the residents and show disregard for the property of others. I would also regulate what has been happening on TV over these past few years, when the largest proportion of those who purchase TV licences (the over 40s) have constantly to suffer the programming mistakes of whiz-kid commissioners who because they have yet to live life long enough to really know what viewers wish to see, transmit mindless garbage called 'reality TV', under the banner of total crap like *Big Brother*, *Celebrity Love Island*, and *I'm A Celebrity, Get Me Out Of Here*, etc., etc. Ah, if only, eh?

Tuesday, 19th July

Stiff and cool westerly wind. Clear skies.

In readiness for an early session after bream this morning, yesterday I popped along to a wide, slow, deep and heavily reed-lined stretch of the River Wensum on the outskirts of Norwich, where giant willows line the opposite bank, to clear a path down to the river (it had not been fished since I caught a nice bag of bream to 9lbs from the same spot last summer) and bait up with a mixture of maize and breadcrumbs. But I needn't have bothered, and have to log up a total blank.

Though I enjoyed the somewhat chilly, dawn start accompanied by 'chattering' from reed warblers and felt great delight at watching numbers of kingfishers zooming along the river making that distinct and high-pitched 'peep' as they pass, not so much as a 'tremble' came to my quiver-tipped bread flake ledgered in a ten foot deep run. Torrential overnight rain followed by much cooler weather than of late, did not I feel help matters, and I was home for breakfast before 8 a.m.

Friday, 22nd – Sunday, 24th July

Overcast and cool with strong winds and persistent rain from Sunday lunchtime.

The CLA Game Fair, held recently in the grounds of Belvoir Castle (pronounced 'Beaver') in Leicestershire over three days, is an event that my wife Jo and I very much look forward to. And this year instead of fighting the lines of cars back to a hotel each evening at the end of the show, we were so glad that we had hired a campervan, and so stayed with friends on site.

In addition to my giving daily casting demonstrations to visitors at the Grand Stand, which overlooks one of the three coarse fishing lakes at Belvoir Castle, it's great to meet up again with many old fishing friends like John Bailey, Hywell Morgan and Michael Evans who were also demonstrating, some of whom I only ever seem to bump into at these occasions. Such is our pace of life I guess.

For my stint this year I demonstrated the basic differences between the 'Nottingham' and 'Wallis' styles of casting using a centre pin reel, which seemed to go down very well, plus some rudimentary tips for tench and carp anglers using the 'lift method' of close-range float fishing. On day three however, when the promised rain started to fall heavily accompanied by strong and gusting winds, just as I started my 'demo', patience was suddenly pushed to the absolute limit. It is of course never 'easy' demonstrating fishing techniques to several hundred people, particularly when they are all seated in a grandstand and perfectly dry, waiting to be entertained, while you are being blown about on a floating pontoon 50 feet out into the lake and getting more soaked by the minute. And when a gust of wind almost blows your six different and carefully-rigged outfits off the pontoon simultaneously tangling the line of the one you're holding around them, you really wish the ground could swallow you up. Moreover due to the super-sensitive radio mike

situated a mere inch from your mouth, you can't even cuss and curse. So it's simply a case of gritting your teeth and making the best of it. A great three days nonetheless.

Tuesday, 26th July

Overcast and cool with a light southwesterly wind.

Despite the miserable weather, today proved most enjoyable in the company of the keenest female angler I have ever known, and a national fishing coach to boot, one Nuala Gray from Milton Keynes. Husband John deposited her at the summer house beside our lakes at 5 a.m., the day's fishing with yours truly being a 50th birthday present from her daughter, and she didn't stop chattering or put the Avon rod down (except for an hour's lunch break down at my local pub) till he came back 12 hours later to collect her. Now that's dedication.

I would have loved Nuala to have found my carp in an aggressive mood, but despite much bubbling going on in some of the swims we fished, they simply were not interested in picking up her hook bait for much of the day, and the common of about 9lbs followed by a chunky mirror of around 15lbs, the first taken using the 'lift-method' on a couple of hair-rigged 10mm boilies, and the second on a floating mixer biscuit, were about par for the course on the day. The roach and rudd however, as is so often the case when the carp are uncooperative, were almost a nuisance, and Nuala took several beauties up to around 1¼lbs, despite the 8lbs test reel line.

On several occasions green woodpeckers identified by their 'drunken sailor' chattering flew overhead and a succession of kingfishers (probably the same two) were working the fry shoals up and down the lakes all morning long. Bumble bee-sized moorhen chicks unsteadily walking across lily pads were fed by their mother on our loose-fed mixer biscuits, while a family of six half-grown mallards and their mum were devouring the rest. As Nuala happened to say on several occasions, the carp were simply a bonus. And she was so right.

LEFT
Demonstrating angling techniques stuck out on a floating pontoon in front of thousands of visitors at the annual CLA Game Fair (held in 2005 at Belvoir Castle) becomes daunting 'only' when things go pear-shaped, which is what happens when rain soaks you through and gusting winds tangle tackle arrangements. At least then, everyone realises that you are only human after all.

Monday, 8th August

Overcast with occasional drizzle.

Yesterday evening my wife Jo and I were invited out to dinner at The Lenwade Country House Hotel, by a group of angling and business friends of 56 year old John Jeffree who comes from Dulwich in south London near Crystal Palace. A lovely guy who several months ago was told he had lung cancer and just a year to live. So they all got together and asked if I would take him fishing, which I was only too pleased to do, and the reason for everyone staying overnight close to our lakes, so I could surprise him in the bar prior to dinner. It turned out to be an evening Jo and I will remember for a very long time, not just for the bottles of red we put away, the fine food, or even the singalong that went on into the early hours (someone in the bar thought we were a rugby club) but mostly for the poignant reason that had brought us all together.

At 8.30 a.m. this morning I collected John from the hotel and within half an hour we were comfortably settled in at the larger of our two lakes with three carp rods fanned out and tight up against a thick bed of lilies on the opposite bank, with a 20mm hair-rigged boilie and bolt rig on each. I don't usually tackle the carp in my own lakes in this way but holding a float rod for the entire morning and quickly striking bites using the 'lift method' was not something John was really up to. So we sat relaxed yet expectantly waiting for a run whilst chewing over the trials of life.

How I would react given the sudden news that confronted an extremely brave John, I simply cannot say, but I doubt I would be so pragmatic. What I can say however is that our fishing session of just a few hours certainly left me emotionally drained, and I have been contemplating our avenues of discussion ever since. I remembered that my brother Dave, who is due round this evening together with his wife Boon, from Thailand where he now lives, used to have a huge poster on his bedroom wall when we were teenagers, saying, 'Today is the first day of the rest of your life'. And of course it is so very true, but not something most of us ever get to contemplate, because we don't know when the end will come.

At around 12 a.m. I suggested to John that prior to him being collected by the group at 1 p.m., why don't we wind the boilies in, which produced not a single bleep on the alarms, and try a last ditch attempt for a carp by presenting floaters amongst the lilies. There was the occasional movement close to the surface amongst the dense floating canopy of pads, (those carp simply didn't want to leave the sanctuary of the lilies in such dank, miserable conditions) and I felt confident that John could induce a take at least. Whether he would then be able to extract the fish from an entanglement of yellow lilies would be up to him. And it truly was. I had no hand in the outcome whatsoever, except reaching out with the landing net to secure a beautifully big 'metallic' carp, easily the better side of 15lbs, (his biggest carp ever incidentally) after it had led John a merry song and dance in and out of the pads for over ten minutes. It was in fact his only bite, and I was praying throughout the hectic battle (because I doubt he would have had a second chance following such a commotion) that the size 10 hook would not pull free. I honestly don't know who was happier, John or I.

Tuesday, 9th August

Clear skies accompanied by a heavy mist at dawn. Light westerly wind.

The last time brother Dave and I fished together was getting on for two years ago when I visited him in Thailand and caught the legendary and unbelievably hard-fighting Mekong catfish to close on 60lbs, plus other weird and wonderfully coloured freshwater battlers from the Cha-am lakes close to where he lives at Hua Hin, some 100 miles south of Bangkok. I am actually due to return for some more action this coming December if all goes well, so we shall see. For the present, Dave is bent on enjoying his first love which are big bream, so this morning we rose at 4.30 a.m. and visited one of my favourite local still waters, a three-lake syndicate fishery in the nearby village of Elsing called Three Bridges Farm Lakes. I last took Dave here in the early 1990s and on one morning (quite unprecedented in those days incidentally) we caught no less than seven doubles, all on ledgered worms and sweet corn. I had five to over 12lbs, but Dave sneaked out the best two weighing 13¼lbs and 13½lbs.

LEFT
Ever smiling, 'big John Jeffree' from Dulwich in south London cradles his largest ever carp, a perfectly proportioned, golden, metallic koi/cross, skilfully extracted from a dense patch of yellow lilies from my two-lake Norfolk fishery after it had sucked down his floating mixer biscuit presented on a controller float rig. Sadly, John passed away, as he bravely knew he soon would, during January 2006. A truly lovely person, whose company left a marked impression upon me.

On arrival the heavy mist was just starting to clear and there was a definite 'nip' in the air, but there, between just 50 and 60 yards out, directly in front of where we intended fishing in the largest of the three lakes were the great, bronze backs of giant bream rolling through the surface film. We couldn't get rigged up quick enough, and within 20 minutes had two feeder rods apiece, presenting a mixture of worms, bread flake and sweet corn fanned out over the area, where great sheets of bubbles were regularly rising to the surface. It was obviously going to be a classical 'bream' morning.

Within minutes we experienced line bites on all four rods, and it was literally only a matter of time before one of the bobbins rose steadily to the butt ring. Three hours later, we were still thinking, "it's just a matter of time," when in truth the bream had moved way across the lake, (I was following their feeding route through binoculars) no doubt browsing upon blood worms over pastures new with not a consideration in the world for our regular introductions of sumptuous feeder food and carefully presented hook baits.

At 11 a.m., feeling totally frustrated, (though watching a pair of grebes repeatedly catch and feed small roach to their two offspring softened the pain) we called it a day, and Dave proclaimed himself winner (we are always competitive when fishing together, even after 50 years) on account of the three, 6oz roach that had gobbled up his worm baits. I immediately declared it was a 'bream only' session. And that was that. In the morning we shall visit a favourite local mill pool, again with big bream in mind, and hope that Dave's second and last day's fishing with me is more productive. I somehow think it will be. On the way back from the lakes we dropped in at the mill pool and introduced several handfuls of stewed maize into the head of the main flush where depth shelves to over ten feet.

Wednesday, 10th August

Overcast and dank following overnight rain. Light northwesterly wind.

I would love to report that brother Dave really got amongst those mill-pool bream this morning, but within minutes of dawn breaking over the pool, when the bream usually characteristically roll and cavort on the surface, I think we both knew that due to a total lack of movement, sport was going to be slow. These continuing heavily overcast conditions accompanied by low barometric pressure are putting the kiss of death on much of my local fishing in both still and running water, and I cannot remember a summer period in recent years to compare the situation

LEFT
Its smiles all round for Brother Dave over in the UK on holiday from Thailand where he now lives, having netted this 6lbs River Wensum bream. Although we had our sights set much higher, on some double figure specimens that we caught from a particular lake when we last fished together.

with. When we returned to the house at 11 a.m. having accounted for just a couple of bream around the 6lbs bracket, one on free lined maize and one on quiver-tipped bread flake, I immediately noticed that my wife Jo had turned the gas fire on in the sun lounge. And here we are in August. I guess that says it all.

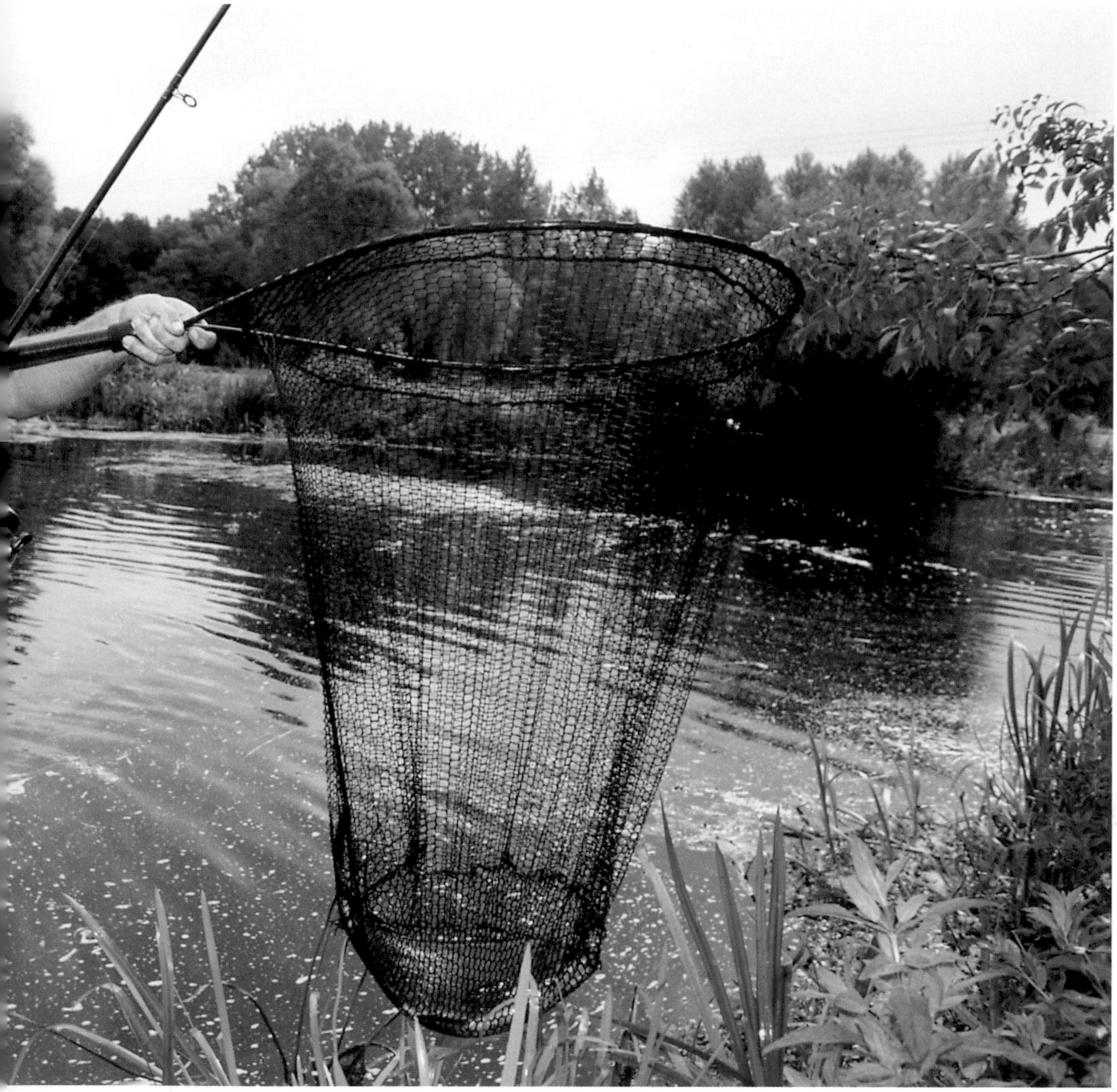

Thursday, 11th August

Hazy sunshine. No wind.

Had a most enjoyable hour's fishing this morning with our ten year old granddaughter Alisha and her three school chums Bethany, Heather and Molly who arrived for a barbeque and 'sleep-over' in the summer house. Alisha had promised them a fishing trip in the boat on the lake in front of the house, and so after clearing up several weeks of fallen leaves and twigs from the bottom of the boat, together with our West Highland Terrier 'Bola', who loves going afloat and wasn't going to miss out on the action for anything, we paddled over to the island and tied up amongst a

dense patch of lilies beside which the roach and rudd can easily be caught on float fished sweet corn in around four feet of water.

To save any arguments and tangles we took just one short rod along rigged up with a simple waggler float and size 12 hook tied direct to the 3lbs line, and the girls took it in turns catching, once each had taken three fish. The fish 'are' that easy to catch, and what roach they were too, (strangely the rudd were not feeding aggressively) averaging around four to ten ounces with two real whoppers that must have weighed getting on for 1½lbs apiece and in the absolute 'mint' of condition. How I would love to return to the days of catching such fish trotting in my beloved River Wensum which flows just 100 yards away from our two lakes, as I did when I first came to live in Norfolk 35 years ago, but where sizeable roach are now as rare as rocking horse droppings. I bet however, that the girls didn't enjoy themselves as much as granddad did.

Wednesday, 17th August

Hazy sunshine, light westerly wind.

Having enjoyed catching those big tope, bass and congers on Dave Nuth's boat *Theseus II* out from St. Helier on the island of Jersey back at the beginning of June, I was really looking forward to returning to the Channel Islands. And this time my destination was the island of Alderney, which was why I left home in Norfolk at 5 a.m. this morning in order to meet up with the rest of the party (following a 270 mile drive) in Weymouth Harbour at lunchtime. I actually arrived ahead of time despite the holiday traffic and popped into Weymouth Angling Centre on the quayside for a couple of blocks of frozen baby squid and some rag worms.

The three day, and three boat 'Alderney get-together' is being organised by Tom Bettle of Southern Motorboats Ltd. in Poole, whom I met at the NEC Angling Show back in April. Local lads Tom and his friend Chris Mazey who are co-owners of one of the boats, *Quest II*, a Merry Fisher 695, which has a 155hp Nanni engine and is 25 feet long with a beam of nine feet, were joined on board by my old mate Dave Lewis from Newport.

The second boat, a Quicksilver 750 which is 26½ feet long, eight foot in beam, and a family/weekender capable of 26 knots from its 220 hp Mercruiser engine was skippered by Steve Chambers of Oceanique who supplied it, with Steve Humpherson and me on board. And the third boat *Aquarius*, a 25 foot Arvor 250, also powered by a Mercruiser 4.3 litre, 220hp engine with skipper/owner Nick Oatway, Bob Musk and Tony Anderson on board, met us in mid channel after their long push up from near Plymouth.

We all stopped en-route to feather up some fresh fish bait in the way of mackerel, which we put on ice, and arrived in Alderney's picturesque Braye Harbour at around 7.30 p.m. And before checking into our guest house accommodation Simerock on the edge of St. Anne's, we enjoyed some wonderful steaks and drinks at The Moorings, just a short walk away from the harbour. Eating out in Alderney is almost as good as the fishing. Believe me.

For yours truly it was lovely to be back on the island again, with fond memories of when I filmed a wrecking programme for cod and ling here with Roddy Hays, in the very first series of my long running Anglia TV production *Go Fishing*, over 20 years ago. And of course I have returned on numerous occasions since, most often with my old mate and skipper of *Sundance II*, Roger Bayzand who pops over from Lymington regularly throughout the summer months. In fact his 'cat' was one of the first boats we saw as we entered the harbour tonight.

Thursday, 18th August

Hot and sunny, light southwesterly wind.

Following a hearty breakfast we left the moorings at around 9 a.m. and headed southwest for some rocky ground in depths varying between 60-120 feet of water to drift for black bream, using two-hook paternoster rigs and size one hooks baited with squid and rag worm. Unfortunately, due to having to refuel following the 50 mile crossing yesterday, we were rather late on the bream and after taking just a dozen or so to around 2½lbs between the three boats, presentation became impossible due to the strength of the spring tide pushing us along at over three knots, and so we motored further around the island to a series of deep-water banks and rips to drift for bass.

BELOW
Steve Chambers (left) of Oceanique Boats brings a Pollack on board for Steve Humpherson. A nice by-product to come from back-drift fishing sand eels over rips intended for bass.

Having been given a good supply of launce, we were into fish almost immediately and Steve Humpherson and I connected with a nice bass each on our first drop down, using 12 ounce leads and plastic booms, with ten foot 12lbs test clear mono traces and 5/0 hooks. This was fabulous fishing in depths varying between 60 and 120 feet where anything might turn up, and in addition to bass up to 7lbs we took some big mackerel plus several nice pollack, the best, a chunky double falling to Steve's rod.

RIGHT

I reckon I spent more time netting out fish for my mates than actually catching myself. Anyway that's my excuse, as I heave out a thick-set double figure Pollack for Steve Humpherson. Again, the successful bait was live sand eel bumped over a deep-water sand bank, whilst on the drift. One of the most fascinating and rewarding techniques perfected by sea anglers.

The other two boats also added black bream and wrasse to their haul of bass and pollack, while right at the end of the day, a conger of around 20lbs, coloured in deep chestnut like the kelp-covered rocks in which it lived, swallowed my mackerel flapper intended for tope. What a great, but incredibly tiring day's fishing, despite the calm seas and bright sunshine. Did we sleep well or what?

Friday, 19th August

Overcast, blustery northwesterly wind force 5.

I'm afraid there is no magical continuation of this story, although last night over a sumptuous
sea food platter dinner we bumped into Roger Bayzand whose party had taken a 75lbs blue shark and some double figure turbot earlier on in the week, because this morning the weather had changed 'big time'. We looked across the harbour entrance at giant, northwesterly waves ripping across, looking more like a force 7 than the predicted 5, and all agreed that in 25 foot long boats in addition to being foolhardy, going fishing off shore would at the very least be
rather unpleasant.

My old mate Roddy Hays who still lives on the island came down to the harbour to commiserate and suggested a coffee at his place, which Dave Lewis, Steve Humpherson and I gladly accepted after popping into the local tackle shop Alderney Angling and Sports, run most enthusiastically by local enthusiast Mark Harding who also runs special fishing classes for youngsters from the end of the breakwater, while the rest of the guys decided to fish in the harbour from their boats and have a baby wrasse and pollack competition. And polish off a few bottles of red.

At 10 a.m. the following morning our three boats set out across the channel with the wind slightly more comfortable, but it was rather hairy over the first few miles of rips directly out from Braye Harbour. I eventually arrived back home in Norfolk on the Saturday evening at 8 p.m. having left on the Wednesday morning at 5 a.m., with just one day's fishing to account for. But that's life, eh? Wouldn't swap it for anything.

Friday, 26th August

Blustery westerly wind with sunny periods.

It's always nice entertaining fellow fishery owners at my own lakes and today my good friend Con Wilson (no relation incidentally) popped across from Northampton with his nephew Paul Matthews for a few hours' carp fishing, aptly broken by a nice lunch and a few drinks along at the village pub. For many years Con researched some of the stillwater fly fisheries all over southern England that I featured in my Anglia TV series *Go Fishing*, and then he went one step further, several years back and actually purchased one of them,

famous Dever Springs Fishery in Barton Stacey, Hampshire, just off the 303 Andover road. It is a day ticket fishery renowned for its monster trout which has produced for yours truly over the years. So I particularly wanted for Con and Paul to experience some exciting fights with my carp.

In recent weeks however they have not really been receptive to my normal ploy of fishing the 'lift-float method', with a 10mm pellet on the hook in conjunction with smaller, loose fed pellets, regularly introduced beside the float. In fact roach and rudd running to well over the pound have almost become a nuisance to anyone float fishing light tackle and small baits for carp.

Of course getting towards the end of the summer season as we are now, both carp and tench do eventually wise up to float fishing and the 'verticle' line, especially in clear water, which along with the bait they purposefully learn to avoid. And for anyone float fishing without experiencing occasional line bites, it simply means that their target species are critically inspecting the terminal rig and consequently not biting. This is why the majority of serious carp anglers go to great lengths, with lead core rig traces and back leads to ensure their hook length and the line

beyond it for several yards, lie flat to the bottom. This enables a carp to approach the bait from any direction without fear of bumping into, or actually seeing the line and spooking.

With my favourite way of catching small-water carp being to 'stalk' them, only rarely do I use the more popular bolt-rig and waiting game approach. I think those who stalk are probably more like 'hunters', while those who put out three or four rods and wait, are akin to 'trappers'. But either way I wanted Con and Paul to catch and so we became 'trappers' for the day by putting out three bolt rigs tight up against a dense line of yellow lilies skirting the two islands in the middle of the largest lake, each with a three ounce lead set up and size 20mm 'marine extreme' boilie hair rigged to a size 6 hook on a ten inch braided hook link. Immediately prior to casting I nicked on a 'quick-dissolving' PVA bag of 6mm halibut pellets onto the hook, and catapulted in a few loose boilies around each hook bait. We then sat back to wait, and have a good natter, our conversation being mostly about how prospects were shaping up for salmon this autumn on Scotland's River Tweed at the famous 'Junction Pool' in Kelso. Con and Paul are fishing this majestic location for a week each in both September and October, and they have invited me along for a few days on their last trip in November. Can't wait.

Every so often a continual bleep from the buzzer interrupted the silence as a carp sucked up one of the hook baits, the first, a nice double figure common came to Paul's rod and the second, a beautiful koi-leather cross, getting on for 15lbs gave Con a real song and dance amongst the lilies. Fish number three and the last of the session which also came to Con's rod was another nice, scale-perfect common of around 9lbs. And my two mates drove back to Northampton with smiles on their faces.

Tuesday, 30th August

Hot and humid, flat calm.

Max Dorling who comes from near Brandon in Norfolk, won a day's carp fishing with me on our lakes through the Quidenham Hospice and I arranged to meet him beside the summer house for a 6 a.m. start. As the weather has eventually turned into what I would now call 'summer' I decided that a return to the 'lift method' of float fishing close in beside the lilies would produce some nice fish, and fortunately it did. Presenting two 10mm halibut pellets on a hair-rigged size 10 hook in conjunction with regular helpings of 6mm pellet loose feed, really had those carp bubbling away, and Max enjoyed banging into five fish to around 14lbs, (his largest carp ever) plus a lost Wels catfish of around 5lbs (which inexplicably got rid of the hook) on the 8lbs test Avon rod outfit prior to lunch.

When we returned in the afternoon the sun had induced most of the carp up to the surface where Max accounted for another two doubles on a floating controller rig and size 11mm floating pellets from amongst dense lilies. As most of the stems and pads are on the point of rotting off now in late summer, there was no chance of him losing either fish which put up incredible scraps. And he finished the day a tired but happy angler, which after all, is what these sessions are all about! Because if my guest has a good day, then so do I.

Friday, 2nd September

Overcast conditions burnt off by the sun from midday. No wind.

My how the time flies. Two thirds of this year gone already, and I still haven't managed to extract a barbel from my local River Wensum. Today would have been a good time to try however, as due to the recent lack of rain and with the river running low now for several weeks, barbel will have moved into the well oxygenated water of the local mill pools. But as they say I've had other fish to fry, in the form of guest Andy Lack from Harlow in Essex, whom I met beside the summer house at 6 a.m. as dawn broke.

Andy fancied a 'split' day's fishing, trying for carp in the morning, followed by some stalking for chub in the Wensum after lunch, which I guessed was a good choice taking the weather prospects into account. Poor Andy however, who turned out to be an accomplished float angler who regularly enjoys catching carp on the 'lift method', endured more than his share of bad luck. After landing a small common of around 2lbs, he went on to pull the hook from three double figure carp in succession from three different swims. So we settled for an early lunch and afterwards popped along to the Wensum Valley Hotel, Golf and Country Club stretch of the river in Taverham, to which I have access.

This fabulous, clear flowing, winding and weedy piece of the Wensum is over a mile long, and is in fact available to any guest spending a minimum of two nights in the Hotel. There are several 'classic' chub swims where great willows preside over the water, and it was into one of these tempting runs Andy free lined his lobworm downstream to a group of huge chub shading themselves beneath a canopy of overhanging branches, the largest looking rather better than 6lbs and immensely thick across its back. But they were far from pushovers, actually parting formation craftily to let his worm drift through the swim (something I could see from halfway up the tree) so I suggested he twitch it back erratically in case one grabbed hold, which it did. But that something was a pike of around 8lbs which thrashed the swim to foam and scaring the chub off, before promptly biting through Andy's 6lbs line.

The next cast into a similar swim produced a perch of around the pound, beautifully coloured and literally 'bristling', which dropped off as it came to the surface. I dare not look at my guest, as he nicked on another lobworm. From the next swim however, an under-cut bank run beneath our feet, Andy landed a modest-sized chub of around 2lbs, and his luck started to change. Casting way downstream to where the river narrowed into an eight foot deep hole with dense marginal growth overhanging both banks, the quiver tip pulled savagely round as something inhaled the lobworm on the drop, literally within seconds of casting, and after a hectic battle Andy slid the net beneath a lovely chub pushing 5lbs. This was more like my local summer chub stalking. But we were fast running out of time, and I suggested to Andy that an option for the last hour of his session, now he had taken some chub, would be to return to the lake and wipe the smiles from the faces of those carp. With the sun shining strongly all afternoon, they would definitely be up on the top in and around the lilies and taking surface baits, which is exactly how we finished the afternoon. Andy's only take, on a mixer biscuit, coming from a superbly shaped and scale perfect common carp of around 12lbs, which provided a thrilling scrap amongst the pads and stalks, allowing my guest to drive back to Essex, a happy bunny after all.

Phew! There are days when all the stops need to be pulled out and those fish really take it out of you. This was one of them.

Monday, 5th September

Bright sunshine and very warm, with force 3 southwesterly winds reducing throughout the day.

I'd hazard a guess that for most anglers, the 741 mile round-trip drive from my house in deepest Norfolk to the southwest coast of Wales would be too far for a day's fishing, but you won't hear me complaining. My old pal Dave Lewis from Newport, who drove the last 100 mile leg yesterday evening accompanied by Rhys Llywelyn of the Wales Tourist Board, together with friends John Mahon and Rob Starr, had arranged a day's fishing for blue sharks out of picturesque Milford Haven, which is actually a fiord, and part of the rugged and stunningly beautiful Pembrokeshire coastline, and I was hoping to research what was on offer for shooting a proposed new TV series next summer.

Our boat was White Water II, a 38 foot Evolution, berthed in the 'Haven' which cruises at 25 knots, and skippered by one of the most successful sharking specialists in the British Isles, Andrew Alsop. Together with mate Simon Davis, he has averaged throughout these summer months a staggering ten blue sharks per trip, with whoppers to 170lbs, plus the occasional porbeagle of similar size, but with a monster estimated at twice the size lost. Heady figures indeed, when like everyone else I honestly thought shark fishing had been on the decline since the heydays off Looe in Cornwall, 30 years back.

Having left Milford Haven which itself is 25 miles long, shelving down to over 70 feet in places and offering excellent sport with a variety of species from bass to conger, we headed due west and ten miles off the heads passed fascinating Grass Holm Island, the second largest gannet colony in Europe and home to over 40,000 pairs of these huge sea birds. We also attracted an enormous school of dolphins which stayed with the boat until they became bored.

Half way out to the sharking grounds we stopped to catch fresh mackerel for hook baits on feathers over the famous 'barrels', a huge reef system where pollack and coalfish can also be taken. And within half an hour, always great fun,

BELOW
With Dave Lewis hidden behind his camera capturing the action, Skipper Andrew Alsop (foreground) and mate Simon Davis haul a nice blue shark over the gunnels of White Water 11, for Rhys Llywelyn (far left) of the Wales Tourist Board.

BELOW RIGHT
Note the incredibly long snout and pectoral fins of this 110lbs blue shark held by Andrew Alsop (left) and Dave Lewis who enjoyed its powerful fight using a sporting, 30lbs outfit.

ANOTHER FISHING YEAR

we had filled a large box. Andrew's final stop for cutting the engine and starting the sharking 'drift' was around 25 miles out, a good five miles into the Gulf Stream where sea temperature was 65°F and the ocean floor dropped away to between 250 and 400 feet deep. Now was the time for mate Simon to earn his keep and, from the 50 gallon tub of pre-mixed and fermented mixture of bran and minced-up mackerel (not something your nostrils want to be immediately down wind of, believe me) fill four onion sacks to hang over the side as 'rubby dubby' to form a slick which encourages the sharks to follow up to the boat drifting along with the tide at around 1½ knots.

Now, at 11 a.m., was the time to put four 30lbs class outfits out, each presenting a fresh mackerel flapper on a 10/0 hook to 15 foot wire traces, beneath partially inflated balloons set at various depths between 20 and 150 feet, and wait. And wait we did for precisely one hour, while several species of sea birds including fulmars, storm petrels, shearwaters and herring gulls fed from the slick, with gannets and the occasional skua overhead. We were also entertained at regular intervals by dolphins play-acting around the boat and twice by basking sharks showing their immense bulk not 50 feet away directly beneath our bobbing balloons.

Then quite suddenly to break the strange trance of silence, one of the reels started screaming like a stuck pig. It was as always, a nerve-shattering experience and indeed a fitting tribute to the film Jaws which this very week celebrated its 30th birthday since we were all scared 'witless' by that classic motion picture back in the mid 1970s.

Airline pilot John Mahon took the first strike and following a spirited fight, (these 'blues' really pull your string) skipper Andrew hauled a 70lbs blue shark over the gunnels, resplendent in bright cobalt blue along its back with a creamy white belly, and that characteristic, long 'pointed' nose. It was John's first shark ever, as was the 80lbs blue subsequently landed by Rhys Llywelyn, and the 150lbs beauty, following a great battle by a well and truly 'knackered' Rob Starr, who is more used to scraps with brown trout on the fly rod in Berkshire, where he is a river keeper on the lovely River Kennet.

ABOVE
Sport was so
hectic; two sharks
were sometimes
being played
simultaneously.
Rhys Llywelyn's fish
is nearly ready for
hauling out near the
stern, while the big
blue hooked by Rob
Starr (foreground) is
over a 100 yards
from the boat and
still going despite a
firm drag setting.

Having caught more than our fair share of sharks over the years from the world's oceans, Dave Lewis and I were only too pleased to stand back and share in our friends' enjoyment. I then took a fish pushing 100lbs followed shortly afterwards by a 110lbs fish for Dave. And quite simply, the action never waned, with sharks following our 'rubby dubby' trail right up to the boat, till Andrew started the engines to head for home at around 4 p.m., by which time we had accounted for no less than 12 blue sharks with another three lost. What a simply unbelievable day. I can't wait to return to capture it all on video.

Tuesday, 13th September

Bright sunshine all day with a gentle southwesterly wind.

Having watched the carp in our two lakes all morning, on the move and definitely in aggressive feeding mode, whilst trimming the foliage back around some of the swims, I decided at around 3 p.m. to spend a couple of hours along at my favourite River Wensum mill pool, in case the barbel were in a similar mood. And literally within minutes of settling in amongst the rushes opposite

ANOTHER FISHING YEAR

the top flush with a 20mm boilie ledgered hard on the gravel bottom, around went the rod tip in a classical 'barbel' bite. As expected however the culprit was an ever hungry chub, and a nice one too which gave a good account of itself in the fast flow, despite my heavy 'barbel' gear, pulling the spring balance down to 5¼lbs.

Nothing else came from the fast water so I moved swims to below the pool where the river narrows and barbel can sometimes be seen moving over the sandy bottom between dense beds of rununculus, along with numerous chub and the odd big bream.

Immediately I spotted a couple of good thick-set doubles which looked all of 12-14lbs apiece, with a few lesser fish in attendance, so I started feeding a mixture of 8mm halibut pellets and large boilies into the head of the run where three swans were feeding, necks down, from the gravel bottom. Unfortunately, the chub (and I ended up with at least 50 of them plus a few small bream and roach moving in and out of the run), decided to go on a mad feeding rampage between the swans, competing for every pellet as they sank and on the bottom. This resulted in the poor old barbel, outnumbered by at least ten to one by the noticeably more aggressive chub, not getting a look in. To add insult to injury a couple of hungry pike of about 8lbs apiece were attracted to the melee, and every so often made savage attacks amongst the smaller fish.

Suddenly, it was the swim from hell. I had obviously overdone the loose feeding big time, and duly suffered by having to place my ledgered boilie several yards downstream where I could not observe which fish took it.

This resulted in one slamming chub bite after another. I thought at first I might be able to wade through them and eventually a barbel would grab hold. But it was not to be, and although they were all from quality fish in the 4-5½lbs range, they were not what I wanted, so I purposefully didn't strike, hoping most would not hook themselves. A couple did however and the resulting commotion made the barbel disappear. So I went home with my tail between my legs, feeling angry with myself and not just a little frustrated.

BELOW
While I enjoy catching big chub from my local River Wensum Weir pool, they can actually become somewhat of a nuisance, gobbling up baits presented on bolt rigs intended for barbel. A nice problem nonetheless.

Wednesday, 14th September

Overcast early, then sunny all day with a fresh southwesterly wind.

I met my guest for the day, Mark Halls, an estate agent from near Ipswich, beside the summer house a little after dawn. Mark had bid for a day's fishing with yours truly (a prize I had donated) at a BT charity bash last summer, and was keen to see if the carp fishing in my two lakes lived up to expectations, and despite the early, overcast conditions, I was confident he would produce at least a couple of doubles, although the first hour, fishing two hair-rigged 10mm pellets on a lift float rig

produced just one missed bite. Strong actions were called for, so we changed tactics and moved position to along the southwestern bank of the largest lake, where a 40 yard cast put both of Mark's ledgered boilies presented on bolt-rigs tight up beside a long bed of yellow lilies skirting the largest of the three islands. A good movement area whatever the weather conditions, as Mark was to find out just before lunch when one of the buzzers sounded.

Suddenly the world seemed a better place, as Mark enjoyed the spirited fight of a 12lbs mirror carp (his largest ever incidentally) which lead him a merry song and dance in and out of the dense lilies. These are all on the point of rotting off now, and Mark soon had his fish in the landing net. With the next run however he was a bit slow off the mark (no pun intended) in lifting the rod, resulting in the fish ploughing straight through the lilies and shedding the hook. This was a good point at which to wind the rods in for lunch and catapult some loose feed plus a few hook baits into the swim for when we returned. A wise move as it happened, because within half an hour of coming back from the pub and casting both baits out again, Mark was into a second 12 pounder, this time, a long, buttery-bronze coloured common carp.

Nothing followed unfortunately, and for the remaining two hours of the day, with the sun now noticeably warm for September, I suggested that we move over to the 'house bank' beneath tall alders, where carp can usually be taken ridiculously close in amongst the lilies on floating baits. Mark's first fish however, using a mixer biscuit super glued onto a size 10 hook set two feet from a floating controller and presented into small gaps amongst a dense mixture of both common yellow and dwarf pond lilies, turned out to be a surprise chub of around 3lbs. He then missed a couple of takes, before hooking into a common carp of around 8lbs which shed the hook on the surface when mere feet from the landing net.

By now the carp were becoming increasingly more suspicious, as close inspections but 'refusals' of his floating bait by several nice fish proved. It was indeed a fascinating experience for my guest who had never before witnessed carp at such close quarters, and certainly not with their open mouths a mere inch from his bait. Suddenly, directly below the roots of the huge alder we were hiding behind, two carp came up to the surface and started to suck down loose floaters which had drifted in close, and the lead fish, a long, thick-set common confidently inhaled Mark's floater down, less than a foot away from the bank.

Wham! The all-through action rod instantly hooped into an alarming full curve around the trunk of the alder as the carp shot off, hooking itself, with the 10lbs test line fair sizzling from the reel. A smiling Mark held on for grim death, hoping the fish would not make the entanglement of submerged marginal roots covering the end of the island opposite around 30 yards away, and he turned it just in time. By now my guest was becoming most competent at his new-found vocation, and after several, progressively less spirited runs, eventually steered the fish

RIGHT

Andy Scott (left) and Tony Policelli from Kent, show the stamp of bass we caught off Orford in Suffolk, whilst drifting over rips 20 miles out on board Stewart Smalley's boat Aldeburgh Angler 11.

expertly through the alder branches into my waiting landing net. And he instantly admitted that before today he would not even have considered casting into such a snaggy swim, let alone contemplating extracting his largest carp ever, a pristine, scale-perfect common which weighed over 14lbs. Well done indeed Mark!

Thursday, 15th September

Heavily overcast, force 4 southwesterly wind accompanied by persistent rain.

Suddenly overnight, it seems as though summer has been replaced in no uncertain terms by autumn, including a drastic drop in temperature, and I was glad that today my target species were bass, and not carp. Bassing enthusiasts Andy Stott and Tony Policelli had made the long drive up to Orford in deepest Suffolk from Kent, and were waiting on the Quay at 7.30 a.m. when I arrived, and shortly afterwards we were on board Stewart Smalley's 25 foot boat Aldeburgh Angler II, (a French-made Arvor) heading along the river beside Orford Island which amongst a horde of wading birds such as curlews, avocets and oystercatchers, is also home to the largest colony of black backed gulls in the British Isles. Not that I could enjoy my 'twitching' interests through binoculars as usual, on account of the slanting, heavy rain which unfortunately persisted on and off all day long.

Soon we were in open sea with the best part of two hours' steaming ahead before reaching a succession of 'rips' where the bottom shelves steeply upwards from over 100 feet to sand and shingle peaks just 60 to 70 feet deep, behind which waited our target species, hard battling bass in the 3-15lbs size range, (Stewart's boat produced a monster of 16½lbs just a few weeks back) ready to pounce upon their staple diet of young mackerel and sand eels as they become disorientated and swirled about by the fierce currents, and thus easy pickings.

Lovely fishing is this, using a technique simply called 'drifting' where the skipper takes the boat 100 yards up tide along varying parts of each rip and drifts back over it, with 20lbs test braided reel lines bumping 8-10oz leads up the slope and down the other side, presenting via a plastic boom and ten foot, clear monofilament trace, a 5/0 hook and a fresh or frozen launce (greater sand eel), and pal Stewart Smalley is a past master at seeking out quality-sized

bass. Over the years he has put several double figure specimens to 12lbs my way from over these very same rips and being the second day of a building spring tide, absolute tip top bassing conditions, with the whole of the ebbing tide ahead of us, by the time we reached the target area our anticipation was literally at fever pitch. Bassing gets you like that, especially as Andy Stott boated a nice fish on the very first drift while I missed a thumping bite.

However, and although we did account for some scrappy bass to around the 4lbs mark, uncharacteristically (most hits usually result in a hooked fish) we experienced numerous half-hearted thumps and knocks, most of which did not materialise into bass. Our baits simply came back crunched or bitten in half.

Were those larger bass affected by the sudden and drastic overnight temperature and barometric drop? Or were our 'tentative' bites purely from small school-bass? I wish I knew.

Monday, 19th September

Light southerly wind. Heavily overcast.

I left my Norfolk home at 4 a.m. this morning to arrive at fellow angling writer, Martin Bowler's house in Chippenham, Wiltshire (a distance of 225 miles) by around 7.30 a.m. for the first of four days' barbel fishing together. Traffic on both the M25 and M4 was moving well, so I actually arrived on time, and after a quick 'cuppa', we headed for one of Martin's favourite local hot spots, a club stretch along the diminutive and delightful, steep-sided River Marden which is a tributary of the Bristol Avon, inhabited by a good stock of dace, chub and barbel from a couple

of pounds upwards to the very occasional double. Its swift flowing, clear and weedy water, interspersed with sandy and gravel runs, for the most part heavily overgrown with beds of ribbon weed and clumps of bulrushes, with overhanging willows and blackthorn bushes providing that all important 'shade', reminded me so much of how Hertfordshire's once lovely, little River Rib used to be back in the 1950s and '60s, where I served my 'stalking apprenticeship', before the ravages of water abstraction took hold.

Unlike the Rib, now a mere memory of its former self, the Marden was a true delight to wander with kingfishers and grey wagtails repeatedly zooming by, and a pair of buzzards high overhead. Catch those barbel however, we could not. The fish seemed surprisingly 'spooky', unnaturally so. Martin however accounted for a small chub on a ledgered 14mm halibut pellet, whilst I blanked despite a double figure barbel feeding from a gravel clearing amongst dense ribbon weed on and off for an hour or so, sometimes mere inches from my hair-rigged pellet. Nevertheless it was as always, truly fascinating to watch.

After lunch we moved to the Bristol Avon itself close to Chippenham, which like all the rivers at present is suffering badly from a lack of rain. I managed to produce a tiny chub from the first of Martin's suggested swims immediately upstream from a huge weed raft that had collected around the branches of a partly submerged willow, and then spent the remainder of the afternoon much further downstream, precariously balanced on a 12 inch wide branch of a fallen willow, literally ten feet above another huge raft, way out in the middle of the river, where within minutes of introducing several handfuls of 4mm pellets, a huge barbel appeared and started to feed from the bottom of a four foot deep, narrow gravel run along the edge of the raft. Had I even managed to hook the monster which looked all of 12lbs plus, actually landing it would have always been in doubt. As it was, after carefully lowering in my hook bait on a bolt rig, the great fish slunk off, never to be seen again, and that was day one.

Tuesday, 20th September

Light southerly wind with sunshine for most of the day.

From Martin's house we headed west along the M4 and then onto the Chepstow road heading upstream along the stunning Wye valley and a limestone gorge of truly unusual beauty, past the ruins of famous Tintern Abbey and into the historic town of Monmouth with its lovely old bridge spanning the majestic River Wye. We passed through Landogo, where I remembered

ABOVE
I've fished few barbel swims to compare in either beauty or majesty with this fast and rocky, mouth watering run immediately downstream of a salmon croy on the River Wye at Symonds Yat. It simply 'screams' barbel. And I'm still screaming.

fishing for salmon along the 'Hardy' beat over 20 years ago with Peter and Paul Thomas, and then finally onto Symonds Yat along the river's eastern, heavily wooded bank (just a 55 mile drive from Chippenham) where we met up with good friend Terry Theobald at the start of the 'Biblings' club stretch, well known for the chub and barbel which inhabit the picturesque fast, and rocky-bottomed runs.

Terry put me in a 'to die for' barbel swim just below a narrow suspension bridge spanning the wide river where a rocky salmon croy, juts 20 feet out into the main flow providing, immediately downstream, a 50 yard long and fast gravel-bottomed run, while he and Martin set off downstream to fish about half a mile below me. I naturally thought I'd died and gone to heaven. This is the barbel swim of all barbel swims. But sadly no one had told the barbel I was coming, and apart from a couple of 'clanging line bites' plus an unmissable bite on a 14mm ledgered halibut pellet, which nearly pulled the rod in, resulting in a barbel of around 5lbs,

ANOTHER FISHING YEAR

which put up a disproportionately powerful scrap (I thought it was twice the size) I then sat there expectantly from late morning through to darkness waiting for the swim to suddenly switch on, which sadly it didn't, apart from the occasional salmon cavorting on the surface midway along the run.

Meanwhile Terry took a couple of chub, and Martin had a field day, bagging no less than ten chub of between 4 and 5lbs plus, all on a method feeder rig and 15mm hair-rigged boilie hook bait, but neither had a barbel from what appeared to be classical barbel runs.

A wonderful day spent along what surely must be one of the most breathtaking river valleys in the British Isles. But why were those barbel not having it?

LEFT
My bolt rig-ledgered halibut pellet did however produce one modest-sized fish, which would have been twice the size, had it come off. The sheer force of flow being so much stronger in the Wye than most other barbel rivers.

Wednesday, 21st September

Southwesterly wind. Hazy sunshine all day.

After breakfast it was back on the M4 again and then the M5 to Worcester where following a leisurely 80 mile drive Martin and I met up with old friends, fellow angling writer Des Taylor and Angling Times photographer Mick Rouse, for a 'sociable' day out barbel fishing on the lower River Severn where it converges with the lovely River Teme, which started with a nice lunch and a few drinks, plus much storytelling at a local hostelry. So we didn't actually get to the river before 2 p.m. Not that it really mattered, because the weather pattern this week together with really low water levels, has really put the kybosh on our barbel fishing. Not only are the fish unusually spooky, they are not inclined to feed aggressively till the light starts to fade, as we were to experience, although Martin did winkle out a 5 pounder from the heavily overgrown River Teme in mid-afternoon.

In fact Martin ended up with a most healthy score of eight barbel (the remainder from the Severn) of between 3 and 6lbs, all on method feeder tactics, while Des and I could not buy a bite till darkness fell over the river. He then took several small chub plus a

5lbs barbel in a mad hour before all went quiet, while I managed a 3 pounder, followed by a lovely, fat fish of around 9lbs, which fought incredibly strongly, despite the sluggish flow.

Martin's method feeder tactics and boilie hook baits, were noticeably more successful for inducing bites than the PVA bag and 14mm halibut pellet hook bait approach of Des and myself. Overall, I guess a total of 11 barbel was a fair result for our excruciatingly long walk down to the

Severn/Teme junction from where we left the cars. Mick Rouse was certainly more than happy with the shots he took of all our fish, though it would have been nice to have secured some 'action' stuff during daylight. But it was not to be. I would certainly like to fish the same stretch when it's higher and moving faster from the first of the winter floods. On past occasions Martin has had numerous doubles in such conditions, mainly from the swim I fished, as large as 14lbs, so I could very well be back sometime.

ANOTHER FISHING YEAR

Thursday, 22nd September

Mist at first. Sunny all day with a southwesterly wind.

We had but a 15 mile drive this morning for the last of my four day visit, to the lovely Bristol Avon between Avon Cliffe and Limpley Stoke. We started in fact at the pool immediately below the river bridge at Limpley Stoke which looked simply mouth-watering. But again those barbel knew better and we moved after lunch, having taken just one small chub, a couple of miles upriver to a winding, nicely overgrown classical barbel beat where the river ran fast and clear between huge beds of bulrushes, and beneath great, overhanging and partly submerged, fallen willows.

Martin put me in a lovely swim where depth dropped away beneath an overhanging willow along the near bank, but though I stuck at it all afternoon, nothing materialised to my PVA bag (filled with 4mm pellets) and hair-rigged 14mm halibut pellet approach, while he took a couple of small chub from a deep run 100 yards further upstream.

Our four day barbel stint had been well and truly scuppered by low water levels and spooky fish. But for me it had been immensely enjoyable nonetheless. I'd caught barbel from rivers where I had not previously fished for them and come to realise why it is in certain parts of the country, silver shoal species in the upper rivers are thankfully still around in catchable numbers, unlike my home counties of Norfolk and Suffolk. In four days I had seen just three cormorants along the Wye, Bristol Avon and the lower Severn, but when I returned home on Friday lunchtime, there were four perched up in the tall, dead tree over on the other side of the lake at the bottom of our garden, not 200 yards away.

Says it all, doesn't it?

Tuesday, 27th September

Baking hot (over 35°C) hazy sunshine, gentle easterly breeze.

Escorting groups of anglers to various 'adventure' locations around the world on behalf of Tailor Made Holidays has got to be the best job I've ever had. I sit writing this for instance, on the veranda of my 'muru-tented' lodge, having just enjoyed a light lunch and a large glass of chilled white wine, with the mysterious Zambezi River, averaging over half a mile across and flowing swiftly along from right to left, its banks shaded by tall hardwood trees, not a cricket pitch length away. The constant bellowing of hippos coming from behind the huge, reedy islands in mid river, is, apart from birds chattering, the only noise I am conscious of. God how I love this spot at Mwambashi River Lodge which is situated within the 100 mile long Lower Zambezi National Park, on the northern (Zambian) bank of the river over a 100 miles downstream from famous Lake Kariba. The Zambezi River is in fact the borderline between Zambia (once North Rhodesia) and Zimbabwe (once South Rhodesia) for several hundred miles.

Elephants and buffalo walk lazily through the camp, whilst after dark, amidst a myriad of animals, lions and hyenas are regular visitors. One reason why when walking back from your evening meal in the restaurant, you need to be escorted by one of the guides. Even after 15

LEFT TOP

Hardly the three wise monkies, but we did each get to enjoy the incredible power of River Severn barbel, even if they were averaging on the small side.

LEFT BOTTOM

The largest, a chunky individual, felt significantly larger (as they do) whilst playing it during darkness, than its 9lbs. Why is that?

OVERLEAF

Two things are virtually guaranteed for those who stay at Mwambashi River Lodge set beside the Legendary Zambezi River which throughout the pristine wilderness of the Lower Zambezi National Park is the borderline between Zambia (north) and Zimbabwe to the south. Breathtaking sunsets, and high-jumping, specimen-sized tiger fish, like this 10 pounder held by local guide Steve Maartens, and caught (his first ever would you believe) by Hussein, 'Moose' Ahmed, left.

SEPTEMBER

RIGHT

With the majestical Zambezi River, over half a mile wide and flowing strongly not a cricket pitch length away, could there be a more inspirational location at which to settle down with a glass of chilled white wine to record the day's events, than at Mwambashi River Lodge?

consecutive years of visiting this mesmeric river valley with its intensity of wildlife, stunning, truly wilderness scenery and unrivalled sports fishing for a variety of weird and colourful species, the main two being the high leaping tiger fish to over 20lbs and the giant vundu catfish which grows over 100lbs, it never ceases to amaze and enthral me. And although I have fished way above Victoria Falls and all the way down into Kariba itself, nowhere do the tiger fish average such a high average size (doubles are commonplace) than in these wide and fast flowing lower reaches.

Following a 9½ hour BA flight yesterday evening from Heathrow's terminal 4 to Lusaka, it took just 30 minutes this morning in a single prop, 12 seater Cessna Caravan, to deposit our seven man party at Kiti, Mwambashi's dirt air strip, where good friend and manager of the lodge Steve Maartens arrived to pick us up in the 'Game-viewing' 4x4, a Land Rover Defender. Night time game viewing is a speciality of the camp for visitors once they have finished their fishing, and on the drive into camp Steve pointed out a pack of wild dogs taking shade beneath a tall tree.

After a quick change and tackle sort-out we set off in beamy 18 foot aluminium boats for a spot of bait catching, followed by a few drifts for tiger before lunch. As always I fished with Steve in his boat, so we can rotate our guests and fish with different anglers each day. Our first two were Paul Dawson and Hussein Ahmed ('Moose' for short as he likes to be called) and within half an hour Steve had anchored us in a deep drop-off immediately below a long, wide sandbar close to a pod of hippos with a view to us catching on ledgered worms and size 8 hooks some free-biting chessa (a bream-like bottom feeder) which when filleted and cut into 3 inch x 1 inch strips makes great bait for tiger fish. And we soon had half a dozen between 12oz and 1½lbs in the live well.

Wherever pods of hippos collect in the drop-offs incidentally, bait fish and vundu catfish, plus tigers of course, are all attracted to their dung and general stirring up of water in what is basically a very clean-flowing river. These are in fact the best 'hot spots' for most species, and provided you don't push the hippos onto shallow water where they might turn towards the boat in panic and thus become an instant danger, they always move away and settle down again. That the hippo is by far the most dangerous animal in Africa because it kills more people through its territorial aggression, is certainly no idle chat.

With an hour to go before lunch Steve suggested we drift for tigers and so we swapped our quiver tip rods for light carp outfits and 6500-sized multiplier reels loaded with 30lbs test braid, with 20 inch, 30lbs test wire traces to which a single size 2/0 Eagle Wave, wide gape hook had been twisted on. Smaller, narrow-gape hooks do not set hold anywhere near so easily behind the tiger fish's awesome dentistry of large, razor sharp canine teeth. There are ten set into the upper jaw and eight in the lower. They even put the gnashers of a piranha to shame.

By drifting with the fish strips worked out the back of the boat as we sped along at a current speed of around two to three knots, (faster than the walking pace incidentally) sideways on, some beautifully coloured but modest-sized tigers came our way. Both Paul and I caught fish to around 5lbs. As always, the tigers fought with incredible speed and ferocity, each repeatedly making acrobatic, tail-walking leaps, several feet clear of the surface. Tarpon apart, I cannot think of a species in fresh or salt water that for, albeit a fairly short but truly explosive battle, can hold a candle to tiger fish. They are simply in an athletic class of their own, and exquisitely enamelled in bright silver scales, overlaid laterally in lines of dark digits, rather like a mullet or striped bass, with beautiful scarlet fins.

On arrival back at the lodge it appeared that everyone had fared well. The largest tiger of the morning at 11lbs exactly, fell to Harry Chamberlain whose previous best, coincidentally, weighed 10lbs and was caught on one of my escorted safaris to Lake Nasser in Egypt, seven years ago. After lunch we all had a siesta, and hit the river again at 3 p.m. (it is far too hot and demanding to stay out all day long in the Zambian sunshine) catching on our boat alone 14 tigers during the afternoon, the best two being a 9½lbs fish for yours truly and a 10lbs beauty for Moose, who also accounted for his first vundu. It scraped well and weighed 15lbs, having sucked up a chessa head from the bottom when we anchored over a drop off, as is the plan most evenings here, to put out ledgered baits on all the heavy outfits (uptide rods and multipliers loaded with 35lbs mono) whilst enjoying our 'sundowners' as the sun literally sets, often, into the most stunning array of colours and cloud formations.

Wednesday, 28th September

Strong westerly wind and hazy sunshine.

I was woken gently from a deep, deep sleep (I always seem to sleep well in tents) by tromboning hippos and an incessant dawn chorus of birds. How lovely it is to be back in Africa again!

Steve and I fished today with Dave Evans and Keith Dellard, both of whom have previously been on my escorted safaris. Dave to Lake Nasser a couple of years back and Keith to both the Upper Zambezi and to Lake Kariba, several years ago before Mugabe's brain became 'fried', when Zimbabwe was arguably one of the most stable economies in Africa.

As usual we spent the first couple of hours ledgering worms for fresh bait amongst fallen trees along the margins, and in addition to some small chessa, Steve hooked a nice nkupe of

ABOVE
Two of the
Zambezi's distinctly
'bream-like' species
Nykupe (left) and
Chessa (right) which
not only provide
great light-tackle
sport, but fresh bait
for tiger fish when
filleted and cut into
strips, are displayed
by my good friend
and manager/guide
at Mwambashi River
Lodge Steve
Maartens.

around 3lbs. The nkupe is also a bream-like species that can attain weights of up to 20lbs, whilst the chessa rarely reaches double figures. When we had caught enough Steve filleted them and we started drifting for tigers. Unfortunately this proved rather slow and having taken just a couple each to around 6lbs, with just an hour left before returning for lunch and a siesta, as we were within sight of a particular island where Steve and I fished successfully for vundu when filming my *Fishing Safari* TV series three years back, I suggested that we change over to vundu tackle with yesterday's chessa heads (the stinkier the better) cast out into the centre of an off-river lagoon situated along the southern side of the island.

This particular spot produced vundu to over 40lbs when filming, and again, it did not let us down, being one of the few deep and still pieces of water along the river at Mwambashi. Keith whacked into a good fish within 20 minutes of the baits being cast out, and whilst playing it my lighter (tiger) outfit screamed off. We were then playing two vundu simultaneously. Unfortunately mine came off before I could catch a glimpse, but it went lazily around the boat (which Steve had now taken out into the middle of the lagoon, having wound all the other rods in) a couple of times before the hook inexplicably pulled free. Keith meanwhile had his vundu hauled on board by Steve using a chain mail glove to get a firm grip around its bottom lip. It was a lovely, superbly proportioned, mahogany-coloured vundu of 45lbs.

We had not settled back into position (tied up beside the island to protruding tree roots) and put all the rods out again for more than ten minutes, before Dave's reel started screaming (most runs from vundu scream off like a bat out of hell) and he duly landed his first vundu ever following an exciting scrap, a fish of around 20lbs. We then missed one more run on Keith's rod, before returning to camp for lunch at 12 noon, marvelling en route at the breathtaking colours of the white fronted bee eaters which have nesting holes in the high sided banking. The plumage along their back, wings and tail is a stunning array of green and shimmering turquoise. The colours of the carmine bee eater however, are even more breathtaking.

In the afternoon we motored way downriver passing a myriad of wading birds on route including both open billed and saddle billed storks, sacred ibis, purple herons, greater egrets and a goliath heron. Along a flattish island where they obviously had their nests, four plovers were noisily mobbing a yellow billed kite, the most common bird of prey along the Zambezi, and a bird which Steve regularly hand-feeds with strips of chessa. It is indeed a sight to be seen, the kite zooming in at incredible speed to take the fish from Steve's outstretched hand.

We stopped to drift some simply mouth-watering glides and drop-offs, but the tiger fish were noticeably 'tetchy', the majority of hits not developing into hittable runs. I must have

ABOVE

The wildlife-rich
Zambezi River
throughout its lower
reaches varies
between several
hundred yards and
one mile across,
interspersed with
reed and tree-
covered sand bars
and islands.

pulled the hook from a dozen or more fish and actually finished the session having landed just one, and that a real baby of 2lbs. Steve and Dave however had three apiece to around 7lbs. During the last hour when we anchored up alongside the heavily wooded northern bank for sundowners, a sudden commotion on land attracted our attention, and we were treated to the unusual sight of an osprey trying to grab one of a dozen or more guinea fowl. It hit into them horizontally, not diving down from above. Foliage of the winter thorn and acacia trees was far too dense, so it must have been perched up deliberately just into the jungle, to swoop down upon the fowl, which it missed anyway. What a spectacle!

Thursday, 29th September

Overcast with light drizzle, followed by hazy sunshine. Strong easterly wind.

I woke to a wonderful dawn chorus with numerous tiny, vervet monkeys jumping about in the tall acacia trees high above my tented lodge. During the night hippos came up onto the bank at the edge of the jungle in front of the lodges, and in the dim light could be seen shuffling about, feeding upon curly seed pods that had fallen from the trees.

SEPTEMBER

After the usual cup of coffee and tackle sort-out immediately after dawn Steve and I set off downriver in the company of Harry Chamberlain and his son-in-law Adam Dunn. We caught sufficient chessa for drifting within an hour and spent the rest of the morning giving the tiger fish a real going over. In all we landed over a dozen, the best two of 12½lbs and 11lbs falling to Steve and me respectively. Steve's actually came on a stinking chessa head ledgered on heavy gear and intended for vundu when we anchored up over a deep drop-off for half an hour's 'static' fishing, which is strange really, because we make a point of catching fresh chessa every morning due to the preference for fresh bait that tiger fish usually show. Come to think of it tiger fish do gobble up some odd offerings. A few years back when out of chessa and my standby vundu bait of good old luncheon meat, I managed to persuade Steve's wife Kerry who organises the food at Mwambashi, to part with a pack of pork sausages. And what did I catch on a ledgered banger first cast? Yes, a double figure tiger.

My 11 pounder today came when on the drift again using tiger gear and provided a truly memorable scrap, including a couple of high leaps. It actually went round the boat three times before it was ready to be 'boga-gripped' out. How on earth we managed to land tigers before 'boga grips' which lock tightly and perfectly behind those wicked teeth, I just don't know. It's as though the device were invented for tiger fishing. I can remember one thing though. The mesh of our landing nets never lasted very long.

After lunch and a short siesta we headed out again at around 2 p.m. and were immediately treated to Steve's 'party piece' when a kite appeared from nowhere ten feet above the boat which was zooming along at over 20 knots, and started whistling at Steve for a piece of chessa. He should have been a bird trainer. Mind he does have a few scars on his fingers to prove that at great speed kites cannot always be trusted to grab only the chessa fillet. Rather him than me. I have enough trouble at home with 'Cheeko' my African Grey parrot, who every now and again tries to take a lump out of my ear.

LEFT
Whilst fishing out with guests Harry Chamberlain (left) and his son in law Adam Dunn (right) Steve Maartens hand-feeds a piece of our tiger fish bait to a Yellow billed kite as it swoops down at truly alarming speed to his 'whistle'. Even using a camera shutter speed of 1/500th of a second (the fastest possible in such overcast conditions with 100 ASA film) it was impossible to freeze the moment.

Following a couple of hours of tiger fishing which produced a dozen fish to around 8lbs, Steve suggested we motor upriver about a mile above the camp into a muddy bay heavily fringed with massive beds of the blue-flowered water hyacinth, for a spot of vundu fishing (we had plenty of stinking chessa heads) whilst enjoying our sundowners. This last hour of the day Steve and I never want to spend drifting for tigers. It is too much like hard work. Besides, chilling out with a G and T or a bottle of wine is such a great end to the day. And Kerry always makes sure we have a box of nibbles like samosas or some biltong to chew on. Yes folks, it can be tough in the African jungle. But like I always say, someone's got to do it.

We had barely been settled bows into the hyacinth for 20 minutes with three rods out, a stinky chessa head on each, and not even on our second G and T, when Adam's vundu reel suddenly out of complete silence, started screaming like the proverbial stuck pig. I'd already explained to him about knocking the reel into gear after turning the ratchet off, and then waiting for the line to become 'humming' tight before slamming the rod back. And he did it to perfection, banging the size 7/0 hook home immediately, into what was, by the power and speed of its initial run, obviously a sizeable fish, which just went and went, half emptying the 10,000 reel of line.

Steve and Harry wound the other rods in whilst I clicked away on the camera, and following an exciting and lengthy battle from by far Adam's largest fish ever, when its wide head finally popped up to the surface, Steve leaned over the side and hauled it out. It was a real beauty and all of 65lbs. It may even have been larger.

When Steve helped Adam to hold it up for a trophy shot however, the shutter on my Nikon F100 suddenly decided to self destruct. Thank goodness for my little back-up digital camera, a Casio 4 M-P, otherwise I would have been totally gutted. Over the years my photography has become equally important as the fishing.

BELOW
If Steve Maartens didn't use a chain mail glove to grip the lower jaw of this 65lbs Vundu, caught by Adam Dunn, (right) the skin across the top of his hand would be immediately 'rubbed' off by the catfish's, abrasion pad situated in the roof of it's huge mouth.

Friday, 30th September

Overcast early on, followed by bright sunshine. Strong westerly wind.

Fished with Paul and Moose again today and started well by snapping one of my telescopic travel rods on a snag whilst bait catching. I followed this up by missing run after run when we started tiger fishing and did not in fact catch a thing all morning, while Paul took fish of 6 and 8lbs and Steve a beauty of 10lbs.

After lunch we continued tiger fishing way upstream along a magnificent mile long tree-clad island close in to the marginal overhanging and fallen trees where several elephants allowed

ANOTHER FISHING YEAR

ABOVE

A 50lbs Vundu, caught by Paul Dawson (left) following an epic battle beneath dense clumps of water hyacinth, is heaved out by Steve Maartens, who has actually landed specimens of the species himself to 100lbs.

our boat to drift by them without spooking, not 30 yards away. A truly emotional experience. I also started to get into the tigers taking a couple of 5 pounders before hooking into a veritable monster which stayed a good 40 yards off the boat in the strongest currents for several minutes without jumping. And the big ones are known for jumping only when they see the boat. But this particular fish I never got to see because the hook suddenly pulled free just when I was getting the upper hand and counting my chickens. Did I curse or what!

For the remaining hour of the afternoon we returned to the shallow bay, and very same spot that produced the big vundu yesterday evening. With both buffalos and elephants trudging through the dense hyacinth behind us, Steve poured out our sundowners, and we settled down to wait with the golden glow of the sun upon everything as it started to set. And again, we were hardly into our drinks, when Paul's stinking chessa head was picked up by what seemed to be yet another good vundu. It certainly fought incredibly strongly as all vundu do, size for size when compared to most other species of fish, making several long runs into the darkness beneath the fringe of hyacinth before Paul eventually worked it back to the boat. Eventually its long whiskers and wide, flat head surfaced beside the boat and Steve hauled it on board using a gloved hand at the first attempt. It was a beauty of around 50lbs and by far Paul's largest catfish.

At around 5.30 p.m. we motored downriver to where Lloyd, one of the other guides, was waiting with the Land Rover 4x4, plus yet more drinks and nibbles, ready for darkness to set in and to take us, plus the other anglers of our group on a game drive through the National Park back to camp. We were the last boat to arrive, due to Steve suddenly cutting the engine en route and telling us to look into the reedy shoreline, for there not 20 yards away was a young male lion squatting down and lapping up water from the margins. What a sight! It was however too dark by now for any serious photography.

During the hour-long game drive we saw impala, by far the most common of all the antelopes here, nightjars, waterbuck, hippos, buffalos, several hyenas, genets, warthogs, and a pair of civets. And we were back in time for a quick shower before dinner at 7.30 p.m. Another wonderful day in paradise.

RIGHT
With our aluminium boat tied up to a fallen tree along the margins of the Zambezi River amongst a huge bed of floating, purple-flowered, water hyacinth, a duo of inquisitive jumbo's approach (L-R) Harry Chamberlain, Steve Maartens and Adam Dunn who are all trying their level best to look unconcerned. And as the elephants approached 'us', and not the other way round, they had good reason to do so. Honestly!

Saturday, 1st October

Clear blue skies, bright sunshine, and a cooling easterly wind.

There were several hippos and elephants wandering between our tented lodges during the night and as usual the vervet monkeys were leaping from branch to branch high in the trees overhead, their acrobatics and squabbling being most comical to watch.

Dave and Keith were back on our boat again today and bait catching proved rather slow as it has for the last couple of days. There are times when chessa are really having it, and times when they bite as delicately and as quick as a dace back home. We eventually managed to catch enough fresh bait however, and the wait was made all the more worthwhile by a superb tiger of 14lbs taken by Dave from a deep drop-off where we decided to anchor up and have a break from drifting.

When we returned for lunch however each having accounted for tigers to 6lbs, and watched a pair of elephants enjoying a mud bath en route, we were given the news that Paul Dawson had enjoyed a marvellous morning's sport with no less than four doubles of 10lbs, 12lbs, 16lbs and 16½lbs. What a remarkable catch of big tigers. Things are certainly hotting up.

After lunch I returned to my lodge as usual to read for an hour and must have dozed off because I woke suddenly from the commotion of an elephant scraping seed pods from the roof of the tent not four feet from where I lay, and he stayed close to the lodge pottering about till I walked down to the boats at 2 p.m. Steve then took Dave, Keith and me way downstream to drift for tigers and what a magnificent afternoon's sport we enjoyed, exploring mile-long, turbulent sections of the Zambezi, sometimes in midstream directly below deep drop-offs, sometimes just 40 yards from the jungle-clad shoreline where the structure-rich holding areas of fallen hardwood trees harboured strong concentrations of fish.

Keith took the largest tiger of exactly 13lbs, while Steve boated an 11 pounder. I lost a fish of similar size right beside the boat, and Dave took fish to 8lbs. As usual all on free lined strips of chessa fillet, and whilst we did battle with the tigers, a myriad of birds were on parade to marvel at. Fish eagles called from the tree tops with that haunting cry of theirs. Storks, egrets and Marabou storks waded the grassy shallows where many a big croc lies wonderfully camouflaged and patiently in wait and vultures circled high in the thermals on the lookout for a recent kill to clean up.

Strangely, our 'sundowner' hour produced not the slightest interest from tigers or vundu, which meant we had more time drinking and we returned to camp in fine fettle, to see that tables and chairs had been set under the trees not five yards from the river. It was barbeque night in the jungle.

Sunday, 2nd October

Clear blue skies and bright sunshine. Light easterly wind.

This is our last full day here in the Lower Zambezi National Park, and it will indeed be a wrench having to depart tomorrow morning, having enjoyed such wonderful hospitality and equally

wonderful fishing. But then I guess it's always best to leave wanting one more cast or one more day, because then you will return.

In the company of Harry and Adam, we went way downstream and got straight into some large chessa and nkupe on ledgered worms from a deep drop-off, along a beautiful stretch of the river interspersed with reed islands where spurwing and Egyptian geese waddled the margins, and by 8 a.m., much earlier than usual, we had enough in the live well for the entire day.

We then motored still further downstream where Steve set up a drift along a very fast run 40 yards off the heavily wooded northern (Zambian) shoreline, the bank heavily overhung by tall, vine-covered hardwood trees where the occasional fish eagle perched on top. We enjoyed great sport with numerous tigers, the best of 10½lbs coming to my rod and experienced a unique and emotional, if not somewhat 'hairy' situation, when two elephants decided to wander up and munch upon the dense rushes not three yards from the boat where we had tied up to a fallen tree for a short spell in order to present static baits along a particularly deep run that was too snaggy to work on the drift.

After lunch we went downriver again for a last play with the tigers and in the late afternoon, having boated fish to 8½lbs and lost what looked to be a much larger fish when it jumped off the hook, I then went and hooked into a real monster, certainly the largest tiger I have ever had on the end of my line. It came zooming towards the boat from where I hooked it 40 yards away directly upstream, and instantly leapt clear of the water not four feet from where Steve and I were standing 'open mouthed'. Steve put it at around 17lbs, but to my eyes it looked even bigger. It was a lost monster indeed.

For sundowners we pushed the bows of the boat into a reedy promontory and cast out bottom baits, chessa and nkupe heads, for vundu, while we sat back to enjoy the setting sun on our last afternoon along this fabulous valley.

Nothing happened for 20 minutes and then would you believe it, I struck into a belting vundu run on my light outfit, only to hook my largest tiger of the entire week. A beauty of 12½lbs, which put up a marvellous scrap. What a lovely end to what has been an exceptional week's fishing. Over dinner Steve, who has been keeping an accurate record of our group's catches all week, said that in all we had accounted for a staggering total of 330 tigers (we must have hooked and lost six times as many) including no less than 30 doubles, for an overall weight topping 1500lbs, Paul's 16½ pounder remaining the largest. We also had a total of ten vundu, the best to Adam at 65lbs, the total aggregate weight for both tigers and vundu amounting to over 1900lbs. Now that is some fishing, as indeed we all so memorably experienced. Everyone to the man said they would return.

Monday, 3rd October

Bright sunshine, clear blue skies and a light westerly wind.

Sadly we left Tiki airstrip at Mwambashi via the 12 seater Cessna Caravan at 8 a.m. (the river looking so much smaller from the air) and upon arrival in Lusaka 30 minutes later met the transfer driver for Chaminuka Wildlife Reserve, our overnight accommodation before flying back to Heathrow the next morning.

     After a light lunch we all enjoyed a game drive around this 10,000 acre reserve, and saw wildebeest, eland, puku, sable, bushbuck, waterbuck, kudu, and impala, plus warthogs, ostriches, elephants, giraffes, lions and hyenas. It was a fitting finale to a simply marvellous adventure.

LEFT TOP
Just look at the length of those wicked, razor-sharp teeth and wide, expandable jaws of this 12½lbs tiger fish I'm holding up on the 'boga-grip'. It was my largest landed of the week.

LEFT BOTTOM
'Sundowner' time on the lower reaches of the Zambezi River. By far my favourite part of the day.

Monday, 10th October

Hot and sunny all day. Northwesterly wind.

Had a most enjoyable day today, spent wandering along a local stretch of the River Wensum in the company of my guest Mick Clubb from Melford in Suffolk, in search of chub. Unfortunately, due to clear, blue skies and bright sunshine, accompanied by copious amounts of floating leaves plus balls of blanket weed tumbling along the river bed, the pursuit of free lining for chub which is usually the most effective technique during both summer and autumn, became frustratingly difficult. From swim after swim, some of them absolute classic chub haunts such as weed rafts around trailing willow branches and dark tunnels beneath overhanging willows and alders, Mick's

ABOVE
Last farewells are made at Mwambashi's 'Tiki' airstrip before boarding the Cessna Caravan returning our party to Lusaka prior to our return flight to the UK.

free lined lobworm induced not the slightest interest. I was even starting to think that we had better change tack completely and return to the house to try for carp in the lakes.

But like a true chubbing enthusiast Mick stuck to his guns and weathered the continual snagging through weed and leaves, by hooking into a clanging bite from a deep under-cut bank swim on the free lined worm. After several seconds however the hook pulled free. Not to be downhearted Mick worked the bait through again, and it was instantly taken by a small chub of around 2lbs. But it was a start at least, against all the odds.

After lunch we resumed our wandering and from the first swim he tried, Mick connected with a nice fat fish of around 4lbs, which fought well in the strong flow. But alas try as he may, and he must have free lined both lobworms and large pieces of bread flake through a good dozen or more runs, all swims from where on past occasions chub have obliged, so we knew they were there, strangely, Mick couldn't buy another bite. What a frustrating day indeed.

Thursday, 13th October

Heavily overcast with continual drizzle, Light westerly wind.

Had my old friend and marketing manager for Masterline International Ltd, Bruce Vaughan not been staying overnight, and had we not finished our 'company' work of discussing new products and looking at the prototypes of a new range of rods by noon, we would never have bothered going fishing. As it was by 1 p.m. we were in the local pub and by 2 p.m. sat side by side opposite the main flush of a local mill pool on the River Wensum. The same pool in fact I last fished on 13th September, exactly one month ago, when I missed out on the chance of contacting with one of the big, double figure barbel in front of me occupying a four foot deep run because I overfed the swim with pellets, sending the chub into a feeding frenzy, which pushed the barbel, and there looked to be at least four good doubles in the swim, way downstream and out of the frame. And if I remember correctly, I went home totally frustrated by my own stupidity that afternoon.

Well, today was a complete turn around in fortunes, although from the main flush an hour of ledgering both halibut pellet and boilie hook baits, produced just a single 2lbs chub for me and nothing for Bruce. So I suggested we moved to the tail end of the pool where an hour before on arrival (contemplating that we might need to change swims) I had introduced several handfuls of 6mm pellets plus a scattering of 20mm boilies, into the very same run where I failed a month back.

In such overcast conditions, just the occasional dark shape of chub could be seen moving through the swim, but it looked promising, and I suggested to Bruce that he flip his boilie close in, tight alongside the edge of a weed raft, virtually beneath the rod tip, while I planned to position mine several yards below, so we covered the entire run. But I never actually got my bait in the water. Literally within 30 seconds of his lead settling on the bottom, (I was in the motion of swinging my bait out), Bruce said "I'm in John," and around went his 1¾lbs test curve rod into an alarming full curve, it couldn't possibly have bent any more, while the 12lbs test line fair screamed from the reel.

Although there was little doubt that Bruce was firmly into a big barbel, as if to toast the occasion, the great fish 'flashed sideways' on to the current as they do, in mid water, before suddenly charging upstream to the shallows opposite where we sat. We could now see it clearly, a long and incredibly thickset beauty, which kept Bruce's heart in his mouth for several minutes longer, as it made still more powerful surges back and forth across the river, testing Bruce's tackle and his nerves to the absolute limit, before I could finally bundle it into the net. And what a superbly proportioned specimen it was, noticeably deep in the body with incredibly large pectorals and noticeably long whiskers. I warmly shook the hand of one of my oldest and closest friends, and shared in the joy of not only his first barbel from the Wensum, but at 13lbs 1oz, by far his largest ever. Nice one Bruce!

ABOVE
No wonder my old pal Bruce Vaughan is sporting an ear to ear grin. He successfully put this superb 13lbs-1 ounce barbel on the bank following a hectic; 'hit and hold' tussle from one of my local River Wensum weir pools. What a beauty, and his largest barbel ever.

Sunday, 16th October

Heavily overcast with rain all day. Chilly westerly wind.

Following a really excellent BA flight of nine hours plus from Heathrow's terminal 4, we arrived safely in Vancouver airport yesterday evening to be met by our transfer driver who two hours later, deposited our eight man party of Brits including yours truly at the fabulous Harrison Hot Springs Resort on the edge of 40 mile long Harrison Lake, 70 miles due east from Vancouver. It was indeed wonderful to be back in Canada again, escorting adventure anglers on behalf of Tailor Made Holidays, to both the mighty Fraser and Harrison rivers which converge near the town of Chilliwack in the picturesque province of British Columbia.

The 1000 mile long Fraser River is the last of the world's great, un-dammed, salmon and sturgeon producing rivers up which phenomenal numbers of salmon migrate to spawn and die. There are over 50 million annually in fact, including five separate species: coho, which average 5-10lbs, pinks, which are around the same size, but only run every two years, sockeye, which are common in the 5-12lbs bracket, chum, which can run anywhere between 10 and 30lbs, and the largest salmon of them all, the mighty chinook which is common in the 15-50lbs range, but can attain weights of 60, 70, 80, and even 90lbs. In addition there are two sea-running trout, the cutthroat and the steelhead, plus of course truly awesome numbers of the enigmatic giant white sturgeon which is commonly caught between 100-250lbs, but can attain weights of over 1000lbs. And it is this dinosaur of a fish, which like the crocodile, dates back millions of years, and which lives to well in excess of 100 years of age, but which only produces eggs every 8-10 years, that we have crossed the Atlantic to the Pacific coast of North America to do battle with. I truly know of nowhere on this planet so 'fish-packed' as here, as indeed English angler Steve Lyons from Kent experienced only this September when he hooked and landed from the Fraser River, following a six hour long battle during which time his boat was towed over two miles and everyone on board had a go at beating the brute, what must surely be every freshwater angler's dream, a 1000lbs plus, 11 foot long giant white sturgeon.

Now I've said it many times before, and following two fabulous weeks amidst the breathtaking river and lakeland wilderness of Canada, which is so enormous there is enough room for everyone to grow in a way that is sadly no longer possible within the diminishing circumstances of the UK, I see no reason for not quoting myself again. If I were a young man at

ANOTHER FISHING YEAR

this point in time, I would have no hesitation in emigrating to this amazing country, British Columbia in particular. But let's return to the fishing.

After breakfast this morning everyone met down at the boat dock immediately in front of the hotel where we sorted out who was fishing with which guides and on what boat. Seeing that I filmed my *Safari* series here, featuring both sturgeon and salmon for Discovery Television three autumns ago with Fred Helmer of Harrison Bay Guided Services, it was only natural for me and our two guests John Howcroft from Lancashire and David Arber from Warwickshire, to fish from Fred's 24 foot aluminium boat. And within minutes we were speeding across Harrison Lake and into the mouth of the Harrison River at over 50 knots. There is then just ten miles of the crystal-blue clear Harrison River, between 100-400 yards across, winding through breathtaking scenery, before it joins forces with the coloured water of the very much wider and mighty Fraser River, which was where Fred intended to start our sturgeon fishing. And en route we were treated to the sight of thousands of seagulls, plus bald eagles and herons devouring freshly dead salmon carcasses that had drifted onto all the gravel bars along the shoreline, the purpose of their life (after spawning) now ended.

At a location in the Fraser River called 'Duncan's Rock', Fred lowered the anchor via an electric winch (I could do with one of these on my boat back home when pike fishing in freezing conditions on the Norfolk Broads) into 14 feet of water, having marked some good sturgeon on the fish finder. Literally five minutes later with only two of our four sturgeon rods out, the size 6/0 barb less hooks (compulsory in Canada) to 150lbs test braided traces and 100lbs braided reel lines presenting three inch sections of lamprey, the first rod buckled over alarmingly in its rest, and David Arber who was on first strike banged the hook home.

Now I think I am correct in saying that his biggest fish until then was a 30lbs vundu catfish from The Zambezi River, caught on one of my escorted 'safaris' to Mwambashi along the lower reaches of the river a couple of years ago. And in no way was David prepared for the animal power of a sturgeon ripping over 200 yards from his multiplier on its initial run. A fish which Fred estimated at over 300lbs when it jumped clear of the surface (as most sturgeon do) following a lengthy battle, within just 20 feet of the boat. And Fred should know, having beaten Fraser River monsters to over 1000lbs. Alas, David was never to see what creature in half an hour had strained his arms and stomach muscles to severe aching point, because just when the great fish was ready to be towed gently towards the nearest sandy piece of beach along the shoreline for some trophy shots, the hook suddenly popped out. Boy was poor David sick as the proverbial parrot.

Throughout the day the rain got steadily worse and the fishing never did reach the giddy heights of that first hook-up, although from a dozen or so bites, most of them on salmon egg balls (a golf ball-sized clump of eggs wrapped in a piece of ladies' tights) I managed a baby sturgeon of just 25lbs, while John Howcroft boated his first ever weighing around 50lbs. It was however a start and I for one was glad to be back on the river again, despite the fact that due to the incessant rain we did not bother fishing for salmon. The other two boats however fared much better, accounting for no less than four sturgeon of between 100-140lbs.

LEFT
The magnificent Harrison Hot Springs Resort situated on the shores of 40-mile long Harrison Lake provided excellent accommodation.
Its boat dock providing easy and quick access to both the Harrison and Fraser Rivers during our stay in Canada's most breathtaking province, beautiful British Columbia.

ANOTHER FISHING YEAR

Monday, 17th October

Blustery westerly wind and heavily overcast conditions, accompanied by heavy rain all day.

Today I fished with guests Rob Burton and carp fanatic Stuart Griggs, both from Essex, on board guide Frank's boat, and again due to the persistent rain we decided to concentrate all day on the sturgeon. Despite mist hugging the mountains the sheer beauty of this 'wilderness environment' along the Harrison River was very much in evidence with the leaves of birch, maple, poplar and cottonwood trees, stacked amongst the conifers, all turning various shades of yellow, red and gold. While along the gravel bars many ravens had joined the gulls and bald eagles in clearing up the dead and dying salmon.

We initially concentrated our efforts along the comparatively narrow section of river immediately below the road bridge where on the eastern bank great machines use thick hawsers to bundle up logs before depositing them in the river where they are guided downstream by tugs. But after three hours with but a handful of missed extremely 'tentative' bites to show for our efforts, Frank motored a mile further downstream to several hundred yards below the railway bridge, which produced our one and only fish of the day to Stuart.

BELOW
Carp fanatic Stuart Griggs from Essex, hauls a 180 lbs white sturgeon to the boat, (by far his largest freshwater fish ever) watched by Rob Burton.

This particular fish made two spectacular jumps then unfortunately zoomed diagonally across the river straight through the lines of two other anchored boats. With over 200 yards of line out Stuart was in a right pickle, so Frank pulled up our anchor to drift way below the two boats in order to untangle all the lines from the far from happy other anglers before finally landing the sturgeon. Fortunately that is what happened, although tempers rose to boiling point throughout the escapade as we eventually (they would not put their reels into free spool and give line) had to cut through all five of the other lines! They were not happy bunnies at all, but Stuart was. His fish turned out to be a 'beacher' (worth towing to the shore for trophy shots where it can be lifted by two to three people, as large fish cannot be man-handled into the boat) estimated by Frank to be around 180lbs – Stuart's largest fish ever by a huge margin. And that is the true value of anglers fishing sturgeon here for the first time. Just about everyone goes home to 'Blighty' having landed their largest fish ever following a spectacular battle. We arrived back at the boat dock completely soaked through at 4.30 p.m., to the expected news that only six sturgeon had been taken from our three boats, including another two over 100lbs.

Tuesday, 18th October

Gentle northerly wind with bright sunshine and clear, blue skies all day.

Today's weather was typical of how anglers envisage British Columbia in the autumn, when the sun picks out the golden red leaves of Canada's emblem tree the maple, amongst the blue-green of tall cedars and pine stacked along the mountain sides. A truly beautiful scene, (and the first time we have seen all the mountain tops, some covered in snow, since arriving) matched only by the quality of the salmon fly fishing in the Harrison River. At least those were the feelings of my two guests 'Dangerous' Dave Johnson, with whom I last fished in Montauk back in June and before that on the Rio Negro in Brazil back in January, and Ross Coker from Essex (I've nicknamed them the 'Essex Mafia') on board guide Tony Nootebos's boat.

Tony helped so much with the making of my TV fly fishing programme here three autumns ago, that I was very much looking forward to fishing with him again. Unfortunately, due to heavy rain over the past few days the river was running three feet above normal, which kind of restricted our shore fishing access spots. Although as I write this my forearms and fingers are decidedly 'cranky' due to a battering from casting to and playing countless chum salmon in the 12-20lbs bracket, on a single handed 10 weight outfit. But let's be honest here, how often do we tire of catching salmon in the UK? Exactly. So when in Canada I inevitably go at it like a bull at a gate and really fill my boots, especially when the weather is nice.

In depths of between four to six feet over a gravel bottom, easily covered by our sink-tip lines with fast sinking leaders and weighted, gold head or barbell size 4 barb less hook flies (pink, red and mauve being the 'taking' colours) Dave, Ross and I simply lost count of the fish we caught which were mostly all chum save for the occasional pink or sockeye. And most on their initial run screamed all the fly line out way into the backing.

I know it looks as though my 20lbs chum salmon has leaped 50 foot into the air. But it's merely an illusion created by the cameras wide angle lens. Ross Coker (right) and I enjoyed double hook ups on numerous occasions whilst fly fishing for salmon in the clear-flowing Harrison River. What a place.

OCTOBER

BELOW
Ross Coker (left)
and guide Tony
Nootebos display
the stamp of hard-
battling chum
salmon with which
the Harrison River is
unbelievably full.
Note the
characteristic purple
and black bars
which distinguish
this particular
salmon from the
other four species
running these fast,
clear water upper
reaches.

A percentage of these were I am afraid foul-hooked, which is an acceptable par for the course here in BC where salmon runs via the mighty, 1000 mile long Fraser River (the Harrison being just one of its many tributaries) are the most prolific on this planet by far. So exactly how many we hooked into (often two and sometimes all three of us would be simultaneously fighting fish) I just don't know. But I guess an estimation of between 20-25 fish each would be on the conservative side. It really is that prolific, which is why my arms are killing me.

ANOTHER FISHING YEAR

LEFT
If you are frustrated and fed up by fish-less weeks in Scotland, then get yourself over to Canada's British Columbia and the fish-packed Fraser River system. Long, powerful battles on a single handed size 9 or 10 weight outfit with chum salmon averaging between 15 and 20lbs apiece, are literally everyday occurrences, particularly in the Harrison River. As Ross Coker (left) and yours truly experienced.

It was a good day for the other two boats also, which accounted for a total tally of 14 sturgeon including four topping the ton. The best was a 200lbs beauty for David Arber, his largest fish ever, which kind of made up for the monster that slipped the hook on day one.

Wednesday, 19th October

Heavily overcast and a blustery westerly wind, accompanied by persistent rain.

Fished with Tony Nootebos again today, in the company of Dave Arber and John Holcroft, concentrating upon the sturgeon in the Harrison River, where from immediately below the road bridge adjacent to the logging yard and after just ten minutes fishing, David hooked and subsequently landed a nice fish of around 120lbs, after a couple of spectacular leaps, 'Polaris-style', completely clear of the surface. It was then my turn on strike and from the most gentle of taps on the rod tip (very few sturgeon give the kind of bite you would expect in the gin clear water of the Harrison where the bottom can be clearly seen ten feet down) I found myself connected with something that ran and ran for over a 100 yards before catapulting itself high into the air. It was enormous and looked all of 300lbs plus, but I was not going to see this particular fish again. It dived straight beneath a sunken log, and no amount of pulling this way and that would free it, so I had to pull for a break. Frustration personified, although that's not what I yelled at the time.

John then caught a 90lbs fish and Dave a 30lbs 'baby' before it was my turn again. And again from a bite no more powerful than a pull round from a chub on a quiver tip, I hooked into an obvious 'beacher', which was estimated at around 180lbs and which had in fact picked up the bait of another rod, though how it managed this without any registrations on the tip of the second rod I simply don't know. The only explanation is that both egg-ball baits had come to lie

ABOVE
Sure, I was smiling as this 180lbs white sturgeon nears the boat. But only minutes before, I had broken off on a monster getting on for twice the size around a sunken log.

on the river bed very close to one another, and when I struck both hooks were already inside its strange, fully protrusible mouth. Just one of life's little mysteries.

In the afternoon we moved downstream, seeing numerous seals on the way (apparently they could well become a real problem in the future) and anchored up in a deep gully where Dave pulled the hook from a big fish while John took one of 60lbs and I, a 70 pounder. I also lost a good fish due to the hook pulling. Incidentally, none of the sturgeon caught are actually weighed. Their weight is estimated from a weight for length chart formulated by the Fraser River Sturgeon Conservation Society, and is surprisingly accurate.

A great day's fishing despite the persistent rain. Our three boats accounted for no less than 19 sturgeon including five over the ton. We also witnessed the unusual sight of two bald eagles fighting in mid air, their talons locked for quite some time as they squabbled over territory.

Thursday, 20th October

Gentle westerly wind. Blue skies and bright sunshine.

After yesterday's battering of steady rain, today's lovely weather was much appreciated by my fly fishing partners Dave Johnson, Ross Coker and guide Tony Nootebos, and as we made our way down the Harrison River from Harrison Hot Springs Resort (lovely accommodation incidentally for the angler, with hot spring pools to ease aching limbs) we could see that John Howcroft on guide Danny's boat, was fast into a huge chinook salmon hooked on a diving plug. So we stopped for a while to watch the ensuing battle and to photograph the huge fish which when finally beaten and drawn into the shallows, Danny estimated at in excess of 40lbs. Now where else do you go for the chance of a 40lbs salmon these days? Canada, that's where.

At that point we were not to know that John's boat partner Dave Arber, two hours later, was to catch an even bigger chinook, a veritable monster of 50lbs. Both of these fish are in fact the largest I have personally witnessed during the six years that I have been escorting trips to the Fraser Valley, and both were caught on single hook (compulsory in BC) diving plugs worked static behind the boat anchored in 18 feet of water, with just the flow to activate them. The current is that fast.

After photographing John's chinook we motored further downriver to the 'Pilons' stretch to fly fish for salmon, and we took a whole bunch of chum to over 20lbs from gravel shallows four to five feet deep, the current being so fast it was difficult to wade against. Amongst the chum were odd groups of coho in the 6-10lbs bracket, but they were rather spooky, and our gaudy size 4 flies to 12lbs test leaders were too much for them. Coho are like bars of bright chrome and do not colour up like the chum, which are easily recognisable by the purple and black bars along their flanks.

While Dave and Ross were filling their boots with chum I decided to wade back to the boat parked on a gravel bar separating the shallows where we were fishing from the main flow, and to bounce a spoon deep down through the rapid water in the hope of a chinook, seeing as though numbers were running upriver, and after just a few casts I struck gold, as a huge fish

BELOW
This chunky, Chinook salmon of 50lbs, hooked on a diving plug and 30lbs test braid, provided Dave Arber from Warwickshire with a truly memorable encounter up and down the Harrison river for over half an hour.

ANOTHER FISHING YEAR

zoomed off downstream leaping several times as it went, screaming 30lbs test braid from the reel. Simultaneously I happen to notice the head of a seal pop up to the surface not 20 feet from where my chinook last jumped and within a few seconds, sadly the inevitable happened. The rod arched over another 20 percent (I would not have believed that possible) and line evaporated alarmingly from the reel till the spool was empty. At which point I clamped my hand around it and cracked off. The only occasion in over 50 years of fishing around the world that I have lost a fish to a seal. It just happened to be by far the largest chinook I have ever hooked, that's all. Boy was I mad.

With so many chinooks running, after lunch we decided to go upriver to where John and Dave had taken their big fish earlier, a deep turbulent run directly opposite a water tower, and put the anchor down so we could work plugs off the stern. Ross hit into a huge chinook within five minutes of Tony getting all four rods out, which he patiently played throughout a magical 20 minute scrap, only for the salmon's teeth to chew through the 15lbs mono leader attached to the 30lbs braided reel line when it was but three feet from the boat. 'Gutted', just does not describe the look on his face.

We then lost another couple due to the single hook pulling out (only barb less single hooks are allowed for both salmon and sturgeon) before I banged into a dark fish of around 25lbs, which fortunately stayed on and gave a powerful tussle. Ross then hit into another biggy. When numbers of big chinook are running they continually jump clear of the surface, so you are in absolutely no doubt whatsoever about their size. The crash sounds and the

ANOTHER FISHING YEAR

LEFT
When your fish is next to spent, the sensible thing to do is steer it into the slower, shallows where it can be tailed out.

BELOW
This 20lbs plus cock chum salmon gave me the run around for a good 20 minutes. Simply magical fishing on the fly rod, in surroundings of stunning beauty.

disturbance looks as though a labrador has jumped in the river, and indeed some of the fish that afternoon probably weighed as much. Unfortunately, for the second time that afternoon Ross had the mono trace bitten through when only five minutes into the fight. What he said afterwards is totally unprintable, as you can imagine.

When drowning our sorrows back at the hotel bar, we found that the only one of our three boats fishing sturgeon (Rob and Stuart)

had accounted for a respectable nine fish including two over 100lbs, from lower down the Harrison River.

Friday, 21st October

Gentle northerly wind. Hazy sunshine all day.

During this the last day for my six guests (they fly home tomorrow when I have a new party arriving from the UK) I fished with guide Mike, plus Rob and Stuart, who fancied signing off with an all out assault after the sturgeon way down in the Fraser River. And we started exceptionally well using lamprey sections for bait (their high blood content seems to attract

ANOTHER FISHING YEAR

sturgeon quicker than egg-balls, in the heavily coloured water of the Fraser River, as indeed it does pike from my local Norfolk Broads) Rob and Stuart both boating sturgeon of around 50lbs apiece, within half an hour of anchoring up.

I then hooked what materialised into the largest of the week, a particularly fat-bellied monster of exactly seven feet long, which Mike estimated at around 240lbs. It fought heavily in the noticeably faster water of the Fraser River and led me a real song and dance for over 30 minutes with the branch of a tree inextricably stuck around its head. Eventually however we were able to beach it in shallow water for some photos, and I immediately noticed (through lifting the fish) the much colder water of the Fraser which was running at around 45°F compared to the Harrison's 56°F, though how this might affect the sturgeon fishing I am not quite sure.

At lunchtime we decided to head way down the Fraser River to the town of Mission, where in years gone by I have seen some whoppers caught to over 500lbs. My own personal best measuring two inches over eight feet long and weighing over 300lbs came from just above Mission, so we were expectant to say the least. But though a further six fish to around 90lbs came our way there were no surprises, except that when back in the bar, we heard about Ross finally taking a big chinook, and a silver fish to boot, weighing over 40lbs, from exactly the same spot where he lost those two biggies yesterday. I shall certainly have to give the 'water tower' swim some consideration next week. Incidentally, our seven man group's tally for the week amounted to 65 sturgeon, including 22 of them over 100lbs, so my promise at the beginning of the trip that everyone would catch a 100lbs plus sturgeon held fast.

Saturday, 22nd October

Bright and sunny with snow on top of the mountains. What a stunning backdrop!

Tired but delighted with such amazing freshwater fishing my group left at noon and I read a book all afternoon whilst 'chilling out' waiting for the second bunch of anglers to arrive, which they did at 7 p.m. accompanied by Christine Slater of Tailor Made Holidays who organises these Canadian angling adventures.

Sunday, 23rd October

Light westerly wind. Heavily overcast with light rain all day.

Fished on guide Mike's boat again with two good friends from Norwich, Nick Beardmore and Simon Lawton who also happen to be my computer gurus. Nick and I also pike fish together on the Norfolk Broads during the cold, winter months. Due to the persistent rain we decided to head down the Harrison and into the Fraser River, so they could cut their teeth on sturgeon, and within an hour of anchoring up both had accounted for a couple of fish apiece up to around 50lbs.

With heavy mist hugging the river valley and hiding the mountains Nick and Simon were unable to appreciate the true wilderness beauty of the area, but I rather think the spectacular fishing will make up for this, if what transpired during the afternoon has anything to do with it.

LEFT
Just look at the propeller on this seven foot, 240lbs white sturgeon. No wonder they take so long to subdue in the fast and coloured water of the mighty Fraser River, even using 100lbs test line and a powerful rod. Guide Mike (left) did a great job in steering the fish into the shallows for this trophy shot, too.

OVERLEAF
A duo of monsters to remember. (L-R), Guide Mike, Simon Lawford and Nick Beardmore with Nick's 275lbs beauty, and Mark Nickolaides from Poole in Dorset and his two guides with his 440lbs whopper, both hooked almost simultaneously from the clear flowing Harrison River during heavy rain. What an outstanding catch. But that's Canada for you.

Because on a hunch, Mike took us back up the Harrison River to fish for sturgeon in the 'water tower' swim, and Nick became connected to what appeared a very large fish almost immediately, a sturgeon which powered off so fast downriver, it took him completely by surprise. Never before had I seen my mate so fired up by something on the end of his line (winter pike simply don't scream off over 200 yards of 100lbs test line on their initial run) and for a while the sturgeon was really making him puff and blow.

Slowly but surely Nick got the better of the great fish (obviously a 'beacher') which could clearly be seen shaking its head deep down near the gravel bottom, (a most wonderful and totally unique experience) as we drifted downstream with it, hoping to tow it into the shallows for a photography session. And that's exactly what transpired after a monumental battle. Nick's third sturgeon ever, measured nearly eight feet and was estimated to weigh around 275lbs by guide Mike. The look on Nick's decidedly 'flushed' face was priceless. He just could not believe the sheer size of the fish. This of course is everyone's reaction to landing such a monster.

But there was even more drama in the rain to come. As I was rattling off the trophy shots, everyone having donned chest high waders for the occasion, Mark Nicolaides from Poole in Dorset who had flown over with my group but who was staying in Chilliwack, came into the shallows mere yards away on board another boat and in the final throes of playing an even larger sturgeon following another monumental battle, starting way upstream from where Nick first hooked his. A fish which subsequently measured getting on for nine feet with an estimated weight of 440lbs.

What an afternoon, and for me, what an unusual opportunity of photographing two huge fish together, despite the rain. Within minutes of motoring back upriver and putting the anchor down again, we were treated to the appearance of a coyote coming down to the water's edge for a drink, and he didn't seem unduly alarmed by our presence. Simon then caught a 40lbs sturgeon which looked decidedly 'tiny' to the fish we had all just witnessed and I finished a quite spectacular and most memorable day with one of around 150lbs, foul-hooked unfortunately, right up the 'jacksy'. Suddenly it was 4 p.m. (where oh where had the time gone) and the bar of Harrison Hot Springs Resort beckoned.

Monday, 24th October

Gentle northerly wind. The early morning mist burnt off by strong sunlight. Thereafter blue skies all day.

Guide today was Merr, and my two guests John Purcell from Kent and Mark Pickering from Birmingham who has been on several of my 'safaris' over the past few years to Lake Nasser in Egypt, where he caught Nile perch of 165lbs and 175lbs on consecutive days. And I've already told him on this trip he is quite likely to catch an even larger freshwater fish. Our first few spots

along the Harrison anchored up for sturgeon however, failed to produce so much as a knock on any of the rod tips, so I suggested a crash course in fly fishing using my 10 weight outfits, (neither had fly fished before) for some hard battling chum salmon.

This was rather chucking them in at the deep end, but with so many salmon about they were soon experiencing the power of Pacific speedsters following half an hour's casting instruction each from guide Merr and me. Both took chum salmon to around 15lbs and lost several more. We then headed downstream to the confluence of the Fraser with the Harrison, a huge, wide bay simply stacked with jumping salmon (those who repeatedly travel to Scotland for a fruitless week's casting, should try Canada) where both John and Mark used single hook spoons to enjoy still more chum into double figures plus a pink salmon of around 8lbs.

In the strong autumnal sunshine the patchwork of yellow, amber, orange, red and gold leaves of deciduous trees, dotted amongst the pines along the steep-sided mountains was absolutely stunning. What truly breathtaking scenery there is in this land, quite literally around every twist and turn of the river with enough local and migratory birds from bald eagles to red-breasted mergansers and grebes, to keep the most ardent of 'twitchers' happy.

In the late afternoon we returned to fishing for sturgeon, John taking a 'beacher' of around 140lbs following a great tussle. It proved to be our only sturgeon of the day. Nick and Simon however in the company of Christine on Fred Helmer's boat, bagged a trio of 'beachers' between 130-175lbs. Another great day in paradise.

Tuesday, 25th October

*Heavy early morning mist burnt off mid-morning by strong sunlight.
Light westerly wind.*

The weather this week is already proving significantly more comfortable than last week's, which is why guide Tony and I suggested to Nick and Simon that today was an ideal time for them to get into salmon fishing with the fly rod along the picturesque and clear-flowing Harrison River. So we spent the first hour teaching them to cast and keep 30 feet of line in the air before shooting a few yards more on the forward cast, which is really all anyone needs in order to catch salmon here, and then to perform a simple 'roll-cast', to start each sequence. We then showed them how important it is to quickly mend a few yards of line upstream by 'flick-rolling' the rod tip, the very second the fly hits the surface, so the sink-tip line is not dragged downstream by the current in a huge 'bow'. And literally within the hour, both our prodigies were casting and hooking their own sockeye and chum salmon, which considering neither had ever wielded a fly rod in anger before, was marvellous and most satisfying for Tony and me.

Later on in the day when our two salmon converts had gorged upon fighting fish, we motored back upstream to the prolific 'water tower' swim where Tony put out two sturgeon rods and two plugs for chinooks. We never did find out whether the sturgeon were in a feeding mood however, because within five minutes one of the plug rods sporting a multiplier loaded with 30lbs test braid arched over and Nick (who was on first strike) found himself attached to an angry 40lbs chinook salmon, which lead him a merry song and dance all over the river for fully 30 minutes. A fish, which when Tony reached over and hauled it on board by the tail, made everyone gasp in sheer awe. By now the middle of the river below us seemed to be stacked with running chinooks, and seldom a minute went by without at least a couple crashing out completely clear of the surface in that characteristic and strange 'horizontal' leap they make. We were all on tenterhooks.

Then it was Simon's turn for some action, when one of the rods suddenly lurched over and initially we thought he had hooked a small fish which merely went back and forward across the stern of the boat only a few yards downstream. It then suddenly woke up and motored off downriver into deeper water at a rate of knots, with Simon completely powerless to control it despite the 30lbs test reel line. But eventually, and we are talking a further 30 minutes here, it did tire sufficiently to be slowly

LEFT
John Purcell (left) who hails from Kent gets assistance from guide 'Merr' in displaying his 140 lbs white sturgeon. Our only sturgeon of the session (we lost count of the salmon we caught however) and by far his largest fish ever.

BELOW
After less than an hours casting tuition, mate Nick Beardmore finds himself connected to a big chum salmon. The fishing here in British Columbia is that prolific, with over 50 million salmon running annually up the Fraser River system.

ABOVE
I think the manic expression on friend Simon Lawfords face says it all. His first ever Chinook salmon supported by guide Tony Nootebos (left) topped 50lbs. Note the green plug in it's huge jaws. Where does he go from here? Perhaps a 60 pounder next year?

pumped upstream beside the boat where Tony leant over and heaved it out. It was a monstrous chinook of over 50lbs. What a creature, and what a day!

What did I catch? Well nothing, until we started to wind the rods in at 4 p.m. to head back to the hotel. Then, after two cranks of the reel handle the rod came alive in my hands and bent over into a throbbing curve. Wilson was fast into a chinook of around 30lbs, hooked unfortunately in the tail, and we had to drift downriver with it (it was so powerful) in order to release the hook. What a memorable afternoon indeed.

Wednesday, 26th October

Bright sunshine all day with a chilly westerly wind.

I fished all day in the Harrison River, again on Tony's boat, in the company of John and Mark, accounting for a total of eight sturgeon whilst Mark landed the best of around 100lbs. The river appears literally to be paved with sturgeon which like the ever increasing numbers of ravens and gulls are all gorging upon dead and dying salmon. Right now with the river dropping rapidly following last week's heavy rainfall, daily, more and more bald eagles crowd onto the gravel bars now exposed along the shoreline where salmon carcasses are stacked up. The smell and sights of death would indeed seem strange to the majority of European salmon anglers, yet the nutrients of millions of dead salmon is nature's way of feeding all the bugs that in turn will go to feeding the young salmon when they eventually hatch from their eggs beneath the gravel. Tony mentioned that in a few weeks' time at the end of the salmon runs when most have died having

LEFT
The pain of a lengthy sturgeon battle starts to set in. But Simon Lawford hangs on while Nick Beardmore (left) hopes there is another spectacular 'jump' in store.

completed their life's work, there will be as many as 4000 bald eagles alone, along the five mile section of the Harrison that we most regularly fish. What a sight that must be.

Making our last move of the afternoon when close to the junction with Harrison Lake and only a few minutes from the hotel, we passed Nick and Simon who were on Chad's boat, a guide who I fished with a couple of years back, and by the bend in Simon's rod and expression on his 'puffing' face, he was obviously hooked up big time. And seeing the big sturgeon come zooming up to the surface and jump 'Polaris' style into the air and crash back in again in the late afternoon sun, was a marvellous spectacle. So we forgot the fishing and hung around to watch the ensuing battle and to take some trophy shots. Fortunately the giant fish stayed on, and 30 minutes later Simon was able to guide his sturgeon into the shallows where it was measured in excess of seven feet long and estimated at around 270lbs. What a week he and Nick are having.

ABOVE
Holding a near 300lbs fish up for the camera, and smiling, is not as easy as it would seem. Captor Simon Lawford however (left) aided by Nick Beardmore (middle) and guide Chad, has no problem with this 275lbs monster white sturgeon.

Thursday, 27th October

Bright sunshine all day accompanied by a chilly northerly wind.

I was back fishing with mates Nick and Simon today on board Tony's boat with sturgeon very much our target species and we motored ten miles (at over 50 knots as usual – these jet boats are something else) down to the wide junction of the Fraser and Harrison Rivers where we anchored up in 18 feet of water and put out four rods each presenting salmon egg-balls. Simon

drew first blood with a sturgeon of 80lbs, from what were most tentative bites. Nick then pulled out of a fish, which put me on strike. And again, from the tiniest of pulls on the rod tip I struck and was immediately rewarded by a big fish leaping high into the air amongst a kaleidoscope of spray and foam. It then belted off downriver, ripping a couple of hundred yards of line from the reel against a firmly set drag before I stood any chance of turning it. Obviously a 'beacher' it then fought powerfully for over 30 minutes in the strong flow before it rolled on the surface and was quiet enough to tow ashore to a sandy beach in order to measure and photograph.

On the way in, friends Ken Sheath and Tony Lees who also came over with Christine's group and were fishing nearby, had simultaneously hooked up with a smaller fish to Ken's rod, and so we all got together for a double trophy shot. My fish incidentally measured around seven feet, which put it better than 200lbs. Things were definitely looking up. But not another bite did any of us get for the rest of the day.

Friday, 28th October

Early morning mist burnt away by strong sunlight, accompanied by a light northerly wind.

Our last day in big fish paradise and the end of my two week bonanza. What fabulous fishing we have all experienced, particularly during this second week in (apart from one day) glorious sunshine. I cannot possibly imagine any other location in the world where so many anglers could have readily taken such a glut of monstrous salmon and sturgeon. Canada, I love you.

With Mark Pickering and John Purcell on board, both bent on finishing in style with monster sturgeon, Tony zoomed us the ten miles down the Harrison River into the coloured water of the Frazer, where he continued motoring upstream for over 20 minutes to a huge, deep eddy situated immediately above a wide road bridge. A truly beautiful spot, close to snow-topped mountains, where I certainly had not fished previously.

Almost within seconds of the last bait (a mixture of egg-balls and lamprey sections) settling on the bottom, one of the rods buckled over in its rest, and, quick off the mark (no pun intended) Mark thumped into a big fish which made a glorious leap before motoring off downstream like a bat out of hell. Within a minute or so, with Mark's reel fast emptying of 100lbs test braid, Tony had no option but to quickly up anchor and give chase. The currents this far up the Fraser were immense, and it took Mark over half an hour, during which time we had drifted over a mile and way beneath the road bridge, to subdue his fish and bring it alongside the

boat, where Tony surprised us all by man-hauling what was obviously a 'beacher' sturgeon (due to there being no beaching spots close by) straight into the specialist sling stretched across the boat's width by two sections of scaffold pole, specifically used for measuring each fish and for injecting (those which have not been fitted) with an electronic chip. Mark's fish measured over seven feet long which put it over 200lbs, easily beating his previous personal best, the 175lbs Nile perch he took from Lake Nasser several years back.

I then lost a fish of around 90lbs which came straight up to the surface not 20 feet away where it leaped magnificently and threw the hook, followed by one in the boat of around 150lbs which also scrapped extremely well, making me puff some while hauling it back upstream to where we were anchored in the deep eddy.

After this we moved several times throughout the day accounting for no less than ten sturgeon, three of them topping 100lbs.

Back in the hotel bar, at story-swapping time, everyone agreed at the end of their last day here, and that includes yours truly, that to the man, they would be back. Simon Lawford had perhaps a better reason than most, because he and Nick fishing with Fred Helmer experienced an unbelievable day's sturgeon fishing. Nick landed three 'beachers' to 175lbs, while Simon took the best fish of the week estimated by Fred at around 425lbs. What an end and follow up to his 50lbs chinook.

Exactly how many sturgeon we took this second week I am not sure. But it must be getting on for 100, with no fewer than five anglers accounting for specimens over 200lbs, and I reckon the amount of fish exceeding 100lbs must be in the region of 40 or so. 'Nuff' said.

LEFT
This 200lbs plus sturgeon started to wake up during the towing-to shore process, in preparation of taking a trophy shot, and gave me another five minutes of excitement and concern (note the logging poles) in shallow water.

BELOW
Yes, on the very last session before flying back to the UK, Simon Lawford goes and hooks our largest sturgeon of the week. A 425lbs monster which he and Nick (right) could not possibly hoist above the surface while guide Fred Helmer took the photo. What a truly memorable week my two friends from Norwich experienced.

Tuesday, 8th November

Blustery southerly wind, intermittent sunshine and cloud.

After trying to catch up with my various family and writing commitments, including this book, following two weeks of solid fishing in Canada, local fishing has been far from my mind. And what with preparing for a lecture and slide show about mahseer fishing in southern India that I am giving this Thursday in London organised on behalf of the Indian Embassy at the Nehru Centre, plus popping off to Lake Nasser in Egypt on Monday next week escorting a party of eight Brits in search of big Nile perch, small wonder the chub and barbel of my local River Wensum have taken a back seat, until today that is.

Due to the mild conditions I fancied a crack at the very same swim where good friend Bruce Vaughan caught a 13lbs 1oz barbel, from the narrow, four foot deep tail end of a local weir pool, prior to my setting off for Canada, so at lunchtime today I popped along to study river conditions and to introduce a carpet of loose feed in the way of several handfuls of 6mm halibut pellets plus a scattering of 20mm boilies. There was a nice tinge of colour to the river now that it has fined down following recent heavy rain, and at 3 p.m. I returned and fished until darkness, hoping a sizeable barbel would find my bolt-rig-ledgered boilie, presented close into the bank alongside an overhanging raft of marginal growth. But I should have guessed that those chub would thwart my intentions. Every single cast produced bang after bang from chub, three of between 4-5lbs managing to hook themselves and scaring off the barbel in the process. But a most enjoyable, if somewhat short session nonetheless.

Tuesday, 15th November

Strong and chilly northeasterly wind. Bright sunshine.

Following an excellent Astraeus five hour charter flight from Heathrow's terminal 3 yesterday afternoon, my party of seven Brits and I arrived safely on Egyptian soil at Aswan airport to start a week's safari after Nile perch on massive Lake Nasser, and checked into the popular Basma Hotel for overnight accommodation. At 8 a.m. this morning we then met up with Tim Baily of The African Angler, and piled into the transfer coach for an hour's run down the west bank of the lake to Garf Hussein where our safari began.

Being a regular on the lake for approaching a decade now I just adore the solitude and spiritual feeling of adventure fishing for huge fish on what is actually the Nubian Desert flooded by the Nile all the way south for a distance of 300 miles to the Sudan, from the high dam in Aswan. The irregular shoreline actually covers a staggering 5000 miles, and I noticed the daunting look on the faces of our guests, each of whom had yet to fish such a massive sheet of still water. I also noticed that the lake is presently around 15 feet lower than most previous

safaris. Apparently, a huge amount of water has been used for irrigation this year. After all, that is what it was designed for, and not an international sports fishing destination.

Within half an hour of boarding the three, 25 foot trolling boats (with *Nubian Queen* our 50 foot supply boat and mobile restaurant in attendance) we were well under way and heading across the lake towards Nabisco, a vast, relatively shallow area with depths averaging between 12 and 20 feet. These are ideal depths for trolling Rapala Shad Rap floating/divers, and whilst my boat, with faithful guide Mohammed at the helm and Eddy Dart and Ken Sleeman from Salisbury on board failed to catch, one of the other boats came up with a fat 70lbs perch for Paul Taylor from Harlow, fishing with his dad Alex. It was by far Paul's largest fish ever and he was justifiably over the moon when we all met up on the supply boat for dinner to swap stories over drinks as darkness loomed over Lake Nasser. Everyone was amazed at the diversity of bird life they had seen in just a few short hours on what was once a desert, including pelicans, kites, goliath herons, Egyptian vultures and a host of smaller birds from wagtails and warblers to terns. It had been a slow, but interesting start to the week.

Wednesday, 16th November

OVERLEAF
The sun sets over the raw beauty of a forgotten desert, now covered by the mysterious waters of the planets longest river. The mystical Nile.

Chilly northeasterly wind. Bright sunshine.

Last night was the chilliest I have ever known on Lake Nasser, due to a full moon and the biting northeasterly blow. But tucked up in our sleeping bags, with all the boats tied up in the lee of a

tall island, once a mountain top of course, we were as snug as bugs in a rug. I was particularly pleased I'd brought along jogging bottoms and a sweatshirt for sleeping in, and a fleece for dinner.

From the camp at Nabisco we moved southeast into Wadi Alaggi, a huge, five mile wide khor (once a valley bordered by mountain ranges on both sides) where we trolled around a cluster of jagged, steep-sided small islands. Great perch-holding spots these for the amount of 'ambush' points they contain, and my two boat partners for the day, a father and son team of Roy and Chris Darwell from Leeds, enjoyed an early 'double hook up' trolling depth-raider plugs in the form of a 35lbs perch for Chris and a 20 pounder for Roy. And what great tail-walking scraps these fish gave them in exceptionally rough water. In fact during the photography session I was worried we might actually run aground on the rocks.

We continued trolling around the same islands for a further 30 minutes without another hit and so made our way along the top of the wadi for lunch at John Wilson Camp (yes, it's rather flattering to have an island named after you even if it is in the middle of nowhere) where we met up with the other boats. Unfortunately, ours were the only perch taken, and fishing at present, due I think to a mixture of cold winds, a full moon and the lake being unnaturally low, is painful and particularly slow. We are simply not contacting any large groups of fish where we expect them to be collecting as an early grouping process prior to their eventual spawning during the months of January and February. After lunch all the boats made their way to a group of tall islands called 'Maharaga' which are situated more or less in the middle of the lake, but nothing was caught.

Fishing on one of the planets most remote locations they may be, but guests of 'African Angler' certainly enjoy their meal times and spicy local dishes on the top deck of 'Nubian Queen'. Furthest right is my good friend Tim Baily who pioneered this totally unique and exciting angling experience over a decade ago.

Thursday, 17th November

Light northeasterly wind. Bright sunshine.

This typical desert-like weather of cold nights and hot sunny days continues, but the wind is easing and last night was decidedly warmer. I rose early and made a long walk along the shoreline before breakfast, joined only by the tweeting and twittering noise of warblers in the scrub bushes and wagtails along the waterline, without another single sound. What a truly serene and spiritual place Lake Nasser is.

Today Mohammed and I headed south towards Abu Simbel in the company of father and son team Alex and Paul Taylor, trolling a huge deep-water gulley on the outskirts of Madig, a favourite hot spot of mine, which incidentally, produced my best ever perch from the lake a couple of years back, a monster of 150lbs. But I don't doubt for one second that there are leviathans here of twice the size.

Only one hit came from deep water to a 'reef-digger' lure being trolled by Alex, and it could well have been from a big fish. It was there for but a brief second and Alex reeled the lure in with scales impaired on one

200   ANOTHER FISHING YEAR

of the trebles. When not really in a feeding mood perch have the habit of nudging the lure with their shoulders and become momentarily hung up as they crash-dive.

After lunch at Madig we decided to spend some time shore fishing a series of islands, where Alex caught his first Nile perch, a scrappy fish of around 25lbs, and though we had several more follows that was the only fish to come our way. I have never known the fishing here so difficult.

Friday, 18th November

Gentle northerly breeze. Very hot with clear blue skies.

The weather now is more like what I expect on the lake for this time of the year, which was proved by the significantly improved sport today. Mohammed and I had on board our boat

Bahati, Ian Tighe from Chesterfield in Derbyshire and we started by trolling along the wall at Madig (the narrowest part of the lake proper) without a hit, despite marking some good groups of perch on the fish finder, although Paul Taylor on one of the other boats took a 35lbs perch using a 'depth-raider' plug.

A theory about fishing during the full moon is that the perch situated in open water, spend much of their time feeding at night (they have glassy, zander-like eyes, purpose built for hunting in low light conditions) and so consequently are disinclined to hunt during daylight. Whereas perch which ambush their prey from beneath overhanging rocks along the shoreline and from behind islands, are more likely to give chase during daylight. And the more safaris I make to Lake Nasser, the more convinced I am that this is in fact what happens.

For instance, on the way to our next location Sabor, we shore fished where following a half hour encounter a couple of years back, I lost what I thought was my largest ever Nile perch after watching it tail-walk twice, a monster close to 200lbs. Nothing so large this time however, but I did slam into three fish today, all within an hour, whilst working a rubber 'bull-dawg' lure close beside a steep-sided wall. The last, a baby of around 15lbs I landed, but the other two, respectably-sized fish of around 40 and 60lbs apiece, both managed to throw the hooks. The smaller of the two stayed on long enough to explode at the surface in a shower of spray before head-shaking itself from my line.

Always nice to witness are these acrobatic jumps, and I really do not mind, once I have seen the fish, whether they stay on or not, unless it's a whopper of course. Then I'm as sick as the proverbial parrot. And today I felt particularly sorry for Ian whose first sizeable Nile perch, a fish of 30lbs plus, also shook the lure out. After lunch at Sabor Island camp, we all carried on heading south, and spent most of the time drift-casting to small islands from the boat. On its day, it is a lethal method of hitting into perch that have become 'spooked' by the sound of an outboard engine. I lost a fish of around 20lbs, while Ian took a couple of 3 and 10lbs. We then camped overnight at Sabor west bank camp.

Saturday, 19th November

Gentle northerly wind. Bright sunshine and clear blue skies.

There were lots of jackal paw prints in the sand close to the boats this morning, plus the deep groove left by the dangling tail of a large monitor lizard. These are regularly seen in the lake as are some huge crocodiles. It is indeed easy to forget that Lake Nasser is nothing other than the River Nile, so all the creatures and fishes of this mysterious watershed also inhabit the lake, such as snapping turtles and the curious freshwater puffer fish which blow themselves up to stop being swallowed, and the even more mysterious bottlenose. It is a fish that can grow to over three feet in length and 30lbs in weight, yet its tapering, almost anteater-like snout, is less than an inch in diameter. I saw a dead one of over three feet long a couple of mornings back in the margins, but it was unfortunately too decomposed to photograph.

The guys from Wiltshire, Eddy and Ken, came back on *Bahati* today as we travelled still further south to a group of islands at Wadi El Arab. And from three separate islands we enjoyed a small measure of success, each catching perch to around 20lbs. Although Ken was particularly unlucky with a fish of possibly 70lbs plus, which severed his 25lbs reel line around a huge rock,

ANOTHER FISHING YEAR

just ten yards out when it made its last bid for freedom. In all we managed to land seven fish during the day to around 25lbs plus a 6lbs tiger fish, and lost eight. Sport is starting at last to pick up, even if the individual size of each perch is not.

Sunday, 20th November

Gusty, northeasterly wind. Bright blue skies.

Today we started heading back towards Garf Hussein with Mohammed's trainee Hanni on board *Bahati* plus Chris Darwell and his dad Roy, who is particularly enjoying the bird life on the lake, and if the truth be known he is probably more of a 'twitcher' than he is an angler. He pointed out a booted eagle to me this morning, plus some crested skylarks and numerous black and white wheatears. We stopped on several islands for shore fishing with just a 5lbs perch to Chris to show for our efforts, so I suggested to Mohammed that as we were going to pass the wall at Sabor, where I lost those two fair fish on Friday, why not try it again.

LEFT
My good friend and top Lake Nasser guide Mohammed. With whom I have fished, joked and filmed with for nearly a decade. If there are any monsters about, he will put you onto them.

BELOW
The pressure on both body and tackle when connected with a big fish whilst precariously perched 20 feet above the lakes surface on a steep-sided rock face has to be experienced to be believed. Mohammed waits expectantly. This one came off.

RIGHT
Mohammed prepares to haul out a 10lbs perch hooked close in amongst the rocks by Chris Darwell from Leeds.

Due to the gusting wind we had to leave the boat some way from the wall in the lee of a small cove and make a tiring walk over the top of the headland, but it proved well worth it, twitching and jigging our rubber artificials from a platform 20 feet above the water, several feet beneath the surface directly beside the steep-sided wall, to attract any perch using the hidden sub-surface caverns as ambush points. After several minutes up came a perch of around 50lbs and sucked in my 'bull-dawg', only to spit it out before I could bang the hook home. Most perch power-dive upon taking an artificial and almost hook themselves in the process. This one did not.

Thinking that these fish might have seen too much of 'bull-dawgs' I swapped over to a heavily weighted bright red, 12 inch long, rubber monstrosity with a twister tail and large single hook, and with close-in prospects looking worse with every cast, I decided to explore the deeper water straight out from the wall. I had noticed on previous occasions whilst trolling here that the bottom shelved away to over 70 feet, a mere 60 yards out, and thinking some fish might have moved further out, I allowed the lure to hit bottom (watching the bow of line in the wind to fall slack) before commencing a gentle 'jigging' retrieve. To do this I point the rod at the lure and

BELOW
Caption to be
written here.

crank the reel handle a turn or two every few seconds. This results in a lifelike action and because the rod is pointed at the lure, (minimal line stretch to be taken up) the hook has the very best possible chance of finding purchase should something grab hold.

A totally invigorating style of fishing this, being buffeted by the strong wind whilst trying to keep your balance on a plateau of rock 20 feet above the surface. And on about my fourth or fifth cast having cranked the lure just off bottom, over went the 11 foot rod into a full curve as 30lbs test mono fair sizzled from my 7001 multiplier.

Immediately I knew this was a big fish and yelled to Roy and Chris to watch out for when it zoomed up to the surface to jump. They were equally as gobsmacked as I, when a 'buffalo' came up and tailed-walked a couple of times before I had it under control following a powerful battle lasting around ten minutes, sufficient for Mohammed to think about climbing down the wall to a shallow ledge in order to hoist the monster ashore. What a satisfying sight after a week of indifference.

Why oh why does everything start to happen on our last full day's fishing of the safari? But a 100lbs perch is always a special occasion for me, especially as this particular fish was my first ever 100lbs freshwater fish hooked and landed from the shore. We then continued on our way to Madig and lunch, without another hit, despite trying a couple of potentially good islands en route. Without question this particular safari has seen the hardest fishing ever for our guests that I have experienced on the lake. That extremely strong and cold northeasterly blow during the first few days really put the kybosh on things. After lunch Chris got into the action with a 10lbs fish from one of the several islands we fished.

Monday, 21st November

Strong northeasterly wind. Bright blue skies and strong sunlight.

Our last morning on the lake before heading north from our overnight camp at Madig to meet up with the transfer bus at Garf Hussein for our return flight from Aswan in the late afternoon, and weather conditions had worsened. Paul, Alex and Ian fished on *Bahati*, without, I am sad to say, so much as another hit. Our seven man safari had experienced the poorest fishing I have ever known on the lake, but to the man they were so unbelievably upbeat and philosophical about the unusual conditions. Most actually caught, (despite the weather and full moon) their largest freshwater fish ever. I hope I get to take some of them again on a more 'prolific' occasion in the future.

ANOTHER FISHING YEAR

Thursday, 1st December

No wind. Baking hot and humid. Bright sunshine with a temperature approaching 100°F.

Here we are into December and I have yet to get my boat out on the Norfolk Broads for a pike fishing session. With such cold weather this last week throughout the UK however, I am rather glad to be back in the Tropics again for the next eight days. I could get used to fishing 'only' in the warm again. I guess it's my age. Incidentally, from 1969 to 71 I lived on the west coast of Barbados.

Following an eleven hour EVA Air flight from Heathrow into Bangkok's Don Mueang airport, a half hour Western Tours southerly shuttle took me into Hua Hin airport, where brother Dave picked me up yesterday evening, bubbling about the fishing prospects for this coming week. Within 15 minutes we arrived at his lovely new house, finally finished only a couple of months ago, set in a half acre garden in which Dave and his Thai wife Boon, have constructed

and landscaped an equally large pond. I am tempted to say 'lake', because no one (except my brother) would build a pond so large that it virtually fills their entire walled garden, leaving a pathway round of just a yard or two on either side. And naturally, it's full of fish. Everything from Pla Buek or Mekong Giant catfish and koi carp to the most colourful of exotic, freshwater oddities. There are so many, I even persuaded Dave to part with half a dozen of his pets in the way of small (bar-dok) catfish and orange-coloured tilapia for bait, which we netted out and put into a large tub in the back of his Nissan truck along with all our rods and other equipment ready for a 5.30 a.m. alarm call.

Now before I start recalling our adventures in this truly fascinating country, let me explain that much of the serious freshwater sport fishing in Thailand is based largely around modest-sized, heavily stocked commercial still waters.

Of course there are still monster catfish of several species, the largest being the Mekong, plus several carp-like fish, some exotic predators both indigenous and from South America, and even giant stingrays to be taken from the enormous network of river and lakeland systems. But by and large, most everything with easy access from the major cities, has been fished-out commercially.

It seemed strange (in fact it blew my mind away) when I first visited brother Dave here a couple of years ago, to have flown best part half way round the world, only to be fishing in what I would (back home) call 'hole in the ground' fisheries. But as they say, 'when in Rome', and throughout my life this has been a principle I have always tried to adhere to. Consequently, this week's fishing is based around three different commercial fisheries. One in Bangkok called Bung Sam Ran, a large lake and Thailand's most famous, monster fish water, and two close to the city of Hua Hin where Dave lives. One is called Cha-am Fish Park, a two-lake complex of four and seven acres (where we concentrated our efforts for an entire week two years back) and Palm Tree Lagoon, a recent find of Dave's, and our first port of call.

We arrived at 8 a.m. following a lengthy drive to find the square-shaped, five acre lake, nicely planted with grasses, shrubs and palms (hence its name) around the margins, without a single person fishing. Local Thai anglers never seem to arrive until late morning. It's only us mad westerners who seem willing to lose sleep for their sport.

Anyway, we soon lugged all the gear round to the southern side of the lake (with big fish rolling everywhere in the coloured water) where Dave had fished previously, only last week in fact, when he caught some large piranhas and lost something much larger, and set up our stall.

Dave had intrigued me with stories about two giant arapaima which inhabit the lake along with, would you believe, an eight foot long crocodile which escaped from its bank side, wire enclosure, where its twin is still on show adjacent to the fishery office, (we passed it when walking round) plus an enormous mixture of both local and imported species including both Mekong and swai catfish, piranhas, Pla Khao, carp and alligator gars etc., etc. And as if to confirm his words, one of the giant arapaima suddenly came up to the surface and rolled

LEFT
Using a three foot deep salmon net to capture a seven foot long arapaima, did I must admit seem daft. But Paul, the owner of Palm tree Lagoon jumped into the lake anyway and performed the impossible at the end of a monumental encounter.

ANOTHER FISHING YEAR

DECEMBER

(displaying its enormous length and width and large bright red scales) not 30 yards out. It was truly massive and at least a couple of hundred pounds. Dave looked at me as if to say "I told you," and for once I was speechless. No, that's not true. I did say something but it simply cannot be repeated here.

I was so glad we had brought the bucket of live baits, and the first outfit I put together was a powerful Masterline, ten foot Nige Williams catfish rod, sporting a multiplier loaded with 50lbs braid and a pike-style sliding float rig with a single 6/0 hook to a three foot trace of 100lbs test mono. On went one of Dave's pond pets (a small, bar-dok catfish) and I walked 50 yards to my left (Dave sat five yards to my right) before plopping it 30 yards out. I then walked back and put the rod down on the ground with the tip pointing at the 'gently bobbing' float set five feet deep and put the reel into free spool with the ratchet on.

Meanwhile, Dave had put together two rods (each presenting peacock quill lift float rigs) and was fishing large lumps of bread flake just five yards out (the lake averages around ten foot deep) over a bed of mashed bread ground bait. As everybody fishes with just bread in Thailand's commercial fisheries (other baits are in many cases frowned upon) consequently, all the species get weaned onto eating it, even predatory oddities like piranhas and of course the algae-eating (in the wild) Mekong catfish.

Within minutes, one of Dave's floats disappeared and he was fast into a good fish by the bend in his carp rod. But whatever it was quickly bit through the 25lbs mono and Dave wound in minus his size 2 hook. He simply muttered something about 'piranhas' and feverishly tied on another hook. I also put together two peacock quill lift float rigs using my all through action 11½ foot Masterline JW Heritage 1¾bs test curve carp rods (little did I know what was in store just 24 hours later) plus my Baitmaster 'free-spool' fixed spool reels loaded with 19lbs test Rapala 'clear' mono. And just in case something 'toothy' grabbed hold, I tied up two 10 inch traces using 25lbs test Cannelle Supatress which is made from high density braided fibres and steel braid, with a size 1/0 hook on the business end. It's as soft as monofilament and can be knotted in the same way. And thank goodness I did.

There then followed one of the most hectic times I've ever had fishing, when for most of the day one of us, or both, were hitting into, losing, playing or missing bites from beautiful swai or striped catfish which are only striped when young, and similar in looks to the Mekong. The lake seemed literally to be paved with them, all beautifully proportioned, silver-sided specimens running from around 18 to 25lbs, providing truly breathtaking, arm wrenching sport especially on the float. Although we did each change one of our rods over to a spiral-in-line feeder rig in order to fish further out after lunch. And that's another benefit of fishing in Thailand. They bring round cold beers and tasty lunches of fried pork or prawns and noodles etc., to wherever you are

ANOTHER FISHING YEAR

ANOTHER FISHING YEAR

fishing. I've heard there are other 'benefits' on offer too, but we won't go into those.

Since my previous visit to fish with Dave, I had forgotten the sheer pulling power of Thailand's pussies. Pound for pound I have yet to catch freshwater fish that can pull as hard or for as long, Mekongs in particular. Their stamina is quite phenomenal, due no doubt to the species' huge and powerful tail and anal fins. A blind man would think they are twice their physical size. A 20lbs Mekong for instance, even on 20lbs line, fights like a 40lbs Wels catfish. They are that tough.

Halfway through the afternoon session Dave suddenly exclaimed, "This is a bigger fish John," and he was so right. Totally unstoppable, it ran 40 yards to his right straight into a scaffold pole arrangement constructed to support a three paddle aerator unit on the surface 30 feet out into the lake, run via a long, scaffold pole prop shaft from an electric motor on the bank. Dave was in a right pickle, but miraculously, after ten minutes of cussing and cursing he managed to coax the fish out again, I don't know how, whereupon the lake's owner Paul came over eventually, after a few more heavy lunges and crash dives, to put the net beneath a huge and incredibly fat red tail catfish, which subsequently pulled Dave's scales round to 72lbs. Not I hasten to add, the indigenous, Thai red tail catfish, but the very same species I caught back in January in Brazil from the Rio Negro, and not for one minute did I expect to see one in Thailand. Boy was Brother Dave over the moon. It would appear that several of the larger and more exotic South American species like arapaima, red tail cats, alligator gars and even peacock bass etc., have become immensely popular sports fish in Thailand's commercial fisheries, though I've no idea when the Thais first started importing and subsequently breeding these beautiful species.

During our unbelievable day of catfishing, we must have taken more than 20 swais apiece averaging over 20lbs, and every now and again something would run off with my live bait. But when I tightened down to strike, whatever it was (and it felt like a 10-20lbs fish, certainly not one of the arapaima that I had set my sights on) came off within seconds. I could only guess they were alligator gars having trouble sucking the live bait past their set of 'crocodile' gnashers.

When darkness loomed over the lake at 6 p.m., and doesn't it happen quickly, Dave and I drove along the

LEFT
The Lake's owner Paul, not only helped brother Dave hoist his magnificent, 72lbs 'Brazilian' red tail catfish onto the scales. He jumped into the lake on my account, twice, when I hooked into one of the fisheries main attractions. Can't imagine many UK fishery owners doing likewise...

road to an air-conditioned motel where we stayed the night, in order to rise at the crack of dawn for a second day at Palm Tree Lagoon. And we slept like babies after a few cold beers and some tasty local food.

Friday, 2nd December

Overcast and humid. No wind and baking hot.

They say no two days' fishing are ever the same. And they (whoever they are) are perfectly right. Yesterday's swai catfish were today, conspicuous by their absence. In fact I doubt we caught half a dozen all day long. But I did play for a minute or two a rather large (well it felt like a 20-30lbs fish) alligator gar which grabbed one of Dave's pond fish. I would have loved to have caught a fleeting glance of it especially as it took our last live bait. (Two weeks later incidentally, Dave rang the UK early one morning having just returned from the lake to tell me he had taken two alligator gars, both around 30lbs apiece). There then followed the most bizarre and fortunate experience I have ever known in over 50 years of fishing in fresh water around the world. And it started when I was walking back from the owner's house just 50 yards away to see if he had any small fish I could purchase to use as live bait, which unfortunately he didn't.

Anyway, as I approached our swim Dave's rod was hooped over alarmingly with his line going into the scaffolding of the aerator paddles, where in the middle of an enormous swirl I momentarily made out the broad back and large greeny-brown scales of what looked like one of the two huge arapaima. The fish here are certainly well aware of the fisheries only snag, and brother Dave was nearly out of his tree with frustration. Then I suddenly noticed that my own rod (float rig with bread flake) lying on the ground to Dave's left was also bent round with the Baitmaster reel singing and the line going past Dave also into the aerator.

Suddenly Dave exclaimed "It's not my fish, it's on your line John," as his tangled hook and swan shot slid up my bowstring-tight line.

The fish had obviously hooked itself on my rod and gone through Dave's float rig providing him with an unmissable bite, so that when he struck and caught my line, he truly thought he'd hooked the monster. Immediately I grabbed my rod and angled it over to Dave so he could cut through his line just above the tangle around mine, which was when Paul the owner appeared, obviously having witnessed our predicament from his window which overlooks the lake. On our behalf and without more ado he waded across the scaffold pole structure which looked like collapsing into the lake at any second, to try and free my line, while I ran towards it winding like mad.

By now the arapaima was at least 50 yards the other side of the aerator crashing angrily on the surface and creating the most enormous swirls, with line hissing from my reel (which I'd now knocked into free spool) and going through the middle of the scaffold pole structure. I was about to strip off and swim out to pass the rod between the poles, when Paul the owner dived in himself to free the line. I instinctively hoped the escaped eight foot croc had not been attracted by all the commotion, but immediately put such preposterous notions out of my mind. The great fish by now must have been over a 100 yards across the lake and my reel was fast emptying of 19lbs test line. I literally threw Paul the rod and he niftily weaved it through the aerator poles, so that within seconds, 'hey presto', the line was free with the fish miraculously still attached

ANOTHER FISHING YEAR

but now trying to bury itself amongst a huge patch of water hyacinth some 150 yards away along the far margins of the lake.

Not for a second did I fancy my chances of ever seeing this awesome fish on the bank. I had no idea about the condition of the line, coupled to the fact that my 1¾lbs test curve carp rod seemed totally unmatched for what was obviously a 100lbs plus arapaima, it being the very same outfit (of my own design for Masterline) that I had loaned to Bruce Vaughan several weeks ago (except that I had replaced the 12lbs test with 19lbs) when he caught that lovely 13lbs barbel from my local River Wensum. And if I remember correctly, the rod took on an alarming bend that day too, with just a barbel on the other end.

It was about this time when Paul the owner nonchalantly mentioned that this was actually the smaller of the lake's two arapaima, neither of which had ever been landed. So how big, I mused, was the largest? I asked Dave to rattle off several shots of my playing the monster on both my little Casio digital and Nikon F100 SLR cameras, because not for a minute did I ever expect to see it up close. But an hour later, following numerous occasions when the great fish surfaced in enormous, oily swirls to take in gulps of air, before lunging off again on 30 to 40 yard runs with line fair screaming from the reel, I actually started to think about the impossible.

Paul the owner even picked up the landing net, which less than half the arapaima just might go into, as step by step the runs became less regular and far less violent. I have always thought that it is indeed surprising what can be done with an all through action carp rod, and here, following one of the most bizarre hook ups in my entire angling career and an hour long battle with an adversary I certainly didn't deserve to still be playing, let alone landing, I was able to steer it close into the bank.

Paul had already waded out chest deep into the lake (again the eight foot escaped crocodile came to mind, but I was too hyped up to dwell on the thought) the second time on my account this morning (courteous and most helpful blokes are Thai fishery owners) and slowly eased the net, an old salmon net that I had given Dave several years ago, along the great fish's head and shoulders. Less than half its length actually went into the mesh, but it was so knackered, it allowed itself also to be cradled along its back end in Paul's arms and brought into the shallows. By now this 'Wilson' was also in the lake, and the impossible had actually happened. A massive predatory fish beaten on carp tackle and size 1/0 hook on float-fished bread flake. A fish which was about as deep in the body as a 100lbs plus tarpon (and I've had my share of those in the Florida Keys) but twice as thick. It must have been fully 14 inches across the back, and could have weighed much more, (Dave's scales only went to 100lbs) but we reckoned a conservative weight would be around 130-140lbs. I marvelled at its strange colouration along the lower half of its fully scaled body, with areas of scales vividly enamelled in bright red, and felt inside the upturned jaws for my comparatively tiny hook, which literally fell

out. Yet another lucky element of capture, but then perhaps my name had been on this fish from the start. Regardless. I was however glad I had tied the hook to Supertress as the row of small but strong and sharp canine teeth just inside the bony jaws, both top and bottom, would have made short work of the 19lbs monofilament.

Was I over the moon or what? In fact very few fish over the years have made me feel as elated as I did at that moment, and I just could not concentrate for the rest of the day (silly old sod), which was just as well really, because as I mentioned earlier, the pussies were not really in a feeding mood. Although I did catch another, a previously un-caught and unseen species in the way of a silver-scaled chub-like fish with a small mouth just like a grass carp, of around 10lbs, again on bread flake. What a day though. Barbel fishing on the Wensum using that same rod, will never seem the same again.

Saturday, 3rd December

Heavily overcast with a gentle southerly breeze.

Today was totally different again, as yesterday was from the previous day. Dave and I decided to fish his favourite local water, Cha-am Fish Park near Hua Hin where we fished together with our old friend Jinx Davey during my first visit two years ago. The larger of the two lakes was our

Dave's stepped-up carp rod is taking a real hammering here at Cha-am Fish Park from the powerful lunges of a Pla Khao (Siamese giant carp) hooked on float-fished bread flake.

choice and to start we both float-fished bread flake (lift-style of course) close in to try and catch one of the lake's biggest attractions (apart from Mekong pussies to 60lbs that is) a big Pla Kaho carp. These are in fact Siamese Giant carp, one of the world's largest cyprinids incidentally, which have been taken to over 100lbs at Cha-am, but which regularly come out between 30-60lbs. Dave's best here weighed a staggering 81¾lbs and was a stunning creature, deep-bodied and immensely thick with blue-black scales and a characteristic and strange ruby-red patch on the rear of its anal fin.

ABOVE
Guide Git (right)
helps Dave display
his 45lbs Pla Khao.
Note the huge,
filter-feeding mouth,
large powerful fins,
huge, black-edged
scales and the
characteristic ruby-
red patch (beneath
Git's left hand) on
the rear of the anal
fin. A truly beautiful
creature.

I was indeed looking forward to experiencing one on the end of my line. But by lunchtime however (when tasty meat and sea food dishes are brought round to wherever you are fishing) our close-in tactics were simply not working, although Dave had accounted for a couple of swai catfish to around 10lbs. So we changed tack completely over to ledgering, using 30lbs reel lines, with in-line spiral feeders, around which is moulded an orange-sized ball of dampened bread crumbs, concealing the short, five inch hook trace and flake-covered size 2/0 hook.

After casting and the bait hits bottom, the line is wound up almost tight and the multiplier is put into free spool with the ratchet on. There then follows a series of taps on the rod tip till the Mekong or swai catfish either knock the hook bait off or zoom off, thus hooking themselves in the process. And the resulting scream of the reel's ratchet is absolute music to the ears.

We bumped into English angler Eric King who hails from Christchurch in Hampshire, who is staying at Cha-am in one of the holiday bungalows for three weeks. He has fished extensively all over Thailand for the last eight years, and often fishes Bung Sam Ran near Bangkok, so we invited him along on our trip there for Monday and Tuesday. His advice will I am sure be invaluable.

Later on this afternoon it started to rain so Dave and I decided to pack up early as the fishing for Mekongs proved unsuccessful, though plenty of swai catfish in the 8-12lbs range were feeding heavily. So we had our strings well and truly pulled.

Sunday, 4th December.

Very humid, hazy sunshine, light southerly wind.

Dave and I arrived at Cha-am lakes shortly after dawn, where numerous night herons and egrets were feeding along the margins, hopefully to capitalise on the chances of catching a big Pla Kaho, by float fishing bread flake close in. But after two hours without so much as a line bite, and when lots of other anglers arrived, we changed over to distance fishing for Mekongs and swai catfish using spiral feeders and sliding pike floats, (set six feet deep in ten feet of water) with the ball of bread ground bait squeezed tightly around the in-line feeder hiding the hook bait covering a size 2/0 hook. By far the best method for Mekong pussies hooking themselves which the float greatly assists in, when they nibble at the ground bait ball around the feeder and subsequently dive down with the hook bait.

And what did brother Dave belt into on his very first cast? Only a 45lbs Pla Khao, that's all. What a fantastically fast and powerful scrap it put up too, for over 15 minutes, before local guide and good friend of Dave's, Git (pronounced Jit) slipped the net under it and hoisted it up onto the grassy bank. But there were no others to follow. Throughout the day on both float-feeder and straight ledger-feeder tactics we caught numerous swai catfish to around 15lbs, and in the late afternoon Dave took our only Mekong of 40lbs following a powerful scrap. Another great day although the Mekongs were decidedly not playing ball.

We left before dark in order to get back to the house and tackle up ready for a trip to Bung Sam Ran in the morning with Eric who's staying at Cha-am. The taxi driver who has a seven seater minibus is due round the house at 7 a.m.

Monday 5th December

Humid and heavily overcast with thunder and lightning. Persistent rain till 10 a.m.

Dave and I woke at 6 a.m. to the sound of heavy rain hitting the metal roof of the house. Wood is not used due to termites. And we got soaked netting about 40 small, orange-coloured live baits out of his pond, (bunning, tap tin and butter pian which are all tilapia-like fish) and putting them into two large tubs, around which we secured two bin liners so they didn't swamp the minibus.

We picked up Eric from Cha-am Fish Park en route and continued on the 130 mile trip to Bung Sam Ran which lies northeast of Bangkok, arriving a little after 11 a.m. We had telephoned ahead to book up bungalow 23 (there are 27 around the fishery)

which Eric said afforded casting into one of the best swims within the entire complex and a fascinating, if somewhat overcrowded fishery, if you call getting on for 200 anglers all hammering 40 acres, crowded.

Popular with both visiting and local anglers alike, the wooden, garden shed-like bungalows on wooden stilts are spread out around one entire length and one complete side of the oblong-shaped fishery, which is apparently an old clay pit where depths shelve to over 20 feet. The centre of the lake is one mass of rolling monsters including Mekong, arapaima, Pla Khao, and swai catfish, plus silver carp, alligator gars and many other exotic species. Four of these,

arapaima, Mekong, Pla Khao and Chao Phray Giant catfish (named after the river running through Bangkok) all grow to over 100lbs, whilst the first three have all been caught to a staggering 200lbs plus. A truly unique and fascinating fishery containing over 50 species of exotica (more than ten IGFA world records were set here in 2001-02) where you soon forget the noise and clatter and ramshackle wooden buildings and rickety bridges around the lake. Here it is a case of 'big fish rule OK!' So it's best to forget the aesthetics.

Every few minutes there are huge crashes out in the middle that would do justice to a donkey jumping in. And I for one could not wait to get bait into the water. Within an hour we had everything loaded onto a wheel barrow and taken round to bungalow 23 where we each put a couple of rods out presenting both bread and live baits. Dave lost a swai catfish of around 25lbs at the net within half an hour of casting and then I hooked into a really huge Mekong on 30lbs mono loaded onto my 7001 big game multiplier, which simply kept going and going to our right straight under a bridge. I put on all the stops but the end was inevitable, and the line suddenly fell back slack having been severed around the bridge supports.

I then decided to walk half way along the same bridge (which goes around 180 yards across from one bank to the other) in order to cast a float-fished live bait out 50 yards on my heavy outfit onto which I had loaded 80lbs braid, before walking back to our bungalow whilst paying out line. I then left the reel in free spool with the ratchet on, and 30 minutes later away screamed the live bait and I struck into what felt like another 100lbs plus arapaima (hooking into two, each from a different water within days of each other is remarkable enough in itself, but how lucky can you get) which I then played hard for a good ten minutes, managing to steer it well clear of the bridge supports, using the power of the heavier outfit. I eventually had it almost under control mere yards from the bungalow, chugging up and down, when the 7/0 hook to a 50lbs test wire trace suddenly decided to pop out. Boy was I gutted, because unlike the arapaima of a few days ago, with this particular fish I had done everything right, but nonetheless still managed to lose another monster. Who said fishing was ever fair anyway?

Shortly afterwards Dave banged into what was obviously a big Mekong using good old bread flake in conjunction with an in-line spiral feeder/ float rig, but the hook pulled when he piled on the pressure to stop it from going under the bridge. The fish here certainly know where the snags are and consequently don't take any prisoners, Dave and I losing four good fish in less than two hours' fishing. At 3.30 p.m. I hooked into another arapaima on the float-fished live bait but the hook pulled within 30 seconds. 15 minutes later I was reeling in my feeder rig when I foul hooked something in mid water (obviously another large Mekong) which ran and ran against a wound down clutch, 180 yards over to the other side of the lake where the 30lbs mono parted just as I was feeling confident.

An hour before darkness set in Dave struck into a nice Mekong of around 60lbs which gave a great account of itself. The power of these catfish never ceases to amaze me; they are simply one awesome mother to horse in. When darkness came I wound in my heavy arapaima outfit to concentrate on a small ledgered live bait cast just 30 yards out, which Eric had said Chao Phray catfish are most likely to be caught on, being out and out predators (how right he was) and float fishing close in on a second rod with a luminous chemical element sleeved onto the long, peacock waggler, in the hope of a big Pla Khao, the depth being 12 feet, just a rod length out. The humid but 'pregnant' silence was broken ten minutes later by my faithful ABU 10.000 screaming into life as something ran away with one of Dave's orange-coloured pond fish.

What a place this is. Bung Sam Ran is a veritable 'Jurassic Park' of the world's angling fisheries, if somewhat 'honky tonk' in appearance, and I just love it. 20 minutes later after a powerful battle, Dave put the net under my first ever Chao Phray catfish, a silver-sided, deep-bodied beauty with the most enormous sail-like dorsal fin and huge deeply forked tail. No wonder it was repeatedly able to rip the 40lbs test mono from my reel in long, unstoppable runs. A whopper no less of 80lbs. Could things get better? Yes, because shortly after the photography session and returning the most beautiful catfish I have ever caught, away went Dave's lift float rig and 20 minutes later in came a 70lbs Mekong, which throughout most of the fight we had all assumed was a big Pla Khao. Well, the species has been caught here to a staggering 245lbs, and the fact that Dave's line became entangled around those of two local Thai anglers fishing from the bungalow to our left, kept everyone guessing till the last minute. Fortunately, everyone who fishes at the lake knows the score and eases off on their clutches when lines become entwined.

At around 9 p.m. I caught a 20lbs Mekong on the float, and for a moment I too thought a Pla Khao was responsible for ripping the line off so speedily. Fortunately, rain had now set in which kept the mosquitoes at bay, but seemed not to dampen the movements of huge bats which continually zoomed back and forward between the bungalows. At 10 p.m. I wound my rods in for some shut eye, (I just couldn't keep awake) while Dave continued bashing out Mekongs between 30-60lbs. He landed 13 in fact.

Tuesday, 6th December

Humid and overcast.

As dawn broke I lifted the bait net up to find that all our live baits, except a lone catfish, were dead. Obviously oxygen problems are common after dark here. And I'm not surprised with such a high stocking density, and the sheer amount of bread that gets thrown in. No wonder there are aerator paddle units situated at several locations around the lake. So I took one of our large, small mesh-landing nets along the dyke running behind the bungalows, and within 20 minutes had scooped out about 20 small, 3-7 inch tilapias to replace our stock of livelies.

I then cast a couple of them out in the hope of contacting another Chao Phray catfish. Having caught that 80lbs beauty during the hours of darkness, I rather fancied one during daylight to be able to study it more closely. And within half an hour I had the opportunity of exactly that when one of the small ledgered live baits got nobbled by a fish of around 35lbs which like the first put up a lively tussle. I immediately noticed the short, rather weak barbels, and the vundu-like 'holding pads' situated just inside both the top and lower jaws, with extra 'crushing-holding pads' in the throat. The fish had a small, low-set eye, long pelvics, and characteristically long dorsal and pectoral fins with tapering extensions. Bright silver and immensely deep in the body with a huge forked tail, they are truly a lovely fish to both catch and behold. Certainly the most beautiful catfish I have ever caught.

At around 7 a.m. I put out a float-fished live bait for arapaima, but there was no interest. Dave then took a 20lbs swai catfish on ledgered bread, followed by a 60lbs Mekong, and then one of 45lbs. At any second within our wide field of view looking out across the lake from bungalow 23, literally hundreds and hundreds of swai and Mekong catfish could be seen rolling on the surface, along with the occasional arapaima. And scarcely a minute went by when someone around the lake was not playing or landing a sizeable fish. What a place.

I then pulled out of a big Mekong on bread after just a few seconds, and shortly afterwards Eric took an 85lbs Mekong which gave him a fantastic scrap for fully half an hour. I then took another swai of 25lbs, followed by one easily over 30lbs, the best swai of our two day trip. What unbelievable sport we were enjoying, and yet Eric said it was actually slow compared to his last few trips.

During all this action a huge snapping turtle, the size of a wheelie bin lid repeatedly swam around the bungalow, but whenever I stood up to capture it on camera, it sunk from view. I then took a whole bunch of swai catfish (I literally lost count) of between 18-25lbs on ledgered bread. Then, at the opposite end of the bridge to my right I suddenly noticed a group of local anglers crowding around someone playing a fish, and upon walking round with my camera, a young lady angler had caught a beautiful pacu, a South American, fruit-eating species. She had in fact used a float-fished chunk of banana to tempt this superb, deep-bodied specimen of around 10-12lbs.

Upon returning to the bungalow (Eric and Dave were by now both snoring loudly having been up all night) I had a really slow run on bread, and out against a tightly set clutch on my 30lbs outfit went over 100 yards of line, the fish veering right and towards the dreaded bridge supports. I managed to turn it just in time however and back across the lake it went. Half an hour later it was under the rod tip with Eric, who had woken up to my calls, ready with the net. Wilson was about to land his first 100lbs plus Mekong catfish, (Eric's estimation not mine) after a monumental battle. Then inexplicably, the hook pulled out. I followed up with another five

swai averaging around 20lbs, and then it was sadly time to go. We left for the long journey, through Bangkok's rush hour traffic back to Hua Hin at 6 p.m., getting back to Dave's house by about 9.30 p.m. What a fantastic couple of days! I cannot ever remember hooking and losing so many big fish. But in the words of 'Arnie', I will be back. Believe me.

Monday, 12th December

Mild and sunny. Gentle northeast wind.

It's back to reality and our British winter again for yours truly, after enjoying so much sun and foreign travel of late. Kevin Green, editor of Improve *Your Coarse Fishing* magazine and his photographer Lloyd were round at the house for 9 a.m. having taken two hours to get here from Peterborough for the purpose of putting together a 'lure-fishing' feature. And being blessed with such nice weather for my first local trip in over a month, I was really confident about producing a few decent pike from a couple of weir pools along my local River Wensum, on the several new ranges of Rapala plugs recently sent to me by Dick Tallents of Masterline International. Unfortunately, with the river pathetically low and clear, the worst I have ever seen it at this time of the year (there has been a complete lack of floods, much needed to flush out the system and raise the water table) those pike were extra 'spooky'. I managed to initiate a dozen or more follows during our five hour session, three were from nice doubles between 12-15lbs, but did they want to grab hold? Did they hell! Actually that is not strictly true, because I did set the hooks into a jack of about 4lbs which gave Lloyd something 'live' to film as I chinned it out, and another, slightly larger, hung on long enough to shake the hooks out at my feet.

The largest fish even made a last minute lunge and momentarily grabbed hold, but without turning away aggressively enough for the hooks to be banged home. And they all behaved similarly in that half-hearted way. What a frustrating session. Although Kevin was pleased that the sunny conditions made for some nice photography which included shooting some pack shots of all the various 'new' lures, and so my guests returned to Peterborough in the late afternoon with the feature completed. But I was still angry with those cute pike and my own inability at putting at least a few on the bank. But so it goes.

Wednesday, 14th December

Overcast with a light northerly wind.

Back in the 1970s I regularly wrote monthly articles for a wonderful magazine called *Angling*, edited by Brian Harris. A magazine which unfortunately unlike any published today, catered especially for the all round angler; those who long trotted, lure anglers, fly fisherman both at home and abroad, sea anglers both at home and abroad, those who explored tropical exotica, be it mahseer fishing in India or catching stingrays and tarpon from the beach in Barbados, and of course fishing domestically for barbel, carp, tench and bream etc., etc. (and was in the opinion of many, light years ahead of its time) the lead writer being Twickenham tackle dealer Dave

LEFT
Small wonder this young lass wears a happy grin, having hooked on a chunk of banana and played skilfully around the woodwork of a bridge, this superbly shaped pacu. Yet another of the fascinating, South American species now regularly caught from Thailand's commercial sports fisheries.

RIGHT
Long trotting
maggots in the fast
waters of
Hampshire's
delightful River Test
produced this scale-
perfect 4lbs plus
chub for my long-
time angling buddy
Bruce Vaughan.
Centre pin fishing at
its finest.

Steuart, whose adventures and writing I enjoyed and admired enormously. Dave in fact wrote for *Angling* throughout an entire decade, which by our peers, was considered by far the most exciting and innovative period in modern angling, from the mid '60s until it was bought by Burlington Publishing in 1977 when Sandy Leventon became editor and Bruce Vaughan his assistant.

Since those years Dave, Bruce and I have become firm friends so it was no coincidence yesterday evening when Bruce and I arrived at Dave and his wife Kay's lovely house which nestles beside the enchanting and famous River Test in Romsey, Hampshire for some serious long trotting. Dave quickly reminded me, although we regularly natter over the phone (and he could talk for England – though he would probably say the same about me) that the last time I came fishing on his piece of the river was 14 years ago. So we had much to catch up on.

I thought that I had done my time, so to speak, having run my tackle shop 'John's Tackle Den' in Norwich for some 26 years, but Dave and Kay ran their shop in Twickenham for a staggering 39 years. After which, they decided to retire down in Hampshire beside the fast flowing River Test, due mostly to the salmon fishing then, being so prolific. And I found this so coincidental to my own life, in that I moved to Norfolk in 1971, for the 'once' marvellous roach fishing, now long ruined by cormorants, while salmon fishing in the Test is also now but a memory of its former glory. Like I said in the introduction of this book, my how things can alter, and sadly, all for the worse, in just 30 years.

Dave and Kay are an extremely rare duo. In my opinion, they are the most successful husband and wife fishing team ever. Their conquests in worldwide pelagic game species alone from marlin to roosterfish and amberjacks, plus their catches of both Atlantic and Pacific salmon from great chinooks to Atlantic salmon approaching 40lbs, will never be equalled. Add to this big carp, barbel, sturgeon, roach, chub, tarpon, pike, and giant common skate etc., and you have a measure of their legacy.

Following an evening of total nostalgia, helped along by a couple of bottles of red, Bruce and I eventually rose at around 7.30 a.m. to the aroma of a full English breakfast cooked to perfection by our man Steuart, which we polished off in his conservatory overlooking the river, not 30 feet away. We then sorted our trotting gear out and enjoyed what to our good friend has been a real labour of love over the past 30 years, turning a rough meadow into almost park-like bank sides beside a twisting, most picturesque and ever-changing River Test.

From the bridge spanning the upstream limit of Dave's fishery to the very end swim, a veritable 'big dace banker', a distance of perhaps 600 yards, there is every imaginable feature from deep narrows and hatch pools, to a weir and several tree-lined bends. It is a veritable long-trotters' paradise, and Bruce and I were like kids in a sweet shop, but with only one day to spend our pennies. Dave even has a special 'hatch pool' full of Jurassic-like monster brownies and chub which he calls his 'pets', and feeds daily. But no one, and rightly so, is allowed to offer them a baited hook.

Hard fighting grayling of between 8oz and 1½lbs formed the bulk of our catches, providing immense trotting pleasure on our 13 foot rods and centre pin reels loaded with 2½lbs test line and five AA chubber floats, with size 16 hooks tied direct presenting two white maggots. Depths varied between three and eight feet in the strong flow, despite water levels being low, as indeed they have been throughout southern England including my local Norfolk rivers of late, particularly the River Wensum.

Along at the 'end' swim where a huge laurel bush overhangs the river immediately upstream of a footbridge, I took several grayling and salmon parr, a single eight ounce roach, plus

My good friends and the most successful angling partnership for catching monster fish all over the world that I know of, Kay and Dave Steuart, share in my pleasure at netting a fine grayling from the River Test which runs through their beautifully landscaped property.

20 or so dace to 14 ounces. Meanwhile, in the late afternoon just before the light started to go Bruce accounted for a nice chub of 4¾lbs and a lovely roach of 2lbs 2oz, plus several nice grayling. What a truly superb day's trotting, punctuated every so often by the antics and flapping tails of grey wagtails flitting from swim to swim. A veritable angling haven has been created here. I won't wait 14 years again Dave, honestly.

Thursday, 15th December

Heavily overcast, gentle northerly wind.

After another superb 'Dave Steuart fry-up' (he really should have been a short-order cook) Bruce and I made our farewells before driving upstream along the beautiful Test Valley to where the diminutive River Anton converges with the mainstream. And what a lovely river this tributary of the Test is. Fast, shallow, winding, ever changing with willows and alders overhanging its banks, it is simply stuffed full of chunky grayling, in depths ranging from two to four feet. In some swims the brownies were a nuisance, if trout to 3lbs can be a problem, and when you are purposefully seeking grayling they are indeed. Ironic really, because any one of those trout hooked on a dry fly or nymph in the spring would be the event of the day.

Nevertheless we were after her ladyship the grayling and not spotties. It is indeed all a matter of preference after all. And the preference of Bruce and me was grayling. Our day started, as always on these southern chalk streams, with our walking upstream to the very top of the fishery (a distance of perhaps two miles) considering and looking intently into each and every swim for signs of fish and what course we needed to work our floats when covering the river on our way back downstream. Unfortunately, poor old Bruce had left his Polaroid glasses in his car, which was almost as bad as leaving the bait at home. You see

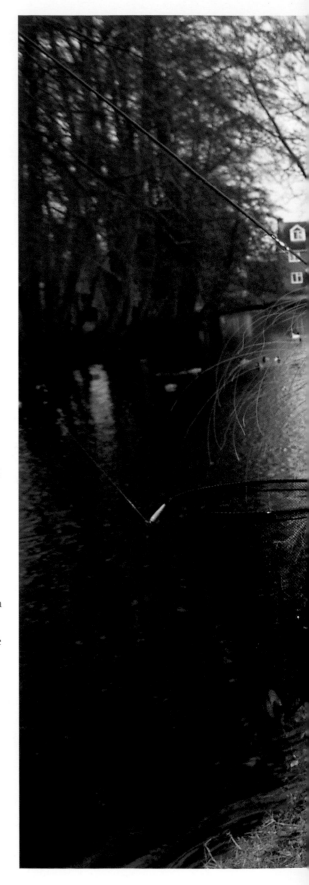

ANOTHER FISHING YEAR

LEFT
Happiness is indeed
grayling-shaped.
Look at the power of
this exquisitely
painted specimen
from the diminutive
River Anton.

in these shallow, exceedingly clear Hampshire chalk streams, unless you can identify where the grayling are 'not', think about this (all the shallow, unoccupied parts of each swim) you have no clear line for working your float downstream. In other words, unless you can identify the deeper, darker, obviously, fish-occupied runs, and yellow, HLT Polaroid glasses are imperative here, you are at a distinct and complete disadvantage.

Nevertheless, Bruce and I had a fantastic day wandering along the River Anton, accounting for around 40-50 grayling apiece with several individuals in the 1½-1¾lbs bracket. What fantastic scraps they put up on light tackle too, sometimes being hooked at the very end of the runs over 40 yards downriver. In these days of 'minimal' big-roach potential, trotting for grayling is the next best thing, believe me, and if you love working a float downstream with the current, then get yourself down to Hampshire and its marvellous chalk streams. The Orvis tackle shop in Stockbridge high street can arrange grayling days during the winter months along some mouth-watering beats of The River Test.

Monday, 19th December

Bright sunshine, gentle northwesterly wind.

As the sixth year of this new millennium rapidly comes to an end I thought it only fitting that I revisited 'The Conifers' lake near Norwich where I started this diary back on 2nd January in the company of Jinx Davey, when despite the cold conditions we nevertheless accounted for several pike to almost 20lbs, my boat partner today being Masterline International representative and

DECEMBER

The very last fish I caught during 2005. This streamlined and nicely marked pike came from the same lake near Norwich where this year's diary started way back at the beginning of January. A most fitting end to a spectacular years fishing.

an old friend, Dave Barnes from Royston, whom I last fished with at Blenheim Palace Lake during the summer.

Fortunately, and although my estate car's outside thermometer gave just 2°C when I met Dave at 7.30 a.m. for an early start, there was next to no wind chill and only a slight ripple on the 15 acre lake by the time we had got the boat out and anchored in a depth of around 12 feet, 60 yards out from the heavily-reeded southern shoreline. We then fanned a selection of smelt and half-lamprey dead baits around the boat on both float fished and free lined rigs, and sat back for the action to happen.

With bright sunshine to illuminate the heavily coloured water of the lake I was most confident of pike moving about and sniffing out our static baits, but alas, the sub-zero overnight temperatures of the past two days had greatly reduced the pikes' metabolism and thus their enthusiasm for feeding, and though we moved several times to help increase our chances of a pick up, we sat there all day till the sun sank below the tall fir trees around the lake in the late afternoon when air temperatures started to drop rapidly, having instigated just two runs, unfortunately, both on my rods. I say unfortunately, because I always hope my guest enjoys the lion's share of any action. The first run came at around 10 a.m. and produced a fish of around 8lbs, and the second four hours later, producing a chunky double of around 18lbs, which actually gave a good account of itself, repeatedly making long crash dives through the cold depths before popping up next to the boat where I chinned her out for a trophy shot.

An enjoyable day nonetheless when we rarely stopped talking about the tackle trade and its characters past and present, Dave being in the industry for 39 long years, 26 of which he regularly called at my tackle shop in Norwich, which was of course how we met.

EPILOGUE

And that 18lbs pike from 'The Conifers' lake, ironically, where this diary started in January, will in fact have to be my last fish of 2005. I sit writing this on my PC in the late morning of Wednesday 28th December, looking out over the snow-covered, iced-up lake at the bottom of the lawn where mallards and young black headed gulls are waddling about, with little chance of an outing till the New Year, if the weather report covering the next few days is anything to go by.

I have just unclipped my 14 foot boat from the tow bar on the estate and re-parked it, having loaded everything up yesterday evening for a pike fishing trip today on the Norfolk Broads with old friends Nick Beardmore and Andy Jubb who would have been awaiting my arrival round at Nick's house in Norwich at 7 a.m. But when I rose at 6 a.m. and considered the conditions, with four inches of overnight snow covering everything and the lakes frozen over, the hour long drive through narrow country lanes to reach a slipway on Hickling Broad seemed a rather foolhardy exercise, so I rang Nick and Andy immediately to call the trip off.

A pity really, because I love the chance of enjoying photography in the snow, whilst it has also just occurred to me that I have not in fact fished with Andy all year, and I so much wanted to fish with all the very same friends who shared that first 'diary book' back in 1976.

Terry Houseago is another old friend of over 30 years standing who appeared in *A Specimen Fishing Year*, and while we still pike fish the Broads and chub fish together along the Wensum, somehow during 2005 we simply have not found the time. Neither have my wife Jo and I been pike fishing together this winter, or my son Lee come to that, and they both love boat fishing for pike. But then you cannot fit everything in. This past year has been unusually and surprisingly busy, though with 15 half hour programmes to film for Discovery Real Time TV during 2006 (starting with boat fishing for giant stingrays off Madeira in February)

next year could be even more hectic. But that 'is' the way I like it. That old cliché, 'if you want something done quickly, give it to a busy man' was probably invented for the likes of me.

When I first started writing this book, and I have my good friend Nick Beardmore to thank for prising me away from the Middle Ages of writing by long hand, and setting me up with a PC, (his job is installing computer systems) it was also my intention to make far more comparisons with the fishing of the mid 1970s to how things are now. That however would have seen me revisiting lakes and stretches of river which now frankly, do not hold the same fascination as they did 30 years ago. Truth is, we all move on in our attitudes and in our aspirations, and I seemed to have followed an adventure trail, first born in the late 1960s and early '70s whilst working and living on a P&O passenger ship for two years and fishing around the world, followed by three years' sea fishing in the Caribbean. And my big fish results for this year which have included personal bests in the form of that 75lbs red tail catfish and 13lbs peacock bass from Brazil, followed by a monster perch of 4lbs 10oz, a tope of 49lbs, tench of 9lbs 5oz and 9lbs 1oz during my first two sessions in June, striped bass to 25lbs off Long Island, New York, blue sharks topping the ton off the Welsh coast, culminating in a Chao Phray catfish of 80lbs and that huge surprise 130lbs arapaima in Thailand, reflect my international, all round preferences nowadays, in game, coarse and sea fishing.

Back in 1976 however, with a young family to bring up and a 'six days a week tackle shop' to run, my present level of swanning off to exotic locations between bouts of domestic fishing could in no way have been possible. I guess it was simply suppressed for many years. Now I am in the ideal position of truly being able to enjoy my work as a full time angling journalist and TV presenter. Perhaps my readers would not even call it work. Perhaps we'll even bump into one another along the way. Who knows?

Whatever happens, may the flow always be with you.

J.W.

Design: Kevin Gardner

Proofreading: Jane Pamenter

Project Editor: Vanessa Gardner

Publishers: Jules Gammond, Tim Exell & Vanessa Gardner

Written By: John Wilson